MODERN IRISH POETRY

An Anthology

•

Edited by

PATRICK CROTTY

THE
BLACKSTAFF
PRESS

BELFAST

In memory of
Tudor Bevan
1933-1944

First published in 2003 by
The Blackstaff Press Limited
4c Heron Wharf, Sydenham Business Park
Belfast BT3 9LE
with the assistance of
The Arts Council of Northern Ireland

ARTS
COUNCIL
of Northern Ireland

Reprinted 1996 (twice), 1997, 1999,
2001, 2003, 2004, 2006
The Acknowledgments on pp, 423-8 constitute an extension
of this copyright page

Typeset by Paragon Typesetters, Queensferry, Clwyd
Printed in Ireland by
Colourbooks Limited
A CIP catalogue record for this book
is available from the British Library

ISBN 0-85640-561-2

www.blackstaffpress.com

CONTENTS

INTRODUCTION

So many strands of poetry in Ireland since the 1920s define themselves against the exhilarating, overbearing example of W.B. Yeats that it might be said that Irish writers make poetry less out of their quarrel with themselves than out of their quarrel with the founder of the Literary Revival. The poets included in this anthology reject the other-worldly pull of the Celtic Twilight, and distrust the plangent, resonant tones Yeats brought to even his most rooted and earthy themes. James Joyce's preference for the everyday and contemporary over the legendary – that first, decisive revision of the Revival aesthetic – is endorsed by all of them. Yet Austin Clarke, John Hewitt, Richard Murphy, Thomas Kinsella, John Montague, Seamus Heaney, Michael Hartnett, Eavan Boland and Tom Paulin extend a characteristically Yeatsian and Revivalist practice insofar as they approach the present through a heroising reading of the past (the Celtic Romanesque period in Clarke, pre-history in Kinsella, radical late-eighteenth-century Ulster in Paulin, and so on). Indeed the very lack of a historical dimension in the work of those poets who take a stand on the primacy of the here-and-now – Patrick Kavanagh, Brian Coffey, Samuel Beckett, Louis MacNeice, Paul Durcan and Medbh McGuckian – offers the indirect homage of counterstatement to the Literary Revival's premiss that only a recovery of the past can effect liberation in the present. The realism of Kavanagh's *The Great Hunger* is to be understood, in part at least, as a response to the Abbey Theatre's pastoralisation of peasant life. Similarly, though MacNeice had little use for Yeats's concept of a specifically Irish tradition in English poetry, he continually relocated himself in relation to the older writer (his *The Poetry of W.B. Yeats*, published in 1941, was the first book-length study of the poet).

It is true, of course, that anxiety about Yeats's influence has been felt by poets everywhere in the English-speaking world over the last three-quarters of a century. Much of the verse of subsequent decades

1

has sought to absorb the implications of the modernist high tide of the 1920s, when Yeats's *The Tower*, T.S. Eliot's *The Waste Land*, Wallace Stevens's *Harmonium*, William Carlos Williams's *Spring and All*, Ezra Pound's *Hugh Selwyn Mauberley* and early *Cantos*, Hugh MacDiarmid's *Sangschaw* and *A Drunk Man Looks at the Thistle* and Hart Crane's *White Buildings* all appeared within a few years of each other. Despite its variety and enhanced social awareness, the poetry of the thirties and later fails to sustain the energy and innovative flair of those volumes. Even as we approach the end of the century Yeats and Eliot survive along with Stevens, Williams and (to a perhaps diminishing degree) Pound as crucial exemplars for anyone wishing to extend the possibilities of English poetic idiom.

The loss of aesthetic optimism in the post-twenties period is perhaps clearer in retrospect than it was at the time, at least in Britain and the United States. In Ireland, however, the sense of anti-climax was immediate and acute, for two reasons. Firstly, the disproportionate contribution of Irish writers to the international modernist movement had a disabling effect on subsequent, less gifted artists, not least because in making the matter of Ireland central to their work, Yeats and Joyce had exhausted many local possibilities of subject matter and attitude. (It is no coincidence that Beckett, eventually installed as the third member of an Irish modernist triumvirate, elides geographical and historical particulars from his writing.) Secondly, the upsurge in literary activity had been connected to the political turbulence which found resolution (of a sort) in the settlement of 1922. From the rise of the Home Rule and Land League movements in the 1870s to the setting up of Northern Ireland and the Irish Free State, cultural identities were rendered problematic as power relations with Britain and between the various population groups within Ireland shifted. Cultural myth-making and self-confrontation in response to rapidly changing needs provided an impetus for texts as diverse as Standish O'Grady's *History of Ireland*, J.M. Synge's *The Playboy of the Western World*, and *Ulysses*. By the time Joyce's novel appeared in 1922 the old Ascendancy class had retreated to the margins of Irish life, and cultural as well as political power had begun to stabilise round new institutions which reflected the triumph of the Gaelic/Catholic sect in the South and its Scots-Irish/Protestant counterpart in the North.

There is a feeling of aftermath in the work of Clarke, Kavanagh and Hewitt, a taking stock as the dust of revolution settles. On both sides of the border the years 1922 to 1960 mark a period of retrenchment and more or less institutionalised Philistinism. In the South contemporary literature was all but outlawed by the Censorship of Publications Act (1929). Yeats's success in cultivating audiences at home and abroad eluded poets of the next generation who chose to live in or write mainly about Ireland. The obscurity and near penury in which Clarke and Kavanagh spent their lives was one consequence of this, the broken trajectory of their careers another. Satire, more than most modes, implies an audience. In a painful paradox, the lack of a domestic public to receive their work helped drive Clarke and Kavanagh to satire, while the lack of an audience for their satire reduced much of what might have been forceful cultural and social commentary to flailing, would-be comic doggerel in the case of Kavanagh, and a species of muttering protest, at once over-topical and arcane, in that of Clarke. The latter's increasing dependence on homonymic rhyme and other stylistic eccentricities suggests an almost wilful self-subversion on the part of a writer who knows his complaints will go unheard. Louis MacNeice's is the only achievement of the period free of a sense of dissipated or misdirected energies, and his work was largely aimed at (and registered by) an audience outside Ireland. Though Clarke, Kavanagh and Seán Ó Ríordáin may equal him in stylistic ingenuity and moral purpose, MacNeice wrote a strikingly greater number of successful poems than they did. (This was brought home to me during the compilation of the present anthology, when shortlists of two dozen poems each by Clarke and Kavanagh, and a slightly smaller number by Ó Ríordáin, rapidly emerged: it took much labour to whittle MacNeice's work down to a shortlist, and then there were well in excess of sixty items on it.)

The achievement of Clarke and Kavanagh is nonetheless considerable. The former recuperated the intricate assonantal patterning of Gaelic verse in a recognisably modernist idiom – as distinctive in its way as William Empson's or Theodore Roethke's – and turned a potentially reactionary regard for the past to the service of a libertarian vision. The latter was the first writer to create wholly out of the vernacular English of Ireland a poetic voice free of whimsy and folksiness. Irish poets after Kavanagh are at last psychologically and technically sure of the resources of their English medium: his example can be said to have made possible the freedom of address of such colloquially rooted contemporary poetries as Heaney's, Durcan's and Muldoon's.

It was not, however, until the 1950s and the emergence of Richard Murphy, Thomas Kinsella and John Montague – a generation born in the first decade of independence – that post-Yeatsian Irish poets began to have professional careers, supported now by grants, literary prizes and the growing institutionalisation of poetry on both sides of the

Atlantic. The cosmopolitan flavour of their work reflects alike the ending of the neutral South's wartime isolation and the significant periods spent by these authors overseas, whether in France, the United States or Sri Lanka. Kinsella's brooding narratives relate the dislocations of psychic, family and national history to universal perspectives on incoherence and loss, while Montague's erotic lyrics deploy a taut, unemphatic line derived from Williams, Kenneth Rexroth and Robert Creeley to challenge the sexual glumness of mid-century Ireland. Their temptation towards bardic commentary on the social and economic changes of the Lemass era reveals the confidence of these poets in their audience. In Murphy's *The Battle of Aughrim* (1968), Kinsella's *Nightwalker* (1967) and such portions of Montague's *The Rough Field* (1972) as had made their appearance by the end of the 1960s, history is a nightmare from which the poetic consciousness has awoken into modernity. For a younger generation north of the border it was by contrast one whose full terrors were about to be disclosed.

Thomas MacGreevy, whose work opens the present anthology, has been identified as the founder of a 'tradition of Irish modernism' which includes his friends Coffey, Beckett and Denis Devlin, along with a number of more recent writers not represented here. The wish is sometimes mistaken for the deed in discussion of this strand of Irish poetic effort: though these poets produced a number of fine individual lyrics, perhaps only Beckett can be said to have succeeded in developing – as opposed to merely seeking – new forms. Indeed, it might be argued that the modernist injunction to 'make it new' is honoured more by Kinsella in pieces like 'Hen Woman' and '38 Phoenix Street' – and by such northern poets as McGuckian and Muldoon – than by any of the self-consciously anti-traditional writers associated with MacGreevy.

The 'Irish modernists' share with the Kinsella/Montague generation an eagerness to accommodate European and American influences. Internationalism and nationalism are close companions in Ireland, as they are in Scotland, where poets from MacDiarmid to Kenneth White have cultivated a cosmopolitan formal lineage to underscore their separateness from an insular English tradition. (Patriotism gets mixed up in the debate about modernism in England, too, of course, albeit in the opposite way: anti-modernism was for Philip Larkin, Kingsley Amis and others in the 1950s a mode of chauvinism, an aesthetic forerunner to the Euro-scepticism of the 1990s.) Many of the writers associated with Liam Miller's Dolmen Press disapproved of what one of the foremost of them, John Montague, called the 'limiting British mode' of the Thomas Hardy/Edward Thomas/Philip Larkin axis. It was perhaps inevitable that the appearance towards the end of the 1960s of a group of Belfast-based, London-published poets who displayed a preference for the tight, traditionally derived forms of Larkin and the Movement should have been greeted with a measure of suspicion south of the border. Seamus Heaney, Michael Longley and Derek Mahon, however, were not offering fifties English poetry at second hand. The tonalities of their version of 'the well-made lyric' involve what Terence Brown has called 'a tense astringency' deeply at odds with the genteel weariness of the parent mode. Renewed rather than merely borrowed, that is to say, the forms of northern poetry in the 1960s and early 1970s were made as adequate to the fraught realities of their new socio-political context as they had been to the *longueurs* of suburban England.

With their fidelity to local speech patterns, Heaney's verses in any case were from the beginning considerably removed from the clipped tones and edges of the Movement lyric. Unease about the procedures of his work is so crucial to this poet's sense of artistic responsibility that one must be wary of reading too much into the manner of his progress towards more open and varied forms. It can nonetheless be noted that Heaney dropped the regular stanzas of his first two books just as his poetry was taking on an explicitly historical character in response to the catastrophic turn of events in Northern Ireland. His adoption of an American-style short unrhymed line for *Wintering Out* (1972) and *North* (1975) may represent a last – and this time largely coincidental – intersection between Irish nationalist politics and international modernism. More recent northern writers have engaged as much with transatlantic as with English examples, and have done so in a manner which undermines the old assumptions about the cultural loyalties implicit in procedural choices. Indeed one can read back from Ciaran Carson's adaptation of the long line of C.K. Williams, or from Paul Muldoon's grafting of Amerindian legend to the stock of the English sonnet sequence, to see in the orderliness of the 1960s work of Heaney, Longley and Mahon an early expression of that vigorous, slightly distrustful formalist eclecticism which has for three decades distinguished northern poetry.

Regional characteristics are exhibited by the poetry of other parts of Ireland too, of course – not least Munster, where the outstanding twentieth-century achievement has been in the Irish language, in the work of Seán Ó Ríordáin and Nuala Ní Dhomhnaill, rather than in the English spoken by the great majority of the population. The fact that the province's leading English-medium poet, Michael Hartnett, spent a decade writing mainly in Irish may be further symptomatic of

5

the vestigial life of the language in the Munster countryside. The Gaelic literary tradition, however, had petered out in misery and doggerel generations before the writers in the present anthology were born. Efforts to resuscitate it began to bear fruit only as hopes of reversing or even arresting the decline of the spoken language were being abandoned. The disappointing actuality of independence broke the link between lyric endeavour and aspirant nationalism, allowing for the emergence of a cautious, introspective, characteristically self-reflexive art. The modernity of Ó Ríordáin and his Connacht contemporary Máirtín Ó Direáin – a matter not only of psychology but of a rhythmic innovation necessarily more fundamental than anything in the Anglophone poetry of Ireland – highlights the unbridgeable nature of the gap separating their work from that of Aodhagán Ó Rathaille and other poets of the eighteenth century.

There is a measure of continuity with the modes of the past in the poetry of Máire Mhac an tSaoi, but it is with *amhráin na ndaoine* – the songs of the folk – rather than the elaborate art that died with Ó Rathaille. An even more remarkable receptiveness to the sub-literary, the instinctual and the communal can be found in the verse of Nuala Ní Dhomhnaill. Women have made an outstanding contribution to poetry in Irish, particularly in the contemporary period. In English their achievement is perhaps slightly less considerable, though a huge increase in literary activity in line with the rise of the women's movement may prove the prelude to a revolution which will render such a judgement invalid by the turn of the century. As yet, however, recognition that a feminist aesthetic demands new forms and cadences has been reflected in the work of few but the more established writers: the poetries of Eiléan Ní Chuilleanáin and Eavan Boland have developed in stature and complexity to embrace issues relating to the absence of women's witness from received versions of history, while Medbh McGuckian has sought to reconstitute the figurative dynamics of the lyric according to a fluid, non-linear logic.

The editorial discriminations of the anthology's closing pages – from Thomas McCarthy onwards – are necessarily tentative. More verse by younger writers is appearing than ever before, both in book form and in a wide range of periodicals. Contemporary Ireland is clearly hospitable to new poetry. Whether it is in any serious sense responsive to it is another matter, however, and there are signs that ease of publication has begun to function as an enemy of promise. This may help to explain why young poets appear to be taking longer to mature than a decade or two ago (though it can hardly account for the fact that two of the strongest debut collections of the 1990s have come from Fergus Allen and Maurice Riordan, writers in their seventies and forties respectively). Pre-fabricated Muldoonesque ironies are the staple of much recent writing from the North, while, south of the border, performance-oriented monologues which flatter rather than challenge their audience have wide currency.

The indifferent quality of such work illustrates the dangers of complacency. And yet it is true that Ireland continues to make an improbably strong contribution to poetry: many of the poems reproduced here bear comparison with the best written anywhere in the English-speaking world since the 1920s. While my focus has been on achievement rather than activity – across the book as a whole and within the individual selections – I have nonetheless sought to highlight the range and variety of modern Irish verse. This has necessitated the inclusion of works longer than it is customary to represent in anthologies. For reasons of space some of these have had to be subjected to a process of excision and I am particularly grateful to the poets and their representatives who granted permission for the resulting cuts. (In no case were these meant as challenges to the integrity of the original text.) The word *modern* in this anthology's title is used in the sense that we speak of modern Ireland, Ireland since the settlement of 1922. *Irish* is similarly intended inclusively, as a term capacious enough to encompass the diversity of cultural identities within the island and to admit the reality of the Irish diaspora in the writing of exiles, expatriates and their offspring. The brief critical commentaries which precede each selection are designed to afford an entry into the poetry: if the more experienced reader takes them as starting points for debate, so much the better.

LLANGAIN, CARMARTHEN
31 AUGUST 1995

7

THOMAS MACGREEVY

Born Tarbert, County Kerry, 1893. Served as officer in British Army in First World War. Army scholarship to Trinity College Dublin. Lived London, 1924–6, Paris, 1926–33. *Lecteur* at École Normale Supérieure, 1926–30. Lectured at National Gallery, London, 1935–41. Chevalier de légion d'honneur, 1948, Officier, 1962. Director of the National Gallery of Ireland, 1950–63. Personally close to Joyce, Beckett and Wallace Stevens. Died 1967.

In MacGreevy's work a modernist poetic serves a strikingly conservative world-view. Nationalist and Catholic pieties are rarely far from the surface of the taut *vers libre* meditations from the 1920s which account for most of his slender output. 'Homage to Hieronymus Bosch' is an allegory based on the failure of the provost of Trinity College Dublin to respond to a request by ex-officer undergraduates to intervene with the authorities on behalf of Kevin Barry, a republican student at University College Dublin captured by the Black and Tans and hanged in 1920. 'Recessional' records a visit to Switzerland in 1925.

HOMAGE TO HIERONYMUS BOSCH

A woman with no face walked into the light;
A boy, in a brown-tree norfolk suit,
Holding on
Without hands
To her seeming skirt.

She stopped,
And he stopped,
And I, in terror, stopped, staring.

Then I saw a group of shadowy figures behind her.

It was a wild wet morning
But the little world was spinning on.

Liplessly, somehow, she addressed it:
The book must be opened
And the park too.

I might have tittered
But my teeth chattered
And I saw that the words, as they fell,
Lay, wriggling, on the ground.

There was a stir of wet wind
And the shadowy figures began to stir
When one I had thought dead
Filmed slowly out of his great effigy on a tomb near by
And they all shuddered
He bent as if to speak to the woman
But the nursery governor flew up out of the well of Saint Patrick,
Confiscated by his mistress,
And, his head bent,
Staring out over his spectacles,
And scratching the gravel furiously,
Hissed –
      The words went *pingg!* like bullets,
      Upwards past his spectacles –
Say nothing, I say, say nothing, say nothing!
And he who had seemed to be coming to life
Gasped,
Began hysterically, to laugh and cry,
And, with a gesture of impotent and half-petulant despair,
Filmed back into his effigy again.

High above the Bank of Ireland
Unearthly music sounded,
Passing westwards.

Then, from the drains,
Small sewage rats slid out.
They numbered hundreds of hundreds, tens, thousands.
Each bowed obsequiously to the shadowy figures
Then turned and joined in a stomach dance with his brothers
    and sisters.
Being a multitude, they danced irregularly.

There was rat laughter,
Deeper here and there,
And occasionally she-rat cries grew hysterical.
The shadowy figures looked on, agonized.
The woman with no face gave a cry and collapsed.
The rats danced on her
And on the wriggling words
Smirking.
The nursery governor flew back into the well
With the little figure without hands in the brown-tree clothes.

RECESSIONAL

In the bright broad Swiss glare I stand listening
To the outrageous roars
Of the Engelbergeraa
As it swirls down the gorge
And I think I am thinking
Of Roderick Hudson.
But, as I stand,
Time closes over sight,
And sound
Is drowned
By a long silvery roar
From the far ends of memory
Of a world I have left
And I find I am thinking:
Supposing I drowned now,
This tired, tiresome body,
Before flesh creases further,
Might, recovered, go fair,
To be laid in Saint Lachtin's,
Near where once,
In tender, less glaring, island days
And ways
I could hear –
Where listeners still hear –

That far-away, dear
Roar
The long, silvery roar
Of Mal Bay.

AUSTIN CLARKE

Born Dublin, 1896. Educated at Belvedere College and University
College Dublin. Lecturer in English at UCD, 1917–21. Relieved of his
post due to official disapproval of his marital circumstances. Worked as
literary journalist in London, 1922–37. Thereafter lived in Dublin until
his death in 1974. Author of verse plays, autobiographies and three
highly regarded prose romances, *The Bright Temptation* (1932), *The
Singing Men at Cashel* (1936) and *The Sun Dances at Easter* (1952).

Clarke's prosodic innovations – his efforts to develop what his mentor
Thomas MacDonagh called 'an Irish mode' – link him both to the
cultural nationalism of the Literary Revival and the modernist localism
of William Carlos Williams and Hugh MacDiarmid. Historical setting
and a Gaelicised metric cloak the early poetry's commentary on the
disenchantments of post-revolutionary Ireland. After a seventeen-year
silence Clarke returned with a more directly satirical and topical voice in
1955. The first seven poems in the selection come from the earlier
career, the last four from the later. In both phases the poet measures the
tawdriness of the present against the splendour of the past, and identifies
spiritual with sexual freedom. His social criticisms derive much of their
force from his sense that the civil and ecclesiastical authorities in modern
Ireland have betrayed their heritage. 'The Lost Heifer' seeks amid
the mayhem of the Irish Civil War (1922–3) to resurrect the old Gaelic
image of Ireland as 'Droimeann Donn Dílis' (faithful brown heifer).
'The Straying Student' rewrites as a paean to sexual emancipation an
eighteenth-century song about a repentant, love-lorn friar. In 'Martha
Blake at Fifty-one' the unilluminating indignities of the life and
death of a pious Dublin spinster are counterpointed by the visions of
Saint Teresa of Avila, Saint Thérèse of Lisieux and Saint John of the
Cross. Eroticism – always for Clarke a mode of political resistance –
emerges in the very late 'Tiresias' (1971) as a celebration of an
achieved personal independence.

THE LOST HEIFER

When the black herds of the rain were grazing
In the gap of the pure cold wind

13

And the watery hazes of the hazel
Brought her into my mind,
I thought of the last honey by the water
That no hive can find.

Brightness was drenching through the branches
When she wandered again,
Turning the silver out of dark grasses
Where the skylark had lain,
And her voice coming softly over the meadow
Was the mist becoming rain.

from THE YOUNG WOMAN OF BEARE

Through lane or black archway,
The praying people hurry,
When shadows have been walled,
At market hall and gate,
By low fires after nightfall;
The bright sodalities
Are bannered in the churches;
But I am only roused
By horsemen of de Burgo
That gallop to my house.

Gold slots of the sunlight
Close up my lids at evening.
Half clad in silken piles
I lie upon a hot cheek.
Half in dream I lie there
Until bad thoughts have bloomed
In flushes of desire.
Drowsy with indulgence,
I please a secret eye
That opens at the Judgment.

I am the bright temptation
In talk, in wine, in sleep.
Although the clergy pray,

I triumph in a dream.
Strange armies tax the south,
Yet little do I care
What fiery bridge or town
Has heard the shout begin –
That Ormond's men are out
And the Geraldine is in.

The women at green stall
And doorstep on a weekday,
Who have been chinned with scorn
Of me, would never sleep
So well, could they but know
Their husbands turn at midnight,
And covet in a dream
The touching of my flesh.
Small wonder that men kneel
The longer at confession.

Bullies, that fight in dramshop
For fluttered rags and bare side
At beggars' bush, may gamble
To-night on what they find.
I laze in yellow lamplight –
Young wives have envied me –
And laugh among lace pillows,
For a big-booted captain
Has poured the purse of silver
That glitters in my lap.

Heavily on his elbow,
He turns from a caress
To see – as my arms open –
The red spurs of my breast.
I draw fair pleats around me
And stay his eye at pleasure,
Show but a white knee-cap
Or an immodest smile –
Until his sudden hand
Has dared the silks that bind me.

See! See, as from a lathe
My polished body turning!
He bares me at the waist
And now blue clothes uncurl
Upon white haunch. I let
The last bright stitch fall down
For him as I lean back,
Straining with longer arms
Above my head to snap
The silver knots of sleep.

Together in the dark –
Sin-fast – we can enjoy
What is allowed in marriage.
The jingle of that coin
Is still the same, though stolen:
But are they not unthrifty,
Who spend it in a shame
That brings ill and repentance,
When they might pinch and save
Themselves in lawful pleasure?

THE PLANTER'S DAUGHTER

When night stirred at sea
And the fire brought a crowd in,
They say that her beauty
Was music in mouth
And few in the candlelight
Thought her too proud,
For the house of the planter
Is known by the trees.

Men that had seen her
Drank deep and were silent,
The women were speaking
Wherever she went –
As a bell that is rung
Or a wonder told shyly,

And O she was the Sunday
In every week.

CELIBACY

On a brown isle of Lough Corrib,
When clouds were bare as branch
And water had been thorned
By colder days, I sank
In torment of her side;
But still that woman stayed,
For eye obeys the mind.

Bedraggled in the briar
And grey fire of the nettle,
Three nights, I fell, I groaned
On the flagstone of help
To pluck her from my body;
For servant ribbed with hunger
May climb his rungs to God.

Eyelid stood back in sleep,
I saw what seemed an Angel:
Dews dripped from those bright feet.
But, O, I knew the stranger
By her deceit and, tired
All night by tempting flesh,
I wrestled her in hair-shirt.

On pale knees in the dawn,
Parting the straw that wrapped me,
She sank until I saw
The bright roots of her scalp.
She pulled me down to sleep,
But I fled as the Baptist
To thistle and to reed.

The dragons of the Gospel
Are cast by bell and crook;

17

But fiery as the frost
Or bladed light, she drew
The reeds back, when I fought
The arrow-headed airs
That darken on the water.

MARTHA BLAKE

Before the day is everywhere
And the timid warmth of sleep
Is delicate on limb, she dares
The silence of the street
Until the double bells are thrown back
For Mass and echoes bound
In the chapel yard, O then her soul
Makes bold in the arms of sound.

But in the shadow of the nave
Her well-taught knees are humble,
She does not see through any saint
That stands in the sun
With veins of lead, with painful crown;
She waits that dreaded coming,
When all the congregation bows
And none may look up.

The word is said, the Word sent down,
The miracle is done
Beneath those hands that have been rounded
Over the embodied cup,
And with a few, she leaves her place
Kept by an east-filled window
And kneels at the communion rail
Starching beneath her chin.

She trembles for the Son of Man,
While the priest is murmuring
What she can scarcely tell, her heart
Is making such a stir;

But when he picks a particle
And she puts out her tongue,
That joy is the glittering of candles
And benediction sung.

Her soul is lying in the Presence
Until her senses, one
By one, desiring to attend her,
Come as for feast and run
So fast to share the sacrament,
Her mouth must mother them:
'Sweet tooth grow wise, lip, gum be gentle,
I touch a purple hem.'

Afflicted by that love she turns
To multiply her praise,
Goes over all the foolish words
And finds they are the same;
But now she feels within her breast
Such calm that she is silent,
For soul can never be immodest
Where body may not listen.

On a holy day of obligation
I saw her first in prayer,
But mortal eye had been too late
For all that thought could dare.
The flame in heart is never grieved
That pride and intellect
Were cast below, when God revealed
A heaven for this earth.

So to begin the common day
She needs a miracle,
Knowing the safety of angels
That see her home again,
Yet ignorant of all the rest,
The hidden grace that people
Hurrying to business
Look after in the street.

THE STRAYING STUDENT

On a holy day when sails were blowing southward,
A bishop sang the Mass at Inishmore,
Men took one side, their wives were on the other
But I heard the woman coming from the shore:
And wild in despair my parents cried aloud
For they saw the vision draw me to the doorway.

Long had she lived in Rome when Popes were bad,
The wealth of every age she makes her own,
Yet smiled on me in eager admiration,
And for a summer taught me all I know,
Banishing shame with her great laugh that rang
As if a pillar caught it back alone.

I learned the prouder counsel of her throat,
My mind was growing bold as light in Greece;
And when in sleep her stirring limbs were shown,
I blessed the noonday rock that knew no tree:
And for an hour the mountain was her throne,
Although her eyes were bright with mockery.

They say I was sent back from Salamanca
And failed in logic, but I wrote her praise
Nine times upon a college wall in France.
She laid her hand at darkfall on my page
That I might read the heavens in a glance
And I knew every star the Moors have named.

Awake or in my sleep, I have no peace now,
Before the ball is struck, my breath has gone,
And yet I tremble lest she may deceive me
And leave me in this land, where every woman's son
Must carry his own coffin and believe,
In dread, all that the clergy teach the young.

PENAL LAW

Burn Ovid with the rest. Lovers will find
A hedge-school for themselves and learn by heart
All that the clergy banish from the mind,
When hands are joined and head bows in the dark.

ST CHRISTOPHER

Child that his strength upbore,
Knotted as tree-trunks i' the spate,
Became a giant, whose weight
Unearthed the river from shore
Till saint's bones were a-crack.
Fabulist, can an ill state
Like ours, carry so great
A Church upon its back?

EARLY UNFINISHED SKETCH

Rosalind, in a négligée,
Began to sketch me as I lay
Naked and soon her serious touch
On sheet delighted me as much
In art as loving. Pencil drew,
Poised, measured again, sped downward, flew
Like love scattering clothes to greet
Itself. The outline was complete.
She pondered. Detail was different,
More difficult. She seemed intent
On what the ancients had adored,
Christian apologists deplored.
'Finish it, pet, how can I wait?'
'But, darling, I must concentrate.'
She failed, fled back to our caresses,
Sat up.
         'What's wrong?'

'The problem presses.'
'I have it! Yes. That group in bronze.'
'The satyrs?'
               'Herrick would call them fauns.'
'Stock-still –'
               'in the fountain spray at Florence.'
'All tourists showing their abhorrence!'
'But if that sculptor dared to limn it –'
'The nude, to-day, must have a limit.'
'And Rosalind –'
               'obey the laws
Of decency.'
               'In the line she draws?'

MARTHA BLAKE AT FIFTY-ONE

Early, each morning, Martha Blake
    Walked, angeling the road,
To Mass in the Church of the Three Patrons.
    Sanctuary lamp glowed
And the clerk halo'ed the candles
    On the High Altar. She knelt
Illumined. In gold-hemmed alb,
    The priest intoned. Wax melted.

Waiting for daily Communion, bowed head
    At rail, she hears a murmur.
Latin is near. In a sweet cloud
    That cherub'd, all occurred.
The voice went by. To her pure thought,
    Body was a distress
And soul, a sigh. Behind her denture,
    Love lay, a helplessness.

Then, slowly walking after Mass
    Down Rathgar Road, she took out
Her Yale key, put a match to gas-ring,
    Half filled a saucepan, cooked

A fresh egg lightly, with tea, brown bread,
    Soon, taking off her blouse
And skirt, she rested, pressing the Crown
    Of Thorns until she drowsed.

In her black hat, stockings, she passed
    Nylons to a nearby shop
And purchased, daily, with downcast eyes,
    Fillet of steak or a chop.
She simmered it on a low jet,
    Having a poor appetite,
Yet never for an hour felt better
    From dilatation, tightness.

She suffered from dropped stomach, heartburn
    Scalding, water-brash
And when she brought her wind up, turning
    Red with the weight of mashed
Potato, mint could not relieve her.
    In vain her many belches,
For all below was swelling, heaving
    Wamble, gurgle, squelch.

She lay on the sofa with legs up,
    A decade on her lip,
At four o'clock, taking a cup
    Of lukewarm water, sip
By sip, but still her daily food
    Repeated and the bile
Tormented her. In a blue hood,
    The Virgin sadly smiled.

When she looked up, the Saviour showed
    His Heart, daggered with flame
And, from the mantle-shelf, St Joseph
    Bent, disapproving. Vainly
She prayed, for in the whatnot corner
    The new Pope was frowning. Night
And day, dull pain, as in her corns,
    Recounted every bite.

23

She thought of St Teresa, floating
   On motes of a sunbeam,
Carmelite with scatterful robes,
   Surrounded by demons,
Small black boys in their skin. She gaped
   At Hell: a muddy passage
That led to nothing, queer in shape,
   A cupboard closely fastened.

Sometimes, the walls of the parlour
   Would fade away. No plod
Of feet, rattle of van, in Garville
   Road. Soul now gone abroad
Where saints, like medieval serfs,
   Had laboured. Great sun-flower shone.
Our Lady's Chapel was borne by seraphs,
   Three leagues beyond Ancona.

High towns of Italy, the plain
   Of France, were known to Martha
As she read in a holy book. The sky-blaze
   Nooned at Padua,
Marble grotto of Bernadette.
   Rose-scatterers. New saints
In tropical Africa where the tsetse
   Fly probes, the forest taints.

Teresa had heard the Lutherans
   Howling on red-hot spit,
And grill, men who had searched for truth
   Alone in Holy Writ.
So Martha, fearful of flame lashing
   Those heretics, each instant,
Never dealt in the haberdashery
   Shop, owned by two Protestants.

In ambush of night, an angel wounded
   The Spaniard to the heart
With iron tip on fire. Swooning
   With pain and bliss as a dart

Moved up and down within her bowels
    Quicker, quicker, each cell
Sweating as if rubbed up with towels,
    Her spirit rose and fell.

St John of the Cross, her friend, in prison
    Awaits the bridal night,
Paler than lilies, his wizened skin
    Flowers. In fifths of flight,
Senses beyond seraphic thought,
    In that divinest clasp,
Enfolding of kisses that cauterize,
    Yield to the soul-spasm.

Cunning in body had come to hate
    All this and stirred by mischief
Haled Martha from heaven. Heart palpitates
    And terror in her stiffens.
Heart misses one beat, two . . . flutters . . . stops.
    Her ears are full of sound.
Half fainting, she stares at the grandfather clock
    As if it were overwound.

The fit had come. Ill-natured flesh
    Despised her soul. No bending
Could ease rib. Around her heart, pressure
    Of wind grew worse. Again,
Again, armchaired without relief,
    She eructated, phlegm
In mouth, forgot the woe, the grief,
    Foretold at Bethlehem.

Tired of the same faces, side-altars,
    She went to the Carmelite Church
At Johnson's Court, confessed her faults,
    There, once a week, purchased
Tea, butter in Chatham St. The pond
    In St Stephen's Green was grand.
She watched the seagulls, ducks, black swan,
    Went home by the 15 tram.

Her beads in hand, Martha became
　　A member of the Third Order,
Saved from long purgatorial pain,
　　Brown habit and white cord
Her own when cerges had been lit
　　Around her coffin. She got
Ninety-five pounds on loan for her bit
　　Of clay in the common plot.

Often she thought of a quiet sick-ward,
　　Nuns, with delicious ways,
Consoling the miserable; quick
　　Tea, toast on trays. Wishing
To rid themselves of her, kind neighbours
　　Sent for the ambulance,
Before her brother and sister could hurry
　　To help her. Big gate clanged.

No medical examination
　　For the new patient. Doctor
Had gone to Cork on holidays.
　　Telephone sprang. Hall-clock
Proclaimed the quarters. Clatter of heels
　　On tiles. Corridor, ward,
A-whirr with the electric cleaner,
　　The creak of window cord.

She could not sleep at night. Feeble
　　And old, two women raved
And cried to God. She held her beads.
　　O how could she be saved?
The hospital had this and that rule.
　　Day-chill unshuttered. Nun, with
Thermometer in reticule,
　　Went by. The women mumbled.

Mother Superior believed
　　That she was obstinate, self-willed.
Sisters ignored her, hands-in-sleeves,
　　Beside a pantry shelf

26

Or counting pillow-case, soiled sheet.
　　They gave her purgatives.
Soul-less, she tottered to the toilet.
　　Only her body lived.

Wasted by colitis, refused
　　The daily sacrament
By regulation, fobidden use
　　Of bed-pan, when meals were sent up,
Behind a screen, she lay, shivering,
　　Unable to eat. The soup
Was greasy, mutton, beef or liver,
　　Cold. Kitchen has no scruples.

The Nuns had let the field in front
　　An an Amusement Park,
Merry-go-round, a noisy month, all
　　Heltering-skeltering at darkfall,
Mechanical music, dipper, hold-tights,
　　Rifle-crack, crash of dodgems.
The ward, godless with shadow, lights,
　　How could she pray to God?

Unpitied, wasting with diarrhea
　　And the constant strain,
Poor Child of Mary with one idea,
　　She ruptured a small vein,
Bled inwardly to jazz. No priest
　　Came. She had been anointed
Two days before, yet knew no peace:
　　Her last breath, disappointed.

from TIRESIAS, II

'Strolling one day, beyond the Kalends, on Mount Cyllene,
What should I spy near the dusty track but a couple of sun-spotted
Snakes – writhen together – flashen as they copulated,
Dreamily! Curious about the origin of species, I touched them.
Tunic shrank. I felt in alarm two ugly tumours

Swell from my chest. Juno, our universal mother, you
Know how easily a child wets the bed at night. Pardon
Frankness in saying that my enlarged bladder let go. "Gods," it
Lamented, "has he become an unfortunate woman, humbled by
Fate, yes, forced twice a day, to crouch down on her hunkers?
Leaf-cutting bee affrights me, Ariadne within her web-rounds."
Timidly hidden as hamadryad against her oak-bark,
I dared to pull up resisting tunic, expose my new breasts –
Saw they were beautiful. Lightly I fingered the nipples
And as they cherried, I felt below the burning answer;
Still drenched, I glanced down, but only a modesty of auburn
Curlets was there. If a man whose limb has been amputated
Still feels the throb of cut arteries, could I forget now
Prickle of pintel? Hour-long I grieved until full moonlight,
Entering the forestry, silvered my breasts. They rose up so calmly,
So proud, that peace – taking my hand in gladness – led me
Home, escorted by lucciole.
. . . .
One fine day
During siesta I gazed in reverence at my naked
Body, slim as a nespoli tree, dared to place my shaving
Mirror of polished silver – a birthday gift from my mother –
Between my legs, inspected this way and that, the fleshy
Folds guarding the shortcut, red as my real lips, to Pleasure
Pass. Next day I awoke in alarm, felt a trickle of blood half-
Way down my thigh.
                    "Mother," I sobbed.
                              "Our bold Penates
Pricked me during sleep."
                         "Let me look at it, Pyrrha."
                                          She laughed,
                                            then
Said:
    "Why it's nothing to worry about, my pet, all women
Suffer this shame every month."
                              "What does it mean?"
                                        "That you are
Ready for nuptial bliss."
                         And saying this, she cleansed, bandaged,
Bound my flowers.
              When I recovered, a burning sensation

28

Stayed. Restless at night, lying on my belly, I longed for
Mortal or centaur to surprise me.
                                        One day during
Siesta, I put on my tanagra dress, tightly
Belted, with flouncy skirt, and carrying a blue mantle,
Tiptoed from our home by shuttered window, barred shop-front,
Local temple, took the second turn at the trivium,
Reached a sultriness of hills.
                                    I went up a mule-track
Through a high wood beyond the pasturage: a shepherd's
Bothy was there before me. I peeped, saw a bed of bracken
Covered with a worn sheep-skin. I ventured in: listened,
Heard far away *clink-clank, clink-clank* as a bell-wether
Grazed with his flock while master and dog were myrtled
Somewhere in the coolness. By now I had almost forgotten
Much of my past, yet remembered the love-songs that shepherds
Piped among rock-roses to pretty boy or shy goat-girl.
Was it a pastoral air that had led me to this bothy?
Surely I was mistaken. Paper-knife, pumice, goose-quill,
Manuscripts, had been piled untidily together,
Inkstand, wax tablets, small paint-brushes on a rustic
Table.
     "A student lives here,"
                                I thought,
                                            and half-undressing,
Wearily spreading my cloak along the sheep-skin,
Lay on blueness, wondered as I closed my eyelids,
"What will he do when he sees me in my deshabille?"
                                                        Soon
Morpheus hid me in undreaming sleep until dusk. I woke up –
Not in the arms of softness but underneath the gentle
Weight of a naked youth.
                            Vainly I called out, "Almighty
Jove," struggled against his rigid will-power.'
                                                'And yielded?'
'Yes, for how could I stop him when I burned as he did?
In what seemed less than a minute, I had been deflowered
Without pleasure or pang. Once more, the young man mounted.
Determined by every goddess in high heaven to share his
Spilling, I twined, but just as I was about to . . . '
                                                'What happened?'

'He spent.

     O why should the spurren pleasure of expectant
Woman be snaffled within a yard of the grand stand?
While he was resting, I asked him:

                        "What is your name?"

                                     "Chelos,
Third-year student in Egyptology. Later
I'll show you rolled papyri, hieroglyphics,
Tinted lettering, sand-yellow, Nilus-brown, reed-green,
Outlined with hawk, horn, lotus-bud, sceptre, sun-circles,
Crescent."

     He told me of foreign wonders, the Colossus
Guarding the harbour of Rhodes, his cod bulkier than a
Well-filled freighter passing his shins, unfloodable
Temples beyond Assuan, rock-treasuries, the Mountains
Of the Moon, Alexandria and the Pharos –
Night-light of shipping.

              Soon in a grotto-spring under fern-drip,
Knee-deep, we sponged one another, back and side, laughing.
Chelos faggoted, tricked the brazier from smoke to flame,
   while I
Found in a cupboard cut of ibex, stewed it with carob
Beans, sliced apple, onion, thyme-sprig. And so we had supper,
Sharing a skin of Aetnian wine until the midnight
Hour, then tiptoed tipsily back to our mantled love-bed.
Drowsily entwined, we moved slowly, softly, withholding
Ourselves in sweet delays until at last we yielded,
Mingling our natural flow, feeling it almost linger
Into our sleep.

         Stirred by the melilot daylight, I woke up.
Chelos lay asprawl and I knew that he must be dreaming of me
For he murmured "Pyrrha". I fondled his ithyphallus,
   uncapped it,
Saw for the first time the knob, a purple-red plum, yet firmer.
Covering him like a man, I moved until he gripped me:
Faster, yet faster, we sped, determined down-thrust rivalling
Up-thrust – succus glissading us – exquisite spasm
Contracting, dilating, changed into minute preparatory
Orgasms, a pleasure unknown to man, that culminated
Within their narrowing circles into the great orgasmos.'

PATRICK KAVANAGH

Born Inniskeen, County Monaghan, 1904. Left school early to work as small farmer and shoemaker. Moved in 1939 to Dublin, where he eked out a living on the fringes of literary journalism. Ran own newspaper, *Kavanagh's Weekly*, for thirteen issues in 1952. Died 1967, the year of his marriage. Two semi-comic prose works, *The Green Fool* (1938) and *Tarry Flynn* (1948), give respectively indulgent and unsparing portraits of the struggles of a poetic young man in an impoverished rural community.

With its subtly heightened colloquial speech rhythms and direct apprehension of experience, unmediated by myth or literary allusiveness, Kavanagh's work has immense appeal in Ireland. The poetry's challenge to the Literary Revival's idealisation of the peasant tends to be read – a shade too comfortably, perhaps – as a vindication of day-to-day Irishness. Kavanagh is grittily realistic about the rural scene alike in his rhapsodic lyrics and in *The Great Hunger* (1942), his impassioned complaint against the miseries of small-farm life. 'Father Mat', derived from an abandoned long poem *Why Sorrow?*, strikes a balance between characteristic impulses towards praise and protest. 'The Twelfth of July' and 'Elegy for Jim Larkin' confront the petit-bourgeois, Catholic values of the southern state while absorbing politics into an edgy, visionary subjectivity. Shifting registers with consummate skill behind its ostentatiously ramshackle exterior, 'The Hospital' is perhaps the most remarkable of ten sonnets written in the wake of an operation for lung cancer in 1954.

TO THE MAN AFTER THE HARROW

Now leave the check-reins slack,
The seed is flying far to-day –
The seed like stars against the black
Eternity of April clay.

This seed is potent as the seed
Of knowledge in the Hebrew Book,

So drive your horses in the creed
Of God the Father as a stook.

Forget the men on Brady's hill.
Forget what Brady's boy may say.
For destiny will not fulfil
Unless you let the harrow play.

Forget the worm's opinion too
Of hooves and pointed harrow-pins,
For you are driving your horses through
The mist where Genesis begins.

STONY GREY SOIL

O stony grey soil of Monaghan
The laugh from my love you thieved;
You took the gay child of my passion
And gave me your clod-conceived.

You clogged the feet of my boyhood
And I believed that my stumble
Had the poise and stride of Apollo
And his voice my thick-tongued mumble.

You told me the plough was immortal!
O green-life-conquering plough!
Your mandril strained, your coulter blunted
In the smooth lea-field of my brow.

You sang on steaming dunghills
A song of cowards' brood,
You perfumed my clothes with weasel itch,
You fed me on swinish food.

You flung a ditch on my vision
Of beauty, love and truth.
O stony grey soil of Monaghan
You burgled my bank of youth!

Lost the long hours of pleasure
All the women that love young men.
O can I still stroke the monster's back
Or write with unpoisoned pen

His name in these lonely verses
Or mention the dark fields where
The first gay flight of my lyric
Got caught in a peasant's prayer.

Mullahinsha, Drummeril, Black Shanco –
Wherever I turn I see
In the stony grey soil of Monaghan
Dead loves that were born for me.

from THE GREAT HUNGER

I

Clay is the word and clay is the flesh
Where the potato-gatherers like mechanised scarecrows move
Along the side-fall of the hill – Maguire and his men.
If we watch them an hour is there anything we can prove
Of life as it is broken-backed over the Book
Of Death? Here crows gabble over worms and frogs
And the gulls like old newspapers are blown clear of the
    hedges, luckily.
Is there some light of imagination in these wet clods?
Or why do we stand here shivering?
                                        Which of these men
Loved the light and the queen
Too long virgin? Yesterday was summer. Who was it promised
    marriage to himself
Before apples were hung from the ceilings for Hallowe'en?
We will wait and watch the tragedy to the last curtain,
Till the last soul passively like a bag of wet clay
Rolls down the side of the hill, diverted by the angles
Where the plough missed or a spade stands, straitening the way.

A dog lying on a torn jacket under a heeled-up cart,
A horse nosing along the posied headland, trailing
A rusty plough. Three heads hanging between wide-apart
Legs. October playing a symphony on a slack wire paling.
Maguire watches the drills flattened out
And the flints that lit a candle for him on a June altar
Flameless. The drills slipped by and the days slipped by
And he trembled his head away and ran free from the world's
    halter,
And thought himself wiser than any man in the townland
When he laughed over pints of porter
Of how he came free from every net spread
In the gaps of experience. He shook a knowing head
And pretended to his soul
That children are tedious in hurrying fields of April
Where men are spanging across wide furrows.
Lost in the passion that never needs a wife –
The pricks that pricked were the pointed pins of harrows.
Children scream so loud that the crows could bring
The seed of an acre away with crow-rude jeers.
Patrick Maguire, he called his dog and he flung a stone in the air
And hallooed the birds away that were the birds of the years.

Turn over the weedy clods and tease out the tangled skeins.
What is he looking for there?
He thinks it is a potato, but we know better
Than his mud-gloved fingers probe in this insensitive hair.

'Move forward the basket and balance it steady
In this hollow. Pull down the shafts of that cart, Joe,
And straddle the horse,' Maguire calls.
'The wind's over Brannagan's, now that means rain.
Graip up some withered stalks and see that no potato falls
Over the tail-board going down the ruckety pass –
And *that's* a job we'll have to do in December.
Gravel it and build a kerb on the bog-side. Is that Cassidy's ass
Out in my clover? Curse o' God –
Where is that dog?
Never where he's wanted.' Maguire grunts and spits
Through a clay-wattled moustache and stares about him from the
    height.

His dream changes like the cloud-swung wind
And he is not so sure now if his mother was right
When she praised the man who made a field his bride.

Watch him, watch him, that man on a hill whose spirit
Is a wet sack flapping about the knees of time.
He lives that his little fields may stay fertile when his own body
Is spread in the bottom of a ditch under two coulters crossed in
    Christ's Name.

He was suspicious in his youth as a rat near strange bread,
When girls laughed; when they screamed he knew that meant
The cry of fillies in season. He could not walk
The easy road to destiny. He dreamt
The innocence of young brambles to hooked treachery.
O the grip, O the grip of irregular fields! No man escapes.
It could not be that back of the hills love was free
And ditches straight.
No monster hand lifted up children and put down apes
As here.
                    'O God if I had been wiser!'
That was his sigh like the brown breeze in the thistles.
He looks towards his house and haggard. 'O God if I had been
    wiser!'
But now a crumpled leaf from the whitethorn bushes
Darts like a frightened robin, and the fence
Shows the green of after-grass through a little window,
And he knows that his own heart is calling his mother a liar
God's truth is life – even the grotesque shapes of his foulest fire.

The horse lifts its head and cranes
Through the whins and stones
To lip late passion in the crawling clover.
In the gap there's a bush weighted with boulders like morality,
The fools of life bleed if they climb over.

The wind leans from Brady's, and the coltsfoot leaves are holed
    with rust,
Rain fills the cart-tracks and the sole-plate grooves;
A yellow sun reflects in Donaghmoyne
The poignant light in puddles shaped by hooves.

Come with me, Imagination, into this iron house
And we will watch from the doorway the years run back,
And we will know what a peasant's left hand wrote on the page.
Be easy, October. No cackle hen, horse neigh, tree sough, duck
    quack.

from III

Poor Paddy Maguire, a fourteen-hour day
He worked for years. It was he that lit the fire
And boiled the kettle and gave the cows their hay.
His mother tall hard as a Protestant spire
Came down the stairs barefoot at the kettle-call
And talked to her son sharply: 'Did you let
The hens out, you?' She had a venomous drawl
And a wizened face like moth-eaten leatherette.
Two black cats peeped between the banisters
And gloated over the bacon-fizzling pan.
Outside the window showed tin canisters.
The snipe of Dawn fell like a whirring stone
And Patrick on a headland stood alone.

The pull is on the traces, it is March
And a cold black wind is blowing from Dundalk.
The twisting sod rolls over on her back –
The virgin screams before the irresistible sock.
No worry on Maguire's mind this day
Except that he forgot to bring his matches.
'Hop back there Polly, hoy back, woa, wae',
From every second hill a neighbour watches
With all the sharpened interest of rivalry.
Yet sometimes when the sun comes through a gap
These men know God the Father in a tree:
The Holy Spirit is the rising sap,
And Christ will be the green leaves that will come
At Easter from the sealed and guarded tomb . . .

XIV

We may come out into the October reality, Imagination,
The sleety wind no longer slants to the black hill where Maguire
And his men are now collecting the scattered harness and baskets.

The dog sitting on a wisp of dry stalks
Watches them through the shadows.
'Back in, back in.' One talks to the horse as to a brother.
Maguire himself is patting a potato-pit against the weather –
An old man fondling a new-piled grave:
'Joe, I hope you didn't forget to hide the spade,
For there's rogues in the townland. Hide it flat in a furrow.
I think we ought to be finished by to-morrow.'
Their voices through the darkness sound like voices from a cave,
A dull thudding far away, futile, feeble, far away,
First cousins to the ghosts of the townland.

A light stands in a window Mary Anne
Has the table set and the tea-pot waiting in the ashes.
She goes to the door and listens and then she calls
From the top of the haggard-wall:
'What's keeping you
And the cows to be milked and all the other work there's to do?'
'All right, all right,
We'll not stay here all night.'

Applause, applause,
The curtain falls.
Applause, applause
From the homing carts and the trees
And the bawling cows at the gates.
From the screeching water-hens
And the mill-race heavy with the Lammas floods curving over
    the weir.
A train at the station blowing off steam
And the hysterical laughter of the defeated everywhere.
Night, and the futile cards are shuffled again.
Maguire spreads his legs over the impotent cinders that wake no
    manhood now
And he hardly looks to see which card is trump.
His sister tightens her legs and her lips and frizzles up
Like the wick of an oil-less lamp.
The curtain falls –
Applause, applause.

Maguire is not afraid of death, the Church will light him a candle
To see his way through the vaults and he'll understand the
Quality of the clay that dribbles over his coffin.
He'll know the names of the roots that climb down to tickle his
    feet.
And he will feel no different than when he walked through
    Donaghmoyne.

If he stretches out a hand – a wet clod,
If he opens his nostrils – a dungy smell;
If he opens his eyes once in a million years –
Through a crack in the crust of the earth he may see a face
    nodding in
Or a woman's legs. Shut them again for that sight is sin.

He will hardly remember that life happened to him –
Something was brighter a moment. Somebody sang in the
    distance.
A procession passed down a mesmerised street.
He remembers names like Easter and Christmas
By the colour his fields were.
Maybe he will be born again, a bird of an angel's conceit
To sing the gospel of life
To a music as flightily tangent
As a tune on an oboe.
And the serious look of the fields will have changed to the leer
    of a hobo
Swaggering celestially home to his three wishes granted.
Will that be? will that be?
Or is the earth right that laughs haw-haw
And does not believe
In an unearthly law.
The earth that says:
Patrick Maguire, the old peasant, can neither be damned nor
    glorified:
The graveyard in which he will lie will be just a deep-drilled
    potato-field
Where the seed gets no chance to come through
To the fun of the sun.
The tongue in his mouth is the root of a yew.
Silence, silence. The story is done.

He stands in the doorway of his house
A ragged sculpture of the wind,
October creaks the rotted mattress,
The bedposts fall. No hope. No lust.
The hungry fiend
Screams the apocalypse of clay
In every corner of this land.

THE TWELFTH OF JULY

The Twelfth of July, the voice of Ulster speaking,
Tart as week-old buttermilk from a churn,
Surprising the tired palates of the south.
I said to myself: From them we have much to learn –
Hard business-talk, no mediaeval babble,
But the sudden knife of reality running to the heart
With experience. The pageantry of Scarva
Recalled the Greek idea of dramatic art.
The horse-dealers from the Moy or Banbridge,
The Biblical farmers from Richhill or Coleraine.
All that was sharp, precise and pungent flavoured –
Ah! an Ulster imagined! For here from the train
At Amiens Street come gin-and-bitter blondes,
The slot machines that give us all the 'answers',
And young men out of Ulster who will dare
To drive a wedge in Dublin's Lounge Bar panzers.

TARRY FLYNN

On an apple-ripe September morning
Through the mist-chill fields I went
With a pitch-fork on my shoulder
Less for use than for devilment.

The threshing mill was set up, I knew,
In Cassidy's haggard last night,

And we owed them a day at the threshing
Since last year. O it was delight.

To be paying bills of laughter
And chaffy gossip in kind
With work thrown in to ballast
The fantasy-soaring mind.

As I crossed the wooden bridge I wondered
As I looked into the drain
If ever a summer morning should find me
Shovelling up eels again.

And I thought of the wasps' nest in the bank
And how I got chased one day
Leaving the drag and the scraw-knife behind,
How I covered my face with hay.

The wet leaves of the cocksfoot
Polished my boots as I
Went round by the glistening bog-holes
Lost in unthinking joy.

I'll be carrying bags to-day, I mused,
The best job at the mill
With plenty of time to talk of our loves
As we wait for the bags to fill.

Maybe Mary might call round . . .
And then I came to the haggard gate,
And I knew as I entered that I had come
Through fields that were part of no earthly estate.

A CHRISTMAS CHILDHOOD

I

One side of the potato-pits was white with frost –
How wonderful that was, how wonderful!

40

And when we put our ears to the paling-post
The music that came out was magical.

The light between the ricks of hay and straw
Was a hole in Heaven's gable. An apple tree
With its December-glinting fruit we saw –
O you, Eve, were the world that tempted me.

To eat the knowledge that grew in clay
And death the germ within it! Now and then
I can remember something of the gay
Garden that was childhood's. Again

The tracks of cattle to a drinking-place,
A green stone lying sideways in a ditch
Or any common sight the transfigured face
Of a beauty that the world did not touch.

II

My father played the melodeon
Outside at our gate;
There were stars in the morning east
And they danced to his music.

Across the wild bogs his melodeon called
To Lennons and Callans.
As I pulled on my trousers in a hurry
I knew some strange thing had happened.

Outside in the cow-house my mother
Made the music of milking;
The light of her stable-lamp was a star
And the frost of Bethlehem made it twinkle.

A water-hen screeched in the bog,
Mass-going feet
Crunched the wafer-ice on the pot-holes,
Somebody wistfully twisted the bellows wheel.

My child poet picked out the letters
On the grey stone,
In silver the wonder of a Christmas townland,
The winking glitter of a frosty dawn.

Cassiopeia was over
Cassidy's hanging hill,
I looked and three whin bushes rode across
The horizon – the Three Wise Kings.

An old man passing said:
'Can't he make it talk' –
The melodeon. I hid in the doorway
And tightened the belt of my box-pleated coat.

I nicked six nicks on the door-post
With my penknife's big blade –
There was a little one for cutting tobacco.
And I was six Christmases of age.

My father played the melodeon,
My mother milked the cows,
And I had a prayer like a white rose pinned
On the Virgin Mary's blouse.

FATHER MAT

I

In a meadow
Beside the chapel three boys were playing football.
At the forge door an old man was leaning
Viewing a hunter-hoe. A man could hear
If he listened to the breeze the fall of wings –
How wistfully the sin-birds come home!

It was Confession Saturday, the first
Saturday in May; the May Devotions
Were spread like leaves to quieten

The excited armies of conscience.
The knife of penance fell so like a blade
Of grass that no one was afraid.

Father Mat came slowly walking, stopping to
Stare through gaps at ancient Ireland sweeping
In again with all its unbaptized beauty:
The calm evening,
The whitethorn blossoms,
The smell from ditches that were not Christian.
The dancer that dances in the hearts of men cried:
Look! I have shown this to you before –
The rags of living surprised
The joy in things you cannot forget.

His heavy hat was square upon his head,
Like a Christian Brother's;
His eyes were an old man's watery eyes,

Out of his flat nose grew spiky hairs.
He was a part of the place,
Natural as a round stone in a grass field;
He could walk through a cattle fair
And the people would only notice his odd spirit there.

His curate passed on a bicycle –
He had the haughty intellectual look
Of the man who never reads in brook or book;
A man designed
To wear a mitre,
To sit on committees –
For will grows strongest in the emptiest mind.

The old priest saw him pass
And, seeing, saw
Himself a mediaeval ghost.
Ahead of him went Power,
One who was not afraid when the sun opened a flower,
Who was never astonished
At a stick carried down a stream
Or at the undying difference in the corner of a field.

The Holy Ghost descends
At random like the muse
On wise man and fool,
And why should poet in the twilight choose?

Within the dim chapel was the grey
Mumble of prayer
To the Queen of May –
The Virgin Mary with the schoolgirl air.

Two guttering candles on a brass shrine
Raised upon the wall
Monsters of despair
To terrify deep into the soul.

Through the open door the hum of rosaries
Came out and blended with the homing bees.
                              The trees
Heard nothing stranger than the rain or the wind
Or the birds –
But deep in their roots they knew a seed had sinned.

In the graveyard a goat was nibbling at a yew,
The cobbler's chickens with anxious looks
Were straggling home through nettles, over graves.
A young girl down a hill was driving cows
To a corner at the gable-end of a roofless house.

Cows were milked earlier,
The supper hurried,
Hens shut in,
Horses unyoked,
And three men shaving before the same mirror.

III

The trip of iron tips on tile
Hesitated up the middle aisle,
Heads that were bowed glanced up to see
Who could this last arrival be.

Murmur of women's voices from the porch,
Memories of relations in the graveyard.
On the stem
Of memory imaginations blossom.

                        In the dim
Corners in the side seats faces gather,
Lit up now and then by a guttering candle
And the ghost of day at the window.
A secret lover is saying
Three Hail Marys that she who knows
The ways of women will bring
Cathleen O'Hara (he names her) home to him.
Ironic fate! Cathleen herself is saying
Three Hail Marys to her who knows
The ways of men to bring
Somebody else home to her –
'O may he love me.'
What is the Virgin Mary now to do?

                        IV
        From a confessional
The voice of Father Mat's absolving
Rises and falls like a briar in the breeze.
As the sins pour in the old priest is thinking
His fields of fresh grass, his horses, his cows,
His earth into the fires of Purgatory.
It cools his mind.
'They confess to the fields,' he mused,
'They confess to the fields and the air and the sky',
And forgiveness was the soft grass of his meadow by the river;
His thoughts were walking through it now.

His human lips talked on:
'My son,
Only the poor in spirit shall wear the crown;
Those down
Can creep in the low door
On to Heaven's floor.'

The Tempter had another answer ready:
'Ah lad, upon the road of life
'Tis best to dance with Chance's wife
And let the rains that come in time
Erase the footprints of the crime.'

The dancer that dances in the hearts of men
Tempted him again:
'Look! I have shown you this before;
From this mountain-top I have tempted Christ
With what you see now
Of beauty – all that's music, poetry, art
In things you can touch every day.
I broke away
And rule all dominions that are rare;
I took with me all the answers to every prayer
That young men and girls pray for: love, happiness, riches –'
O Tempter! O Tempter!

V

As Father Mat walked home
Venus was in the western sky
And there were voices in the hedges:
'God the Gay is not the Wise.'

'Take your choice, take your choice,'
Called the breeze through the bridge's eye.
'The domestic Virgin and Her Child
Or Venus with her ecstasy.'

ELEGY FOR JIM LARKIN
died February 1947

Not with public words can his greatness
Be told to children, for he was more
Than labour agitator, mob orator
The flashing fiery sword merely was witness
To the sun rising. Cried Larkin: Look!

The fields are producing for you and the trees;
And beyond are not the serf stockland, but seas
Rolling excitement in God's Poetry Book.
When the full moon's in the river the ghost of bread
Must not be in all your weary trudgings home.
The masts of once black galleys will become
Fir forests under the North's glittering Plough,
And the rusty gantries, the heroic ahead
With man the magician whom the gods endow.

It was thus I heard Jim Larkin shout above
The crowd who would have him turn aside
From the day's shocking reality. Their morphine pride
Hid in the fogs of unhope and would not move –
The smoke and the drug of the newspaper story;
And with mouths open they were glad to stare
Not at a blackbird, but a millionaire
Whose two-year-olds ran off with all their worry –
Though batoned by policemen into Dublin's garbage.
Jim Larkin opened a window wide
And wings flew out and offered to slow rising things
A lift onto high altars with proud carriage.
And they swayed above the city in young knowledge
And they ate the loaf that nourishes great kings.

EPIC

I have lived in important places, times
When great events were decided, who owned
That half a rood of rock, a no-man's land
Surrounded by our pitchfork-armed claims.
I heard the Duffys shouting 'Damn your soul'
And old McCabe stripped to the waist, seen
Step the plot defying blue cast-steel –
'Here is the march along these iron stones'.
That was the year of the Munich bother. Which
Was more important? I inclined
To lose my faith in Ballyrush and Gortin

Till Homer's ghost came whispering to my mind
He said: I made the Iliad from such
A local row. Gods make their own importance.

INNOCENCE

They laughed at one I loved –
The triangular hill that hung
Under the Big Forth. They said
That I was bounded by the whitethorn hedges
Of the little farm and did not know the world.
But I knew that love's doorway to life
Is the same doorway everywhere.

Ashamed of what I loved
I flung her from me and called her a ditch
Although she was smiling at me with violets.

But now I am back in her briary arms
The dew of an Indian Summer morning lies
On bleached potato-stalks –
What age am I?

I do not know what age I am,
I am no mortal age;
I know nothing of women,
Nothing of cities,
I cannot die
Unless I walk outside these whitethorn hedges.

KERR'S ASS

We borrowed the loan of Kerr's big ass
To go to Dundalk with butter,
Brought him home the evening before the market
An exile that night in Mucker.

We heeled up the cart before the door,
We took the harness inside –
The straw-stuffed straddle, the broken breeching
With bits of bull-wire tied;

The winkers that had no choke-band,
The collar and the reins . . .
In Ealing Broadway, London Town
I name their several names

Until a world comes to life –
Morning, the silent bog,
And the God of imagination waking
In a Mucker fog.

THE HOSPITAL

A year ago I fell in love with the functional ward
Of a chest hospital: square cubicles in a row
Plain concrete, wash basins – an art lover's woe,
Not counting how the fellow in the next bed snored.
But nothing whatever is by love debarred,
The common and banal her heat can know.
The corridor led to a stairway and below
Was the inexhaustible adventure of a gravelled yard.

This is what love does to things: the Rialto Bridge,
The main gate that was bent by a heavy lorry,
The seat at the back of a shed that was a suntrap.
Naming these things is the love-act and its pledge;
For we must record love's mystery without claptrap,
Snatch out of time the passionate transitory.

PADRAIC FALLON

Born Athenry, County Galway, 1905. Educated at the Cistercian
boarding school in Roscrea, County Tipperary. Worked as a customs
official in Cavan, Wexford and Dublin. A prolific radio dramatist,
he retired to Cornwall, 1967, then to Kinsale, County Cork, 1971.
Died 1974.

If a taste for the exotic and a tendency to overwrite spoils some of
Fallon's poems, at his best he is capable of meditative stamina and
pictorial vividness. 'Yeats at Athenry Perhaps' is the sturdiest of a series
of troubled explorations of the relevance of the Literary Revival
and its Olympian leader to the ordinary life of Ireland; like 'Gurteen',
it builds its effects on a colloquial naturalism. All but the opening poem
in the selection come from the last decade and a half of Fallon's career.

A FLASK OF BRANDY

You, said the Lionwoman,
Pliz, this errand, a snipe of brandy
From the first shop. Here's money;
And for you this penny.

And on my way I saw:
Item, a clown who waltzed on stilts;
A bear saluting with a paw;
Two pairs of dancing dogs in kilts;
Eight midget ponies in a single file,
A very piccolo of ponies;
Then the princess far off in her smile;
And the seven beautiful distant ladies:
And then –

Facing after the big bandwagon, he
The boy in spangles, lonely and profound:
Behind him the Ringmaster, a redfaced man,

Followed by silence heavy as a wound,
And empty.

Quickly as two feet can did I come back
To the Lionwoman with her cognac.

You, said the Lionwoman;
Pliz to the window, said foreign gutterals in
The cave of the caravan.
I waited, errand done.

And waiting on one foot saw:
Item: a twitching coloured chintz
Moved by a lemontaloned claw:
And after a woman with her face in paints,
A throat thickened in its round of tan
On shoulders sick and white with nature;
Behind was a pair of bloomers on a line,
Blue; a table with a tin platter:
More else:

A black electric cat, a stove, a pot
Purring, and a wild Red Indian blanket
Crouching sidewise on a bunk;
And some exciting smell that stunk
Till the Lionwoman rising blotted out
All but a breast as heavy as a sigh
That stared at me from one bruised eye.

KILTARTAN LEGEND

Penelope pulls home
Rogue-lord, artist, world wanderer,
Simply by sitting in a house,
Its sturdy genius;
Of all sirens the most dangerous.

She'll sit them out,
The curious wonders, the ventriloquial voices,

Spacious landfalls, the women, beds in the blue;
Her oceanography
The garden pond, her compass a knitting needle.

The arc-lamped earth, she knows,
Will burn away and she
Still potter among her flowers waiting for him;
Apollo runs before
Touching the blossoms, her unborn sons.

Knitting, unknitting at the half heard
Music of her tapestry, afraid
Of the sunburned body, the organs, the red beard
Of the unshipped mighty male
Home from the fairy tale;

Providing for him
All that's left of her she ties and knots
Threads everywhere; the luminous house
Must hold and will
Her trying warlord home.

Will she know him?
Dignity begs the question that must follow.
She bends to the web where her lord's face
Glitters but has no fellow
And humbly, or most royally, adds her own.

YEATS AT ATHENRY PERHAPS

1

We had our towers too, a large
Stone soldiery at bridge and gateway, they
Were the whole town once;
And I could have nodded to him from the top
Tendril of ivy or a jackdaw's nest;
But I'd never heard of him, the famous poet,
Who lived as the crow flies fifteen miles away.

Certainly he'd have touched us changing trains
For Gort, have hours to idle, shared
The silence of our small town shell;
Maybe he passed me by
In a narrow-gutted street, an aimless
Straying gentleman, and I
The jerseyed fellow driving out the cows.

Ours was a sightseeing place that had
Exhausted history, but old wars had left
A dead king and a moat
And walls still half alive that watched
From towers with broken rims. I doubt
He bothered with us, all his sight turned in;
Some poems come better waiting for a train.

And that winged footprint could have jarred
The peasant metres of a street given over
To baker, grocer, butcher and
The treadmill of the till. What would he think
Of our outcropping sheds, the architecture
Of the very necessary animal?
And little better our weathered Famine chapel?

But on the eve of May he might have found
Things near his heart, Fertilities
Dropping in;
For then from consecrated ground we moved
The Virgin to the leafing trees
With bonfires, chanting children, the whole works;
The Canon hadn't read the latest books
On golden boughs and odd divinities.

Or would he have looked superior, been difficult
About Our Lady's face, the soft Italian
Look of the milking mother, not the sort
That strings the whole air like a catapult?
This was no moon in women, no
Unpredictable lady sailing
Her wavy shell;
Ours kept the house and answered the chapel bell.

Or so we thought or didn't think at all.
Diana has her secrets from the oak;
The nunlike night commits itself in strokes
Of barbarous shorthand when the candles die.
What's fifteen miles? We could have read together
The same nightscript, felt the vibrations run,
Boughs singing, with the whole south moving up
To stand in a dripping arch of spring.

2

I'd like to think how over the sheep and crops,
The nut-creggs and the loose stone walls we met
In a mutual hazard of burning arrows, but
I was too small then, my wavelengths caught
In anything low-down as a hawthorn tree
And jammed there for a day or all the summer,
Time no object, profession poetry.

Anyway he wouldn't have dared a town
Where every peeling window was an eye;
We smiled of course at strangers, proud
Of a dead king, the lordly
Dung that simmered in the ground. But I could
Have walked him round the moat, in Kingsland shown the rock
Where the crown toppled from the last Irish head
And a royal footsole left a bloody track.

No, he'd have sat down by the line and waited
Melting his bits of ore or watched the sky
Jolt from the saltmills of the Atlantic over
A town that died so often of the rain;
Why muddy a feathered foot when a great house waited
Over in Coole among the trees
(He liked his heraldry alive, well baited)
With all the amenities for Muse and man,
Leda's kingbird on a lake, a lawn
For Juno's peacock, tranquil as a frieze.

from THREE HOUSES

1 GURTEEN

I had no gift for it.
It hung out in the welter of the moor;
A black-faced country staring in

All day. Never did the sun
Explode with flowers in the dark vases
Of the windows. The fall was wrong

And there was uplifted the striking north
Before the door.
We lived in the flintlights of a cavern floor.

It was enemy country too, the rafts of the low
Fields foundering. Every day the latch
Lifted to some catastrophe, such as

A foal dead in an outfield, a calf lost
In a mud-suck, a hen laying wild in the rushes,
A bullock strayed, a goose gone with the fox;

The epic, if any, going on too long.
Nil the glory in it, null the profit;
It was too big for me and full of threat.

A place that glugged green in the vast egg
Of the weather, too littered with rains
And with minor stone-age tragedies like getting wet

Feet in the goose paddock watching
An angel, yes, in the air, in the dusk, taking
A rose petal face out of nothing in particular,

Just happening big out of a glitter,
Unaware of me or the black-avised country where
The half-wheel of the day was bogging down.

Certainly it could have been the moon.
And though I prefer to think otherwise
Nothing happened in the way of ecstasy.

And I took indoors my gawky childhood, still
Unmeasured, through mud and the yard midden
That was acting up and coming into the kitchen

With the milkers, with the men, with the weather,
Feeling as ever that the earth is outside matter
Trying to get in, to get into the very centre

Swamp the sunflowers and stone circles
And all that spirals and wings up, to bring
The tiller back on the old compost heap,

Dung value. Petering out
Like this father-figure at the fire
Crumbling into space, who was something once,

Who was the sage here and the reason, who raised
The roof, begot the tree,
Hedged the apple and built the causeway down

For the postman who never comes, who touched
The harsh sex of the earth that never blooms,
And was gentled by this woman who stands in the door now,

The mistress of a few iron pots,
With the bogface looking in and the barbarous furrows.
I tell of my angel and the bright thing is lost

In the cud of cows, in the farming day,
Never to bloom again and wash the air
Towards Clonkeen Carle. I sit down by the fire

And build my nightly stockade in the ash
With an old catalogue, Army & Navy Stores,
And polish two pennies bright

While earth and day go under. Buoyed up
In their bundles on the nightwave are the plovers,
Blown with the sweet pith of their bones over, the men

Drift off to visit other outposts of
Man in nameless townlands, moon-swollen damps.
The two old people sit it out,

And humped in the very posture of the womb
On a small stool I ride it too,
The dull incessant siege, on the black orb –
The epic, if any, going on too long.

A BIT OF BRASS

A horn hung on an oak;
And he, the big overplus, the hero
Destined, sounds the famous note, invokes
Cascading Gods and
His own death boat.

I did lift
A bit of battered brass once to my mouth,
May 1915, after
A day's rain
In the townwalled field where the Volunteers
Drilled;

That evening the wet overhang had daunted all,
Bugler and mate
Gossiped under a leaking branch, sounding
An occasional call,
Joe Egan, Josie Rooney;
Dear Posterity, I was there.

Echoes hung
Solidly in the drowned green beechtrees,
Hardly swinging;
Call after call brought no one to the field,

That is no man alive;
The mates gave up and I purloined the thing;

Squawk, a couple of fancy tootles,
Then out of Me minus
It came, the soaring
Thing;
Just once.

It could be it still hangs
In the May over
Leonards and the Pound Walk, just waiting
Those fellows, the long striders
Gods or men
To take the field.

BRIAN COFFEY

Born Dun Laoghaire, County Dublin, 1905. Educated at Clongowes
Wood College and University College Dublin. Abandoned science for
philosophy in Paris in early 1930s. Lived in England during the
Second World War. Doctorate in philosophy from Institut Catholique,
Paris, 1947. Lectured in philosophy at the University of St Louis,
Missouri, from that year until 1952, when he returned to England.
Taught mathematics in London schools until 1972. Lived in
Southampton until his death in 1995.

Formally, Coffey was perhaps the most anti traditional of the group of
polyglot young poets – Beckett, Coffey, Devlin, George Reavey, Niall
Sheridan and Niall Montgomery – who gathered round MacGreevy in
the 1930s. The best of his early work shakes off echoes of Eliot and
Pound to pioneer the minimalist lyric mode perfected by Beckett after
the Second World War. Eschewing what he called 'the aeolian
flatulence of tail-end rhyme', Coffey explores philosophical aspects of
themes such as exile, interpersonal responsibility and the artistic act
in a rhythmically chaste free verse. The selections come from
the 1970s and 1980s, the most various and prolific decades
of a lengthy career.

from DEATH OF HEKTOR

6

Homer   where born where buried of whom the son
what journeys undertaken not known   His work
abides witness to unfaltering sad gaze constrained
A harp he uses   background for verses sung
He pared no fingernails not indifferent   not masked
Light we suppose once had entered eyes to brand memory
with noon's exact flame of sun mirrored in wind-stirred sea
Black night for death   Colours of morning evening for life
the rose the glaucous the amethystine wave-work carpeting
maimed anatomy black white red of man at war
screams the women keening patience the emptied hearts

His ears open to spoken word and words down time like
    wind-blown sand
words of triumph unsleeping enmities wound-up spells
    malice
swirl of sound continual mixed in a perfect ear
surfacing coherent truer than history all and everything

Prudent Homer who survived to make his poems
did he keep unsaid wordly in innermost anguished heart
what would not have pleased his client banqueters
not reached by resonance the hearts of self-approving
    lords
yet at last might reach our raddled selves

from FOR WHAT FOR WHOM UNWANTED

1

And where no snow had
fallen
to cover just sleeping earth
where no green awakening
promised highway with sun
dance laughter
in such a matt grey place
of unexpectant waiting
backward staring
those saffron white and purple
reflected from bright eyes
lit up that dust and patience
waste and empty game
for what it was
Suddenly he was a snow field
suddenly bright flowers stirred
suddenly a world was ready
for her walking through.

8

Consider his song

Never to have seen
never to have given
never to have taken

Ever vain homing
ever what is new
and not her

Ever the torn heart
scribed 'You'

Never enough seen
never enough given
never enough taken

Never departure
never what is new
and not her

Ever no change
saying all ways
'You'

SAMUEL BECKETT

Born Foxrock, Dublin, 1906. Educated at Portora Royal School,
Enniskillen, and Trinity College Dublin. Succeeded MacGreevy as
Trinity *lecteur* at École Normale Supérieure, Paris, 1929. Taught modern
languages at Trinity, 1930–2. Abruptly left Ireland, 1932. Settled Paris,
1937. Involved in Resistance. Fled to south of France, 1942, returning
to Paris after the war. The major fiction (*Molloy, Malone Dies,
The Unnameable*) and drama (*Waiting for Godot, Endgame*) written first in
French, then in English, 1946–56. Nobel Prize for Literature, 1969.
Died 1989.

Beckett's earliest poems play grotesque variations on modernist
allusiveness. A sparer, more elliptical idiom makes its appearance in the
mid-1930s in pieces like 'Cascando'. That poem's uncharacteristic
afflatus finds no echo in the austere (originally French) lyrics of the later
1940s, though even these are notably free of the bleak irony of the
novels and plays. The radio playlet *Words and Music* was composed in
English in 1961, and 'Roundelay' in 1976.

CASCANDO

1

why not merely the despaired of
occasion of
wordshed

is it not better abort than be barren

the hours after you are gone are so leaden
they will always start dragging too soon
the grapples clawing blindly the bed of want
bringing up the bones the old loves
sockets filled once with eyes like yours
all always is it better too soon than never
the black want splashing their faces
saying again nine days never floated the loved

nor nine months
nor nine lives

2

saying again
if you do not teach me I shall not learn
saying again there is a last
even of last times
last times of begging
last times of loving
of knowing not knowing pretending
a last even of last times of saying
if you do not love me I shall not be loved
if I do not love you I shall not love

the churn of stale words in the heart again
love love love thud of the old plunger
pestling the unalterable
whey of words

terrified again
of not loving
of loving and not you
of being loved and not by you
of knowing not knowing pretending
pretending

I and all the others that will love you
if they love you

3

unless they love you

'my way is in the sand flowing'

my way is in the sand flowing
between the shingle and the dune
the summer rain rains on my life

63

on me my life harrying fleeing
to its beginning to its end

my peace is there in the receding mist
when I may cease from treading these long shifting
                                        thresholds
and live the space of a door
that opens and shuts

'what would I do without this world faceless incurious'

what would I do without this world faceless incurious
where to be lasts but an instant where every instant
spills in the void the ignorance of having been
without this wave where in the end
body and shadow together are engulfed
what would I do without this silence where the murmurs die
the pantings the frenzies towards succour towards love
without this sky that soars
above its ballast dust

what would I do what I did yesterday and the day before
peering out of my deadlight looking for another
wandering like me eddying far from all the living
in a convulsive space
among the voices voiceless
that throng my hiddenness

from WORDS AND MUSIC

Age is when to a man
Huddled o'er the ingle
Shivering for the hag
To put the pan in the bed
And bring the toddy
She comes in the ashes
Who loved could not be won
Or won not loved

Or some other trouble
Comes in the ashes
Like in that old light
The face in the ashes
That old starlight
On the earth again.

ROUNDELAY

on all that strand
at end of day
steps sole sound
long sole sound
until unbidden stay
then no sound
on all that strand
long no sound
until unbidden go
steps sole sound
long sole sound
on all that strand
at end of day

JOHN HEWITT

Born Belfast, 1907. Educated at Methodist College and Queen's
University Belfast. Worked for twenty-seven years in Belfast Museum
and Art Gallery. Passed over for post of director in 1953, apparently
because of his left-wing, anti-sectarian politics. Moved to Coventry as
director of the Herbert Art Gallery and Museum, 1957. Retired 1972
and returned to Belfast. Died 1987.

Hewitt's assiduously crafted, if formally unadventurous verse counters
the grand narratives of imperialism and nationalism with a democratic,
secular and yet recognisably Protestant empiricism. 'I may appear
Planter's Gothic,' he wrote in 1953, 'but there is a round tower
somewhere inside, and needled through every sentence I utter.'
Identifying with the radicalism of the Presbyterian United Irishmen and
of the eighteenth- and nineteenth-century Rhyming Weavers of Antrim
and Down (whose work he anthologised), Hewitt struggles to keep
viable a submerged Ulster tradition of tolerance and faith in human
progress. His Georgian manner is deceptive: he is capable of
considerable tough-mindedness, as in 'The Colony', where he sustains
an elaborate analogy between Roman colonists and the planters of
Ulster. He can also disarm criticism: 'A Local Poet' offers itself
alternatively as a wry critique of the neat closures of his style or as a self-
rebuke for the reticence of his work on the discrimination against
Catholics in the years leading up to the Troubles.

from FREEHOLD

from II THE LONELY HEART

Once in a seaside town with time to kill,
the windless winter-daylight ebbing chill,
the cafés shut till June, the shop blinds drawn,
only one pub yet open where a man
trundled his barrels off a dray with care,
and two men talking, small across the square,
I turned from broad street, down a red-brick row,
past prams in parlours and infrequent show

of thrusting bulbtips, till high steps and porch
and rigid statue signalised a church.
I climbed the granite past Saint Patrick's knees,
saw cross in stone, befingered, ringed with grease,
and water in a stoup with oily skin,
swung door on stall of booklets and went in
to the dim stained-glass cold interior
between low pews along a marble floor
to where the candles burned, still keeping pace
with ugly-coloured Stations of the Cross.
Two children tiptoed in and prayed awhile.
A shabby woman in a faded shawl
came hirpling past me then, and crumpled down,
crossing herself and mumbling monotone.

I stood and gazed across the altar rail
at the tall windows, cold and winter pale;
Christ and His Mother, Christ and Lazarus,
Christ watching Martha bustle round the house,
Christ crowned, with sceptre and a blessing hand.
I counted seven candles on the stand;
a box of matches of familiar brand
lay on a tray. It somehow seemed my right
to pay my penny and set up my light,
not to this coloured Christ nor to His Mother,
but single flame to sway with all the other
small earnest flames against the crowding gloom
which seemed that year descending on our time,
suppressed the fancy, smiled a cynic thought,
turned clicking heel on marble and went out.

Not this my fathers' faith: their walls are bare;
their comfort's all within, if anywhere.
I had gone there a vacant hour to pass,
to see the sculpture and admire the glass,
but left as I had come, a protestant,
and all unconscious of my yawning want;
too much intent on what to criticise
to give my heart the room to realise
that which endures the tides of time so long
cannot be always absolutely wrong;

not even with a friendly thought or human
for the two children and the praying woman.
The years since then have proved I should have stayed
and mercy might have touched me till I prayed.

For now I scorn no man's or child's belief
in any symbol that may succour grief
if we remember whence life first arose
and how within us yet that river flows;
and how the fabled shapes in dream's deep sea
still evidence our continuity
with being's seamless garment, web and thread.

O windblown grass upon the mounded dead,
O seed in crevice of the frost-split rock,
the power that fixed your root shall take us back,
though endlessly through aeons we are thrust
as luminous or unreflecting dust.

THE RAM'S HORN

I have turned to the landscape because men disappoint me:
the trunk of a tree is proud; when the woodmen fell it,
it still has a contained ionic solemnity:
it is a rounded event without the need to tell it.

I have never been compelled to turn away from the dawn
because it carries treason behind its wakened face:
even the horned ram, glowering over the bog hole,
though symbol of evil, will step through the blown grass with
   grace.

Animal, plant, or insect, stone or water,
are, every minute, themselves; they behave by law.
I am not required to discover motives for them,
or strip my heart to forgive the rat in the straw.

I live my best in the landscape, being at ease there;
the only trouble I find I have brought in my hand.

See, I let it fall with a rustle of stems in the nettles,
and never for a moment suppose that they understand.

THE COLONY

First came the legions, then the colonists,
provincials, landless citizens, and some
camp-followers of restless generals
content now only with the least of wars.
Among this rabble, some to feel more free
beyond the ready whim of Caesar's fist;
for conscience' sake the best of these, but others
because their debts had tongues, one reckless man,
a tax absconder with a sack of coin.

With these, young law clerks skilled with chart and stylus,
their boxes crammed with lease-scrolls duly marked
with distances and names, to be defined
when all was mapped.
                          When they'd surveyed the land,
they gave the richer tillage, tract by tract,
from the great captains down to men-at-arms,
some of the sprawling rents to be retained
by Caesar's mistresses in their far villas.

We planted little towns to garrison
the heaving country, heaping walls of earth
and keeping all our cattle close at hand;
then, thrusting north and west, we felled the trees,
selling them off the foothills, at a stroke
making quick profits, smoking out the nests
of the barbarian tribesmen, clan by clan,
who hunkered in their blankets, biding chance,
till, unobserved, they slither down and run
with torch and blade among the frontier huts
when guards were nodding, or when shining corn
bade sword-hand grip the sickle. There was once
a terrible year when, huddled in our towns,
my people trembled as the beacons ran

from hill to hill across the countryside,
calling the dispossessed to lift their standards.
There was great slaughter then, man, woman, child,
with fire and pillage of our timbered houses;
we had to build in stone for ever after.

That terror dogs us; back of all our thought
the threat behind the dream, those beacons flare,
and we run headlong, screaming in our fear;
fear quickened by the memory of guilt
for we began the plunder – naked men
still have their household gods and holy places,
and what a people loves it will defend.
We took their temples from them and forbade them,
for many years, to worship their strange idols.
They gathered secret, deep in the dripping glens,
chanting their prayers before a lichened rock.

We took the kindlier soils. It had been theirs,
this patient, temperate, slow, indifferent,
crop-yielding, crop-denying, in-neglect-
quickly-returning-to-the-nettle-and-bracken,
sodden and friendly land. We took it from them.
We laboured hard and stubborn, draining, planting,
till half the country took its shape from us.

Only among the hills with hare and kestrel
will you observe what once this land was like
before we made it fat for human use –
all but the forests, all but the tall trees –
I could invent a legend of those trees,
and how their creatures, dryads, hamadryads,
fled from the copses, hid in thorny bushes,
and grew a crooked and malignant folk,
plotting and waiting for a bitter revenge
on their despoilers. So our troubled thought
is from enchantments of the old tree magic,
but I am not a sick and haunted man . . .

Teams of the tamer natives we employed
to hew and draw, but did not call them slaves.

Some say this was our error. Others claim
we were too slow to make them citizens;
we might have made them Caesar's bravest legions.
This is a matter for historians,
or old beards in the Senate to wag over,
not pertinent to us these many years.

But here and there the land was poor and starved,
which, though we mapped, we did not occupy,
leaving the natives, out of laziness
in our demanding it, to hold unleased
the marshy quarters, fens, the broken hills,
and all the rougher places where the whin
still thrust from limestone with its cracking pods.

They multiplied and came with open hands,
begging a crust because their land was poor,
and they were many; squatting at our gates,
till our towns grew and threw them hovelled lanes
which they inhabit still. You may distinguish,
if you were schooled with us, by pigmentation,
by cast of features or by turn of phrase,
or by the clan names on them which are they,
among the faces moving in the street.
They worship Heaven strangely, having rites
we snigger at, are known as superstitious,
cunning by nature, never to be trusted,
given to dancing and a kind of song
seductive to the ear, a whining sorrow.
Also they breed like flies. The danger's there;
when Caesar's old and lays his sceptre down,
we'll be a little people, well outnumbered.

Some of us think our leases have run out
but dig square heels in, keep the roads repaired;
and one or two loud voices would restore
the rack, the yellow patch, the curfewed ghetto.
Most try to ignore the question, going their way,
glad to be living, sure that Caesar's word
is Caesar's bond for legions in our need.
Among us, some, beguiled by their sad music,

make common cause with the natives, in their hearts
hoping to win a truce when the tribes assert
their ancient right and take what once was theirs.
Already from other lands the legions ebb
and men no longer know the Roman peace.

Alone, I have a harder row to hoe:
I think these natives human, think their code,
though strange to us, and farther from the truth,
only a little so – to be redeemed
if they themselves rise up against the spells
and fears their celibates surround them with.
I find their symbols good, as such, for me,
when I walk in dark places of the heart;
but name them not to be misunderstood.
I know no vices they monopolise,
if we allow the forms by hunger bred,
the sores of old oppression, the deep skill
in all evasive acts, the swaddled minds,
admit our load of guilt – I mourn the trees
more than as symbol – and would make amends
by fraternising, by small friendly gestures,
hoping by patient words I may convince
my people and this people we are changed
from the raw levies which usurped the land,
if not to kin, to co-inhabitants,
as goat and ox may graze in the same field
and each gain something from proximity;
for we have rights drawn from the soil and sky;
the use, the pace, the patient years of labour,
the rain against the lips, the changing light,
the heavy clay-sucked stride, have altered us;
we would be strangers in the Capitol;
this is our country also, nowhere else;
and we shall not be outcast on the world.

SUBSTANCE AND SHADOW

There is a bareness in the images
I temper time with in my mind's defence;
they hold their own, their stubborn secrecies;
no use to rage against their reticence:
a gannet's plunge, a heron by a pond,
a last rook homing as the sun goes down,
a spider squatting on a bracken-frond,
and thistles in a cornsheaf's tufted crown,
a boulder on a hillside, lichen-stained,
the sparks of sun on dripping icicles,
their durable significance contained
in texture, colour, shape, and nothing else.
All these are sharp, spare, simple, native to
this small republic I have charted out
as the sure acre where my sense is true,
while round its boundaries sprawl the screes of doubt.

My lamp lights up the kettle on the stove
and throws its shadow on the whitewashed wall,
like some Assyrian profile with, above,
a snake, or bird-prowed helmet crested tall;
but this remains a shadow; when I shift
the lamp or move the kettle it is gone,
the substance and the shadow break adrift
that needed bronze to lock them, bronze or stone.

AN IRISHMAN IN COVENTRY

A full year since, I took this eager city,
the tolerance that laced its blatant roar,
its famous steeples and its web of girders,
as image of the state hope argued for,
and scarcely flung a bitter thought behind me
on all that flaws the glory and the grace
which ribbons through the sick, guilt-clotted legend
of my creed-haunted, godforsaken race.
My rhetoric swung round from steel's high promise

to the precision of the well-gauged tool,
tracing the logic in the vast glass headlands,
the clockwork horse, the comprehensive school.

Then, sudden, by occasion's chance concerted,
in enclave of my nation, but apart,
the jigging dances and the lilting fiddle
stirred the old rage and pity in my heart.
The faces and the voices blurring round me,
the strong hands long familiar with the spade,
the whiskey-tinctured breath, the pious buttons,
called up a people endlessly betrayed
by our own weakness, by the wrongs we suffered
in that long twilight over bog and glen,
by force, by famine and by glittering fables
which gave us martyrs when we needed men,
by faith which had no charity to offer,
by poisoned memory, and by ready wit,
with poverty corroded into malice,
to hit and run and howl when it is hit.
This is our fate: eight hundred years' disaster,
crazily tangled as the Book of Kells;
the dream's distortion and the land's division,
the midnight raiders and the prison cells.
Yet like Lir's children banished to the waters
our hearts still listen for the landward bells.

A LOCAL POET

He followed their lilting stanzas
through a thousand columns or more,
and scratched for the splintered couplets
in the cracks on the cottage floor,
for his Rhyming Weavers fell silent
when they flocked through the factory door.

He'd imagined a highway of heroes
and stepped aside on the grass
to let Cuchullain's chariot through,

and the Starry Ploughmen pass;
but he met the Travelling Gunman
instead of the Galloglass.

And so, with luck, for a decade
down the widowed years ahead,
the pension which crippled his courage
will keep him in daily bread,
while he mourns for his mannerly verses
that had left so much unsaid.

LOUIS MacNEICE

Born Belfast, 1907, to County Galway parents. Childhood in Carrickfergus, County Antrim, where father, later bishop of Down, Connor and Dromore, was rector. Educated at Sherborne Preparatory School, Marlborough School and Merton College, Oxford. Lecturer in classics at University of Birmingham, 1930–6; in Greek at Bedford College, University of London, 1936–40. Worked in features department of BBC, London, 1941–61. Freelanced at the BBC until death in 1963. A distinguished critic and radio dramatist, MacNeice left an unfinished autobiography, *The Strings Are False* (1965).

Perhaps as a consequence of early exposure to the divergent influences of Ulster, Connacht and England, MacNeice was distrustful of political abstractions and incapable of the commitment of the English 'Thirties poets' with whom he has been too strongly identified. His verse combines delight in the colour and variety of the physical world – 'the drunkenness of things being various' – with a stoical melancholy. His almost Platonic dualism can be seen alike in the early love poem 'Mayfly' and in *Autumn Journal*, where he orchestrates a rich flow of comment, memory, anecdote, speculation and opinion round a moral core of concern for the inadequacy of the contemporary response to the Munich crisis. Section XVI, the most energetic of MacNeice's many attempted valedictions to Ireland, achieves the 'impure poetry' he advocated in *Modern Poetry: A Personal Essay* (1938); its inaccuracies and injustices – flattery of English prejudice about de Valera's Ireland among them – are ultimately less important than its flexibility and its accommodation of areas of feeling and experience scanted by High Modernism. *Autumn Sequel* is a less animated performance, though Canto XX's account of the funeral of Dylan Thomas ('Gwilym') deserves to be better known. In 'Western Landscape' the topography of Ireland serves MacNeice as a correlative for the indeterminacy to which he was inclined, both intellectually and psychologically. The lyrics written in the years leading up to his death after a few days' illness at the age of fifty-five are the most delicate and daring of MacNeice's career.

Barometer of my moods today, mayfly,
Up and down one among a million, one
The same at best as the rest of the jigging mayflies,
One only day of May alive beneath the sun.

The yokels tilt their pewters and the foam
Flowers in the sun beside the jewelled water.
Daughter of the South, call the sunbeams home
To nest between your breasts. The kingcups
Ephemeral are gay gulps of laughter.

Gulp of yellow merriment; cackle of ripples;
Lips of the river that pout and whisper round the reeds.
The mayfly flirting and posturing over the water
Goes up and down in the lift so many times for fun.

'When we are grown up we are sure to alter
Much for the better, to adopt solider creeds;
The kingcup will cease proffering his cup
And the foam will have blown from the beer and the heat
    no longer dance
And the lift lose fascination and the May
Change her tune to June – but the trouble with us mayflies
Is that we never have the chance to be grown up.'

They never have the chance, but what of time they have
They stretch out taut and thin and ringing clear;
So we, whose strand of life is not much more,
Let us too make our time elastic and
Inconsequently dance above the dazzling wave.

Nor put too much on the sympathy of things,
The dregs of drink, the dried cups of flowers,
The pathetic fallacy of the passing hours
When it is we who pass them – hours of stone,
Long rows of granite sphinxes looking on.

It is we who pass them, we the circus masters
Who make the mayflies dance, the lapwings lift their crests,

The show will soon shut down, its gay-rags gone,
But when this summer is over let us die together,
I want always to be near your breasts.

SNOW

The room was suddenly rich and the great bay-window was
Spawning snow and pink roses against it
Soundlessly collateral and incompatible:
World is suddener than we fancy it.

World is crazier and more of it than we think,
Incorrigibly plural. I peel and portion
A tangerine and spit the pips and feel
The drunkenness of things being various.

And the fire flames with a bubbling sound for world
Is more spiteful and gay than one supposes –
On the tongue on the eyes on the ears in the palms of one's
    hands –
There is more than glass between the snow and the huge roses.

from AUTUMN JOURNAL

XVI

Nightmare leaves fatigue:
    We envy men of action
Who sleep and wake, murder and intrigue
    Without being doubtful, without being haunted.
And I envy the intransigence of my own
    Countrymen who shoot to kill and never
See the victim's face become their own
    Or find his motive sabotage their motives.
So reading the memoirs of Maud Gonne,
    Daughter of an English mother and a soldier father,

I note how a single purpose can be founded on
    A jumble of opposites:
Dublin Castle, the vice-regal ball,
    The embassies of Europe,
Hatred scribbled on a wall,
    Gaols and revolvers.
And I remember, when I was little, the fear
    Bandied among the servants
That Casement would land at the pier
    With a sword and a horde of rebels;
And how we used to expect, at a later date,
    When the wind blew from the west, the noise of shooting
Starting in the evening at eight
    In Belfast in the York Street district;
And the voodoo of the Orange bands
    Drawing an iron net through darkest Ulster,
Flailing the limbo lands –
    The linen mills, the long wet grass, the ragged hawthorn.
And one read black where the other read white, his hope
    The other man's damnation:
Up the Rebels, To Hell with the Pope,
    And God Save – as you prefer – the King or Ireland.
The land of scholars and saints:
    Scholars and saints my eye, the land of ambush,
Purblind manifestoes, never-ending complaints,
    The born martyr and the gallant ninny;
The grocer drunk with the drum,
    The land-owner shot in his bed, the angry voices
Piercing the broken fanlight in the slum,
    The shawled woman weeping at the garish altar.
Kathaleen ni Houlihan! Why
    Must a country, like a ship or a car, be always female,
Mother or sweetheart? A woman passing by,
    We did but see her passing.
Passing like a patch of sun on the rainy hill
    And yet we love her for ever and hate our neighbour
And each one in his will
    Binds his heirs to continuance of hatred.
Drums on the haycock, drums on the harvest, black
    Drums in the night shaking the windows:

King William is riding his white horse back
    To the Boyne on a banner.
Thousands of banners, thousands of white
    Horses, thousands of Williams
Waving thousands of swords and ready to fight
    Till the blue sea turns to orange.
Such was my country and I thought I was well
    Out of it, educated and domiciled in England,
Though yet her name keeps ringing like a bell
    In an under-water belfry.
Why do we like being Irish? Partly because
    It gives us a hold on the sentimental English
As members of a world that never was,
    Baptised with fairy water;
And partly because Ireland is small enough
    To be still thought of with a family feeling,
And because the waves are rough
    That split her from a more commercial culture;
And because one feels that here at least one can
    Do local work which is not at the world's mercy
And that on this tiny stage with luck a man
    Might see the end of one particular action.
It is self-deception of course;
    There is no immunity in this island either;
A cart that is drawn by somebody else's horse
    And carrying goods to somebody else's market.
The bombs in the turnip sack, the sniper from the roof,
    Griffith, Connolly, Collins, where have they brought us?
Ourselves alone! Let the round tower stand aloof
    In a world of bursting mortar!
Let the school-children fumble their sums
    In a half-dead language;
Let the censor be busy on the books; pull down the Georgian
      slums;
    Let the games be played in Gaelic.
Let them grow beet-sugar; let them build
    A factory in every hamlet;
Let them pigeon-hole the souls of the killed
    Into sheep and goats, patriots and traitors.
And the North, where I was a boy,
    Is still the North, veneered with the grime of Glasgow,

Thousands of men whom nobody will employ
    Standing at the corners, coughing.
And the street-children play on the wet
    Pavement – hopscotch or marbles;
And each rich family boasts a sagging tennis-net
    On a spongy lawn beside a dripping shrubbery.
The smoking chimneys hint
    At prosperity round the corner
But they make their Ulster linen from foreign lint
    And the money that comes in goes out to make more money.
A city built upon mud;
    A culture built upon profit;
Free speech nipped in the bud,
    The minority always guilty.
Why should I want to go back
    To you, Ireland, my Ireland?
The blots on the page are so black
    That they cannot be covered with shamrock.
I hate your grandiose airs,
    Your sob-stuff, your laugh and your swagger,
Your assumption that everyone cares
    Who is the king of your castle.
Castles are out of date,
    The tide flows round the children's sandy fancy;
Put up what flag you like, it is too late
    To save your soul with bunting.
Odi atque amo:
    Shall we cut this name on trees with a rusty dagger?
Her mountains are still blue, her rivers flow
    Bubbling over the boulders.
She is both a bore and a bitch;
    Better close the horizon,
Send her no more fantasy, no more longings which
    Are under a fatal tariff.
For common sense is the vogue
    And she gives her children neither sense nor money
Who slouch around the world with a gesture and a brogue
    And a faggot of useless memories.

Time was away and somewhere else,
There were two glasses and two chairs
And two people with the one pulse
(Somebody stopped the moving stairs):
Time was away and somewhere else.

And they were neither up nor down;
The stream's music did not stop
Flowing through heather, limpid brown,
Although they sat in a coffee shop
And they were neither up nor down.

The bell was silent in the air
Holding its inverted poise –
Between the clang and clang a flower,
A brazen calyx of no noise:
The bell was silent in the air.

The camels crossed the miles of sand
That stretched around the cups and plates;
The desert was their own, they planned
To portion out the stars and dates:
The camels crossed the miles of sand.

Time was away and somewhere else.
The waiter did not come, the clock
Forgot them and the radio waltz
Came out like water from a rock:
Time was away and somewhere else.

Her fingers flicked away the ash
That bloomed again in tropic trees:
Not caring if the markets crash
When they had forests such as these,
Her fingers flicked away the ash.

God or whatever means the Good
Be praised that time can stop like this,
That what the heart has understood

Can verify in the body's peace
God or whatever means the Good.

Time was away and she was here
And life no longer what it was,
The bell was silent in the air
And all the room one glow because
Time was away and she was here.

AUTOBIOGRAPHY

In my childhood trees were green
And there was plenty to be seen.

Come back early or never come.

My father made the walls resound,
He wore his collar the wrong way round.

Come back early or never come.

My mother wore a yellow dress;
Gently, gently, gentleness.

Come back early or never come.

When I was five the black dreams came;
Nothing after was quite the same.

Come back early or never come.

The dark was talking to the dead;
The lamp was dark beside my bed.

Come back early or never come.

When I woke they did not care;
Nobody, nobody was there.

Come back early or never come.

When my silent terror cried,
Nobody, nobody replied.

Come back early or never come.

I got up; the chilly sun
Saw me walk away alone.

Come back early or never come.

THE LIBERTINE

In the old days with married women's stockings
Twisted round his bedpost he felt himself a gay
Dog but now his liver has begun to groan,
Now that pick-ups are the order of the day:
O leave me easy, leave me alone.

Voluptuary in his 'teens and cynic in his twenties,
He ran through women like a child through growing hay
Looking for a lost toy whose capture might atone
For his own guilt and the cosmic disarray:
O leave me easy, leave me alone.

He never found the toy and has forgotten the faces,
Only remembers the props . . . a scent-spray
Beside the bed or a milk-white telephone
Or through the triple ninon the acrid trickle of day:
O leave me easy, leave me alone.

Long fingers over the gunwale, hair in a hair-net,
Furs in January, cartwheel hats in May,
And after the event the wish to be alone –
Angels, goddesses, bitches, all have edged away:
O leave me easy, leave me alone.

So now, in middle age, his erotic programme
Torn in two, if after such a delay
An accident should offer him his own
Fulfilment in a woman, still he would say:
O leave me easy, leave me alone.

WESTERN LANDSCAPE

In doggerel and stout let me honour this country
Though the air is so soft that it smudges the words
And herds of great clouds find the gaps in the fences
Of chance preconceptions and foam-quoits on rock-points
At once hit and miss, hit and miss.
So the kiss of the past is narcotic, the ocean
Lollingly lullingly over-insidiously
Over and under crossing the eyes
And docking the queues of the teetotum consciousness
Proves and disproves what it wants.
For the western climate is Lethe,
The smoky taste of cooking on turf is lotus,
There are affirmation and abnegation together
From the broken bog with its veins of amber water,
From the distant headland, a sphinx's fist, that barely grips the sea,
From the taut-necked donkey's neurotic-asthmatic-erotic
    lamenting,
From the heron in trance and in half-mourning,
From the mitred mountain weeping shale.

O grail of emerald passing light
And hanging smell of sweetest hay
And grain of sea and loom of wind
Weavingly laughingly leavingly weepingly –
Webs that will last and will not.
But what
Is the hold upon, the affinity with
Ourselves of such a light and line,
How do we find continuance
Of our too human skeins of wish
In this inhuman effluence?

O relevance of cloud and rock –
If such could be our permanence!
The flock of mountain sheep belong
To tumbled screes, to tumbling seas
The ribboned wrack, and moor to mist;
But we who savour longingly
This plenitude of solitude
Have lost the right to residence,
Can only glean ephemeral
Ears of our once beatitude.
Caressingly cajolingly –
Take what you can for soon you go –
Consolingly, coquettishly,
The soft rain kisses and forgets,
Silken mesh on skin and mind;
A deaf-dumb siren that can sing
With fingertips her falsities,
Welcoming, abandoning.

O Brandan, spindrift hermit, who
Hankering roaming un-homing up-anchoring
From this rock wall looked seawards to
Knot the horizon round your waist,
Distil that distance and undo
Time in quintessential West:
The best negation, round as nought,
Stiller than stolen sleep – though bought
With mortification, voiceless choir
Where all were silent as one man
And all desire fulfilled, unsought.
Thought:
The curragh went over the wave and dipped in the trough
When that horny-handed saint with the abstract eye set off
Which was fourteen hundred years ago – maybe never –
And yet he bobs beyond that next high crest for ever.
Feeling:
Sea met sky, he had neither floor nor ceiling,
The rising blue of turf-smoke and mountain were left behind,
Blue neither upped nor downed, there was blue all round the
    mind.
Emotion:

One thought of God, one feeling of the ocean,
Fused in the moving body, the unmoved soul,
Made him a part of a not to be parted whole.
Whole.
And the West was all the world, the lonely was the only,
The chosen – and there was no choice – the Best,
For the beyond was here . . .

                                                    But for us now
The beyond is still out there as on tiptoes here we stand
On promontories that are themselves a-tiptoe
Reluctant to be land. Which is why this land
Is always more than matter – as a ballet
Dancer is more than body. The west of Ireland
Is brute and ghost at once. Therefore in passing
Among these shadows of this permanent show
Flitting evolving dissolving but never quitting –
This arbitrary and necessary Nature
Both bountiful and callous, harsh and wheedling –
Let now the visitor, although disfranchised
In the constituencies of quartz and bog-oak
And ousted from the elemental congress,
Let me at least in token that my mother
Earth was a rocky earth with breasts uncovered
To suckle solitary intellects
And limber instincts, let me, if a bastard
Out of the West by urban civilization
(Which unwished father claims me – so I must take
What I can before I go) let me who am neither Brandan
Free of all roots nor yet a rooted peasant
Here add one stone to the indifferent cairn . . .
With a stone on the cairn, with a word on the wind, with a
    prayer in the flesh let me honour this country.

from CANTO XX

To Wales once more, though not on holiday now;
Glued to my seat, whirled down a ruthless track
To Wales once more, grasping a golden bough,

Key to the misty west. I am wearing black
Shoes which I bought with Gwilym in Regent Street
To travel to Drumcliff in, five years back;

Drumcliff was wet, those new shoes cramped my feet
At Yeats's funeral; they are not so smart
Nor yet so tight for Gwilym's. From my seat

I see my night-bound double, slumped apart
On a conveyor belt that, decades high
In emptiness, can neither stop nor start

But just moves on for ever till we die.
It is too late for questions; on this belt
We cannot answer what we are or why . . .

Then on to Swansea for the night, benighted
In black and barren rain. But night must end,
And ending banishes the rain. Delighted

Morning erupts to bless all Wales and send
Us west once more our sad but sunlit way
Through hills of ruddy bracken where each bend

In the road is another smile on the face of day.
We stop at random for a morning drink
In a thatched inn; to find, as at a play,

The bar already loud with chatter and clink
Of glasses; not so random; no one here
But was a friend of Gwilym's. One could think

That all these shots of whisky, pints of beer,
Make one Pactolus turning words to gold
In honour of one golden mouth, in sheer

Rebuttal of the silence and the cold
Attached to death. The river rolls on west
As proud and clear as its best years have rolled

And lands us at the village, which is dressed
In one uncanny quiet and one kind
Blue sky, an attitude of host to guest

Saying: Come share my grief. We walk behind
The slow great heaps of flowers, the small austere
And single laurel wreath. But the numbed mind

Fails to accept such words as tempt the ear –
The Resurrection and the Life; It knows
Only that Gwilym once was living here

And here is now being buried. A repose
Of sunlight lies on the green sloping field
Which should hold goats or geese. My fingers close

On what green thoughts this acre still can yield
Before we leave that deep, that not green, grave,
That letter to be superscribed and sealed

Now that it has no contents; wind and wave
Retain far more of Gwilym. What he took
From this small corner of Wales survives in what he gave.

The green field empties, with one tentative look
Backwards we move away, and then walk down
To where he lived on a cliff; an open book

Of sands and waters, silver and shining brown,
His estuary spreads before us and its birds
To which he gave renown reflect renown

On him, their cries resolve into his words
Just as, upon the right, Sir John's just hill
Looks now, and justly, Gwilym's. We leave the curds

And crimps of flats and channels and through the still

Evening rejoin the mourners. If a birth
Extends a family circle and glasses fill

Confirming its uniqueness and the worth
Of life, I think a death too does the same,
Confirming and extending. Earth to earth,

But to the whole of it. In Gwilym's name
We talk and even laugh, though now and then
Illusions (surely illusions?) rise, to shame

My reason. Three illusions. One: that when
We left that grassy field, we also left
Gwilym behind there, if not able to pen

One word, yet able perhaps to feel bereft
Or maybe to feel pleased that such a place
Remains to him. Then was it gift or theft,

This burial? More rational thoughts efface
Such whims, but the second illusion comes: perhaps
Gwilym has slipped off somewhere, into the grace

Of some afterlife where free from toils and traps
He revels for ever in words. These fancies too
Flicker like Will o' the Wistfuls, and collapse;

Since, even if an afterlife were true,
Gwilym without his body, his booming voice,
Would simply not be Gwilym. As I or you

Would not be I or you and, given the choice,
I, for one, would reject it. Last, the third
Illusion, which gives reason to rejoice

Or rather strong unreason: what we have heard
And seen today means nothing, this crowded bar
Was one of Gwilym's favourites, it is absurd

He should not join us here, it was always going too far
To expect him on the dot but, late or soon,
He will come jaunting in, especially as there are

So many of his friends here to buffoon
And sparkle with. However, if not tonight,
We need not wait for leap year or blue moon

Before we run across him. Moons are white
In London as in Wales and by tomorrow
We shall be back in London where the sight

And sound of him will be welcome, he may borrow
A pound or two of course or keep us waiting
But what about it? In those streets of sorrow

And even more of boredom, his elating
Elated presence brings a sluice of fresh
Water into dim ponds too long stagnating.

This is the third illusion, a fine mesh
Of probable impossibles; of course,
Of course, we think, we shall meet him in the flesh

Tomorrow or the next day, in full force
Of flesh and wit and heart. We close the door
On Wales and backwards, eastwards, from the source

Of such clear water, leave that altered shore
Of gulls and psalms, of green and gold largesse.
November the Twenty-fifth. We are back once more

In London. And will he keep us waiting? . . . Yes.

from A HAND OF SNAPSHOTS

THE ONCE-IN-PASSING

And here the cross on the window means myself
But that window does not open;
Born here, I should have proved a different self.
Such vistas dare not open;
For what can walk or talk without tongue or feet?

91

Here for a month to spend but not to earn,
How could I even imagine
Such a life here that my plain days could earn
The life my dreams imagine?
For what takes root or grows that owns no root?

Yet here for a month, and for this once in passing,
I can imagine at least
The permanence of what passes,
As though the window opened
And the ancient cross on the hillside meant myself.

HOUSE ON A CLIFF

Indoors the tang of a tiny oil lamp. Outdoors
The winking signal on the waste of sea.
Indoors the sound of the wind. Outdoors the wind.
Indoors the locked heart and the lost key.

Outdoors the chill, the void, the siren. Indoors
The strong man pained to find his red blood cools,
While the blind clock grows louder, faster. Outdoors
The silent moon, the garrulous tides she rules.

Indoors ancestral curse-cum-blessing. Outdoors
The empty bowl of heaven, the empty deep.
Indoors a purposeful man who talks at cross
Purposes, to himself, in a broken sleep.

SOAP SUDS

This brand of soap has the same smell as once in the big
House he visited when he was eight: the walls of the bathroom
    open
To reveal a lawn where a great yellow ball rolls back through
    a hoop
To rest at the head of a mallet held in the hands of a child.

And these were the joys of that house: a tower with a telescope;
Two great faded globes, one of the earth, one of the stars;
A stuffed black dog in the hall; a walled garden with bees;
A rabbit warren; a rockery; a vine under glass; the sea.

To which he has now returned. The day of course is fine
And a grown-up voice cries Play! The mallet slowly swings,
Then crack, a great gong booms from the dog-dark hall and the
    ball
Skims forward through the hoop and then through the next and
    then

Through hoops where no hoops were and each dissolves in turn
And the grass has grown head-high and an angry voice cries Play!
But the ball is lost and the mallet slipped long since from the
    hands
Under the running tap that are not the hands of a child.

THE SUICIDE

And this, ladies and gentlemen, whom I am not in fact
Conducting, was his office all those minutes ago,
This man you never heard of. There are the bills
In the intray, the ash in the ashtray, the grey memoranda stacked
Against him, the serried ranks of the box-files, the packed
Jury of his unanswered correspondence
Nodding under the paperweight in the breeze
From the window by which he left; and here is the cracked
Receiver that never got mended and here is the jotter
With his last doodle which might be his own digestive tract
Ulcer and all or might be the flowery maze
Through which he had wandered deliciously till he stumbled
Suddenly finally conscious of all he lacked
On a manhole under the hollyhocks. The pencil
Point had obviously broken, yet, when he left this room
By catdrop sleight-of-foot or simple vanishing act,
To those who knew him for all that mess in the street
This man with the shy smile has left behind
Something that was intact.

Forty-two years ago (to me if to no one else
The number is of some interest) it was a brilliant starry night
And the westward train was empty and had no corridors
So darting from side to side I could catch the unwonted sight
Of those almost intolerably bright
Holes, punched in the sky, which excited me partly because
Of their Latin names and partly because I had read in the
    textbooks
How very far off they were, it seemed their light
Had left them (some at least) long years before I was.

And this remembering now I mark that what
Light was leaving some of them at least then,
Forty-two years ago, will never arrive
In time for me to catch it, which light when
It does get here may find that there is not
Anyone left alive
To run from side to side in a late night train
Admiring it and adding noughts in vain.

DENIS DEVLIN

Born Greenock, Scotland, of Irish parents, 1908. Lived Dublin,
1920–30. Educated at Belvedere College and University College
Dublin. Travelled widely in Europe, 1930–3, studying in Munich and
Paris. Lectured in English at UCD before joining Irish diplomatic service,
1935. Posted to Rome (1938), New York (1939), Washington (1940)
and London (1947). Minister plenipotentiary to Italy, 1950, and
Turkey, 1951. Ambassador to Italy, 1958. Died Dublin, 1959.

Devlin's poems have been championed by such Irish admirers as Brian
Coffey, Samuel Beckett, Thomas Kinsella and John Montague, and by
Allen Tate and Robert Penn Warren in the United States. Other readers
have found them stilted and showy. Manifestly ambitious, his work has a
tendency to lapse into bathos: it is arguable that he only intermittently
achieved a style that fully accommodated his intellectual interests. The
four selected pieces reveal Devlin's characteristic concern with exile
as the true condition of human life, and with the inscrutable
nature of sexual and divine love.

ANK'HOR VAT

The antlered forests
Move down to the sea.
Here the dung-filled jungle pauses

Buddha has covered the walls of the great temple
With the vegetative speed of his imagery

Let us wait, hand in hand

No Western god or saint
Ever smiled with the lissom fury of this god
Who holds in doubt
The wooden stare of Apollo
Our Christian crown of thorns:

There is no mystery in the luminous lines
Of that high, animal face
The smile, sad, humouring and equal
Blesses without obliging
Loves without condescension;
The god, clear as spring-water
Sees through everything, while everything
Flows through him

A fling of flowers here
Whose names I do not know
Downy, scarlet gullets
Green legs yielding and closing

While, at my mental distance from passion,
The prolific divinity of the temple
Is a quiet lettering on vellum.

Let us lie down before him
His look will flow like oil over us.

LITTLE ELEGY

I will walk with a lover of wisdom
A smile for Senator Destiny
But I shall gladly listen.

Her beauty was like silence in a cup of water
Decanting all but the dream matter.
The figures of reality
Stood about, Dantesque and pitiful.
Can anyone tell me her name?
I will love her again and again
Girl on skis, arrow and bow in one,
Masked in glass, graceful,
Hard as a word in season.

I saw a round, Bavarian goodman
And a Harvard student with a Mohican's lope

Colliding with huge nosegays
Then laughter burst above their flowers:
Absent of mind, they had their wits about them
I laughed at them both outright

And at simpering, peasant statues
Graces and gods would they be!
It was a heady springtime in Munich
Many I knew confided in me
Popu, the champion cyclist
Sigmund, deriding tyrants
And Carlos, who made love shyly
To a furtive, gentle girl
And came to my door, stammering,
'She loves me, you know.'
'She loves me, you know.'

But geography separated them
And geography keeps them apart
Now they live forgotten in each other's heart.

II

The sun was full on, the bird-breed
Gradually found their wings.
The baroque churches glowed like the Book of Kells.
We two, with butterbrot and sweetmilk
Over the snow beneath blue winds
Went far and wide.
Busy, alone, we all go far and wide
Who once listened to each other's
Fair vows and counsel.

Of those that go out of the cafés and the gardens
Some lie in prisons
Some die of unhappiness
Indeed, it is so!

This is all I can remember
Quarrelling, gusts of confidence
The class climbing through faun nights

And her I would meet
As though I were unconscious
In vacant, bright-columned streets
And beings in love's tunic scattered to the four winds
For no reason at all
For no reason that I can tell.

from MEMOIRS OF A TURCOMAN DIPLOMAT

OTELI ASIA PALAS, INC.

Evenings ever more willing lapse into my world's evening,
Birds, like Imperial emblems, in their thin, abstract singing,
Announce some lofty Majesty whose embassies are not
    understood,
Thrushes' and finches' chords, like the yellow and blue skies
    changing place.
I hold my stick, old-world, the waiters know me,
And sip at my European drink, while sunlight falls,
Like thick Italian silks over the square houses into the Bosphorus.
Ladies, I call you women now, from out my emptied tenderness,
All dead in the wars, before and after war,
I toast you my adventures with your beauty!
Where the domes of Sinan shiver like ductile violets in the rain
    of light.

To the Franks, I suppose it's ugly, this brick and oblong,
When a rare sunlight, rare birdsong,
Compose the absolute kingdom far in the sky
The Franks must ask how it was known, how reached, how
    governed, how let die?

This woman who passes by, sideways, by your side:
There was one you loved for years and years;
Suddenly the jaw is ugly, the shoulders fall,
Provoking but resentment, hardly tears.

RENEWAL BY HER ELEMENT

The hawthorn morning moving
Above the battlements,
Breast from breast of lover
Tears, reminds of difference
And body's raggedness.

Immune from resolution
Into common clay
Because I have not known you;
Self-content as birdsong
Scornful at night-breakage
You seem to me. I am
Fresh from a long absence.

O suave through surf lifting
My smile upon your mouth;
Limbs according to rhythm
Separating, closing;
Scarcely using my name,
Traveller through troubling gestures,
Only for rare embraces
Of prepared texture.
Your lips amused harden
My arms round you defiant,
You shirk my enwreathing
Language, and you smile,
Turning aside my hand
Through your breath's light leafage,
Preferring yourself reflected
In my body to me,
Preferring my image of you
To you whom I achieved.
Noise is curbed attentive,
The sea hangs on your lips:
What would I do less?

It is over now but once
Our fees were nothing more,
Each for use of the other

In mortgage, than a glance.
I knew the secret movements
Of the blood under your throat
And when we lay love-proven
Whispering legends to sleep
Braceleted in embrace
Your hands pouring on me
Fresh water of their caresses,
Breasts, nests of my tenderness,
All night was laced with praise.

Now my image faded
In the lucid fields
Of your eyes. Never again
Surprise for years, years.

My landscape is grey rain
Aslant on bent seas.

W. R. RODGERS

Born Belfast, 1909. Educated at Queen's University Belfast and the
Presbyterian Theological College. Ordained 1935 and appointed
minister in Loughall, County Armagh. Introduced to modern poetry by
John Hewitt. Began writing, 1939. Resigned ministry and moved to
London to work in BBC features department, 1946. Elected member of
Irish Academy of Letters, 1951. Series of college appointments in
California from 1966. Died Los Angeles, 1969.

Rodgers's work belongs to the New Romantic moment in British poetry
when younger writers reacted against what they saw as the desiccating
ironies of T.S. Eliot's brand of modernism. And yet his verse has a
specific Irish context too, as a Presbyterian manifestation of what
Austin Clarke called 'our racial drama of conscience', it marks a
milestone in the conflict between sensuality and Christian asceticism
which runs from the dialogues of Oisín and Patrick in the Fenian cycle
to Kavanagh's 'Father Mat'. Like many of Rodgers's early poems,
'Snow' celebrates sound and movement, relishing its own reckless
ebullience under the shadow of the encroaching war. 'Lent' is one of a
number of unorthodox Christian meditations written after he left his
ministry. The other two poems explore aspects of sexual love – a subject
to which Rodgers turned with the zeal of a convert.

SNOW

Out of the grey air grew snow and more snow
Soundlessly in nonillions of flakes
Commingling and sinking negligently
To ground, soft as froth and easy as ashes
Alighting, closing the ring of sight. And,
Silting, it augmented everything
Furring the bare leaf, blurring the thorn,
Fluffing, too, the telephone-wire, padding
All the paths and boosting boots, and puffing
Big over rims, like boiling milk, meekly
Indulging the bulging hill, and boldly

Bolstering the retiring hole, until
It owned and integrated all. And then
Snow stopped, disclosing anonymity
Imposed, the blank and blotless sea in which
Both dotted tree and dashing bird were sunk,
And anchored ground and rocking grass engrossed.

And soon the knock and hiss of cistern ceased as
Gradually with inklings and wrinkling strings
Of ice the thickening cold anchored the skin
And slow core of water, gluing and glossing
All leaks, niggling or great, naked or guarded.
Long snaughters of ice at the tap's snout hung
Jagged and stiff like straw-ends this hard morning.
At every vent things hesitated; here,
In conforming holes and huts, the shy creatures
Shrank from issuing, and, rooted together,
Stood arrested and irresolute at doors,
Peppering with peepings the surprising fields –
Fox in knoll, fowl in house, heifer in hovel.
Only the bull, dubious and delicate, stalked
In his paddock, distrust spiking his blind steps.
His spinning eye, his spoked glances, glinted and
Tilted. His horn gored and scorned the ground, and scored
The oak, and fans of vapour jetted and jumped
Stiffly from nostrils, incensing the loose snow
Like smoke, and powdering his knees. Noisily
On the sleeked lake onlookers lingered in ring
Round the single and deferent skater lean-
    ing over in flight, like grass slanted by wind,
Foot-engrossed, locked in his own looking-glass
Of conscious joy and evident finery
Of movement, forgetful of outer voices.
Forgetful of venom, of fame, of laughter,
Of flouting Evil and of touting Good that
Waited woodenly for him like tormentors
At the end and edge of his dream, to waken
And claim him. So he slid on, as we all do,
Forgetting the morrow, forgetting too
The marrow of water in the bone of ice
(Like the worm in the wood), the liquefaction

And friction in all fixed things, virtue in vice,
The bomb domanial in the dome of blue.

LENT

Mary Magdalene, that easy woman,
Saw, from the shore, the seas
Beat against the hard stone of Lent,
Crying, 'Weep, seas, weep
For yourselves that cannot dent me more.

'O more than all these, more crabbed than all stones,
And cold, make me, who once
Could leap like water, Lord. Take me
As one who owes
Nothing to what she was. Ah, naked.

'My waves of scent, my petticoats of foam
Put from me and rebut;
Disown. And that salt lust stave off
That slavered me – O
Let it whiten in grief against the stones

'And outer reefs of me. Utterly doff,
Nor leave the lightest veil
Of feeling to heave or soften.
Nothing cares this heart
What hardness crates it now or coffins.

'Over the balconies of these curved breasts
I'll no more peep to see
The light procession of my loves
Surf-riding in to me
Who now have eyes and alcove, Lord, for Thee.'

'Room, Mary,' said He, 'ah make room for me
Who am come so cold now
To my tomb.' So, on Good Friday,

Under a frosty moon
They carried Him and laid Him in her womb.

A grave and icy mask her heart wore twice,
But on the third day it thawed,
And only a stone's-flow away
Mary saw her God.
Did you hear me? Mary saw her God!

Dance, Mary Magdalene, dance, dance and sing,
For unto you is born
This day a King. 'Lady,' said He,
'To you who relent
I bring back the petticoat and the bottle of scent.'

THE NET

Quick, woman, in your net
Catch the silver I fling!
O I am deep in your debt,
Draw tight, skin-tight, the string,
And rake the silver in.
No fisher ever yet
Drew such a cunning ring.

Ah, shifty as the fin
Of any fish this flesh
That, shaken to the shin,
Now shoals into your mesh,
Bursting to be held in;
Purse-proud and pebble-hard,
Its pence like shingle showered.

Open the haul, and shake
The fill of shillings free,
Let all the satchels break
And leap about the knee
In shoals of ecstasy.

Guineas and gills will flake
At each gull-plunge of me.

Though all the angels, and
Saint Michael at their head,
Nightly contrive to stand
On guard about your bed,
Yet none dare take a hand,
But each can only spread
His eagle-eye instead.

But I, being man, can kiss
And bed-spread-eagle too;
All flesh shall come to this,
Being less than angel is,
Yet higher far in bliss
As it entwines with you.

Come, make no sound, my sweet;
Turn down the candid lamp
And draw the equal quilt
Over our naked guilt.

STORMY NIGHT

Is this the street? Never a sign of life,
The swinging lamp throws everything about;
But see! from that sly doorway, like a knife
The gilt edge of inviting light slides out
And in again – the very sign
Of her whose slightest nod I lately thought was mine;

But not now.
Knock! and the night-flowering lady
Opens, and across the brilliant sill
Sees me standing there so dark and shady
Hugging the silences of my ill-will;
Wildly she turns from me – But no, my love,
This foot's within the door, this hand's without the glove.

Well may you tremble now, and say there was nothing meant,
And curl away from my care with a 'Please, my dear!',
For though you were smoke, sucked up by a raging vent,
I'd follow you through every flue of your fear,
And over your faraway arms I'll mountain and cone
In a pillar of carolling fire and fountaining stone.

O strike the gong of your wrong, raise the roof of your rage
Fist and foist me off with a cloud of cries,
What do I care for all your footling rampage?
On your light-in-gale blows my larking caresses will rise,
But – Why so still? What? are you weeping, my sweet?
Ah heart, heart, look! I throw myself at your feet.

MÁIRTÍN Ó DIREÁIN

Born Inishmore, Aran Islands, 1910. Worked in Central Post Office,
Galway, 1928–37. Moved to Dublin, where he was employed as a civil
servant until 1975. Began writing poetry in 1938, publishing nine
collections between 1942 and 1980. D.Litt. from National
University of Ireland, 1977. Died Dublin, 1988.

Uniquely among Irish-language poets of the modern era, Ó Direáin
grew up in a monoglot Gaelic environment, learning English only in his
teens. His poems typically view Inishmore from the vantage of middle-
class, Anglophone, suburban Dublin, and contrast the material
impoverishment of the one with the spiritual privations of the other.
Small, rhythmically cunning lyrics of swift pace and extreme
compression, at their best they make Aran a symbol of the lost unity of
modern life. The three poems reprinted here come from the 1950s. The
first two are perhaps the most forceful of Ó Direáin's direct evocations
of Inishmore. 'Cranna Foirtil' combines memory, folklore, allusion,
neologisms, and both colloquial and dictionary-drawn idioms in a
sombre but verbally playful meditation on the difficulty of maintaining
artistic integrity in a hostile culture.

DEIREADH RÉ

Fir na scéal mo léan!
Is an bás á leagadh,
Mná na seál á leanacht
Is mise fós ar marthain
I measc na bplód gan ainm,
Gan 'Cé dhár díobh é?' ar a mbéal
Ná fios mo shloinne acu.

Ní háil liom feasta dar m'anam
Dáimh a bhrú ar chlocha glasa!
Ní fáilteach romham an charraig,
Mé ar thóir m'óige ar bealach,
Mé i m'Oisín ar na craga,
Is fós ar fud an chladaigh,
Mé ag caoineadh slua na marbh.

CUIMHNE AN DOMHNAIGH

Chím grian an Domhnaigh ag taitneamh
Anuas ar ghnúis an talaimh
San oileán rúin tráthnóna;
Mórchuid cloch is gannchuid cré
Sin é teist an sceirdoileáin,
Dúthaigh dhearóil mo dhaoine.

Chím mar chaith an chloch gach fear,
Mar lioc ina cló féin é,
Is chím an dream a thréig go héag
Cloch is cré is dúthaigh dhearóil,
Is chímse fós gach máthair faoi chás
Ag ceapadh a háil le dán a cuimhne.

ERA'S END

My grief on the men of the stories
And the death that fells them!
The shawled women following
And I still alive
Anonymous amid the throng,
Without 'Who's he?' on their lips
Or knowledge of my surname.

Never again will I try
To press friendship on grey stones!
There's no welcome for me on the rock,
Hunting my youth on the way
Like Oisín on the crags,
Nor again along the foreshore
Lamenting the host of the dead.

translated by Patrick Crotty

MEMORY OF SUNDAY

I see the Sunday sun beating
Down on the face of the ground
In the beloved island all afternoon;
Much stone, little clay
That's the bleak island's testimony,
The wretched inheritance of my people.

I see how the stone has cast each man,
And bruised him into its own shape.
And I see the crowd who forsook forever
Stone and clay and wretched inheritance,
And I see too each put-upon mother
Composing her brood like a poem to memorise.

translated by Patrick Crotty

Coinnigh do thalamh a anam liom,
Coigil chugat gach tamhanrud,
Is ná bí mar ghiolla gan chaithir
I ndiaidh na gcarad nár fhóin duit.

Minic a dhearcais ladhrán trá
Ar charraig fhliuch go huaigneach;
Mura bhfuair éadáil ón toinn
Ní bhfuair guth ina héagmais.

Níor thugais ó do ríocht dhorcha
Caipín an tsonais ar do cheann,
Ach cuireadh cranna cosanta
Go teann thar do chliabhán cláir.

Cranna caillte a cuireadh tharat;
Tlú iarainn os do chionn,
Ball éadaigh d'athar taobh leat
Is bior sa tine thíos.

Luigh ar do chranna foirtil
I gcoinne mallmhuir is díthrá,
Coigil aithinne d'aislinge,
Scaradh léi is éag duit.

STRONG BEAMS

Stand your ground, soul:
Hold fast to everything that's rooted,
And don't react like some pubescent boy
When your friends let you down.

Often you've seen a redshank
Lonely on a wet rock;
If he won no spoil from the wave
That was no cause for complaint.

You brought from your dark kingdom
No lucky caul on your head
But protective beams were placed
Firmly round your cradle.

Withered beams they placed round you,
An iron tongs above you,
An item of your father's clothes beside you
And a poker in the fire below.

Put your weight to your strong oar-beams
Against neap-tide and low water;
Preserve the spark of your vision –
Lose that and you're finished.

translated by Patrick Crotty

SEÁN Ó RÍORDÁIN

Born Ballyvourney, County Cork, 1917. Moved to Inniscarra, a few
miles outside Cork city, 1932. Educated at the North Monastery, Cork.
Clerk in Cork City Hall, 1936–65. Part-time position in Irish
department, University College Cork, 1969–76. D.Litt. from National
University of Ireland, 1976. Died Cork, 1977. Ó Ríordáin wrote a
weekly column for the *Irish Times*, 1967–75. His near legendary diaries
remain unpublished.

The tuberculosis which blighted Ó Ríordáin's youth is reflected in his
poetry's frequent references to illness and, crucially, in its characteristic
projection of the estranged, resigned, too fervid perspective of the
invalid. Anguish of one sort or another – grief, guilt, religious terror
provides the starting point of many of the poems but the writing is
never merely expressive. Startling imagery and an undercurrent of
anarchic, self-deprecating humour play against the grimness of
Ó Ríordáin's themes. No twentieth-century Irish poem in either
language issues from as deep within Catholic religious consciousness
as 'Cnoc Melleri' (based on a retreat in the Cistercian abbey in
County Waterford). Neither has the Oedipal intensity of the son's
relationship to the mother – a fact of life in rural Ireland – ever been
presented as hauntingly (or with as little embarrassment) as in
'Adhlacadh Mo Mháthar'. That poem extracts a pained artistic credo
from its unlikely materials, and is perhaps the first fully modern lyric in
Irish. The short pieces represent an equal order of achievement.
'Claustrophobia' adapts the rhetoric of the War of Independence
(most fiercely fought in the poet's native west Cork) to the struggle
against despair, while 'Siollabadh' gives free rein to the playful
impulse never entirely absent from Ó Ríordáin's work.

ADHLACADH MO MHÁTHAR

Grian an Mheithimh in úllghort,
   Is siosarnach i síoda an tráthnóna,
Beach mhallaithe ag portaireacht
   Mar screadstracadh ar an nóinbhrat.

Seanalitir shalaithe á léamh agam,
   Le gach focaldeoch dar ólas
Pian bhinibeach ag dealgadh mo chléibhse,
   Do bhrúigh amach gach focal díobh a dheoir féin.

Do chuimhníos ar an láimh a dhein an scríbhinn,
   Lámh a bhí inaitheanta mar aghaidh,
Lámh a thál riamh cneastacht seana-Bhíobla,
   Lámh a bhí mar bhalsam is tú tinn.

Agus thit an Meitheamh siar isteach sa Gheimhreadh,
   Den úllghort deineadh reilig bhán cois abhann,
Is i lár na balbh-bháine i mo thimpeall
   Do liúigh os ard sa tsneachta an dúpholl,

Gile gearrachaile lá á céad chomaoine,
   Gile abhlainne Dé Domhnaigh ar altóir,
Gile bainne ag sreangtheitheadh as na cíochaibh,
   Nuair a chuireadar mo mháthair, gile an fhóid.

Bhí m'aigne á sciúirseadh féin ag iarraidh
   An t-adhlacadh a bhlaiseadh go hiomlán,
Nuair a d'eitil tríd an gciúnas bán go míonla
   Spideog a bhí gan mhearbhall gan scáth:

Agus d'fhan os cionn na huaighe fé mar go mb'eol di
   Go raibh an toisc a thug í ceilte ar chách
Ach an té a bhí ag feitheamh ins an gcomhrainn,
   Is do rinneas éad fén gcaidreamh neamhghnách.

Do thuirling aer na bhFlaitheas ar an uaigh sin,
   Bhí meidhir uafásach naofa ar an éan,
Bhíos deighilte amach ón diamhairghnó im thuata,
   Is an uaigh sin os mo chomhair in imigéin.

114

MY MOTHER'S BURIAL

June sun in an orchard
   And a whispering in the afternoon's silk,
A malicious bee's drone
   Scream-tearing the day's fabric.

An old soiled letter in my hand:
   With every word that I drank
A venomous pain stung my breast,
   Each word bruised out its individual tear.

I recalled the hand that did the writing,
   A hand as recognisable as a face,
A hand that dealt out old Biblical kindness,
   A hand that was like balm when you were ill.

And June collapsed back into winter:
   The orchard was a white cemetery by a river
And from the heart of the silent whiteness all about me
   The black hole roared in the snow.

The whiteness of a girl on her first Communion Day,
   The whiteness of the wafer on a Sunday altar,
The whiteness of milk drawing free from the breasts,
   When they buried my mother, the whiteness of the sod.

My mind was scourging itself in the attempt
   To savour the burial entire
When there gently flew into the bright silence
   A robin, unflustered, unafraid.

It hovered above the grave as if it knew
   The reason for its coming was hidden from all
But the one lying waiting in the coffin:
   I resented their extraordinary exchange.

The air of Heaven landed on that grave,
   A terrible, saintly merriment held the bird:
I was barred from the mystery like a layman
   And the grave, though right before me, was miles away.

Le cumhracht bróin do folcadh m'anam drúiseach,
  Thit sneachta geanmnaíochta ar mo chroí,
Anois adhlacfad sa chroí a deineadh ionraic
  Cuimhne na mná d'iompair mé trí ráithe ina broinn.

Tháinig na scológa le borbthorann sluasad,
  Is do scuabadar le fuinneamh an chré isteach san uaigh,
D'fhéachas-sa treo eile, bhí comharsa ag glanadh a ghlúine,
  D'fhéachas ar an sagart is bhí saoltacht ina ghnúis.

Grian an Mheithimh in úllghort,
  Is siosarnach i síoda an tráthnóna,
Beach mhallaithe ag portaireacht
  Mar screadstracadh ar an nóinbhrat.

Ranna beaga bacacha á scríobh agam,
  Ba mhaith liom breith ar eireaball spideoige,
Ba mhaith liom sprid lucht glanta glún a dhíbirt,
  Ba mhaith liom triall go deireadh lae go brónach.

MALAIRT

'Gaibh i leith,' arsa Turnbull, 'go bhfeice tú an brón
  I súilibh an chapaill,
Dá mbeadh crúba chomh mór leo sin fútsa bheadh brón
  Id shúilibh chomh maith leis.'

Agus b'fhollas gur thuig sé chomh maith sin an brón
  I súilibh an chapaill,
Is gur mhachnaigh chomh cruaidh air gur tomadh é fá dheoidh
  In aigne an chapaill.

D'fhéachas ar an gcapall go bhfeicinn an brón
  'Na shúilibh ag seasamh,
Do chonac súile Turnbull ag féachaint im threo
  As cloigeann an chapaill.

The freshness of sorrow washed my lascivious soul,
  Pure snow fell on my heart:
In my white heart now I will bury the memory
  Of she who carried me three seasons in her womb.

The labourers came with a harsh sound of shovels
  And roughly swept the earth into the grave.
I looked away, a neighbour was brushing his knees;
  I looked at the priest and there was worldliness in his face.

June sun in an orchard
  And a whispering in the afternoon's silk,
A malicious bee's drone
  Scream-tearing the day's fabric.

Little halting verses I'm wilding,
  I'd like to catch the tail of a robin,
I'd like to vanquish the spirit of the knee-brushers,
  I'd like to fare in sorrow to the end of day.

translated by Patrick Crotty

SWITCH

'Come here,' said Turnbull, 'till you see the sadness
  In the horse's eyes,
If you had such big hooves under you there'd be sadness
  In your eyes too.'

It was clear that he understood so well the sadness
  In the horse's eyes,
And had pondered it so long that in the end he'd plunged
  Into the horse's mind.

I looked at the horse to see the sadness
  Obvious in its eyes,
And saw Turnbull's eyes looking in my direction
  From the horse's head.

D'fhéachas ar Turnbull is d'fhéachas air fá dhó
Is do chonac ar a leacain
Na súile rómhóra bhí balbh le brón –
Súile an chapaill.

CNOC MELLERÍ

Sranntarnach na stoirme i Mellerí aréir
Is laethanta an pheaca bhoig mar bhreoiteacht ar mo chuimhne,
Laethanta ba leapacha de shonaschlúmh an tsaoil
Is dreancaidí na drúise iontu ag preabarnaigh ina mílte.

D'éirigh san oíche sidhe gaoithe coiscéim,
Manaigh ag triall ar an Aifreann,
Meidhir, casadh timpeall is rince san aer,
Bróga na manach ag cantaireacht.

Bráthair sa phroinnteach ag riaradh suipéir,
Tost bog ba bhalsam don intinn,
Ainnise naofa in oscailt a bhéil,
Iompar mothaolach Críostaí mhaith.

Do doirteadh steall anchruthach gréine go mall
Trí mhúnla cruiceogach fuinneoige,
Do ghaibh sí cruth manaigh ó bhaitheas go bonn
Is do thosnaigh an ghrian ag léitheoireacht.

Leabhar ag an manach bán namhdach á léamh,
Go hobann casachtach an chloig,
Do múchadh an manach bhí déanta de ghréin
Is do scoilteadh an focal 'na phloic.

Buaileadh clog Complin is bhrostaigh gach aoi
Maolchluasach i dtreo an tséipéil;
Bhí beatha na naomh seo chomh bán le braitlín
Is sinne chomh dubh leis an daol.

I looked at Turnbull one last time
   And saw on his face
Outsize eyes that were dumb with sadness –
   The horse's eyes.

translated by Patrick Crotty

MOUNT MELLERAY

The snoring of the storm in Melleray last night
And days of soft sin on my memory like sickness,
Days that were life's beds of ease
With fleas of lust hopping in them in their thousands.

A fairy wind of footsteps rose in the night
– Monks going to Mass,
Gaiety, turning about and dancing in the air,
The chanting of sandals.

A brother in the dining-hall dispensing supper,
A silence so soft it was balm for the mind,
The saintly poverty of his speech
And unaffected demeanour of a good Christian.

Deformed sunlight was slowly poured
Through the hive-like window
Until it took the shape of a monk from head to toe,
A shape that began to read.

The white malevolent monk was reading a book
When a bell suddenly coughed –
The sun-monk was obliterated
And the word lost from his cheeks.

Compline was rung and every guest
Hurried, subdued, towards the chapel;
These saints' lives seemed sheet-white
Where ours were beetle-black.

119

Allas ar phaidrín brúite im láimh,
Mo bhríste dlúth-tháite lem ghlúin,
Ghluais sochraid chochallach manach thar bráid,
Ba shuarach leat féachaint a thabhairt.

Ach d'fhéachas go fiosrach gan taise gan trua
Mar fhéachadar Giúdaigh fadó
Ar Lazarus cúthail ag triall as an uaigh
Is géire na súl thart á dhó.

Do thiteadar tharainn 'na nduine is 'na nduine,
Reilig ag síorphaidreoireacht,
Is do thuirling tiubhscamall de chlúimh liath na cille
Go brónach ar ghrua an tráthnóna.

'Tá an bás ag cur seaca ar bheatha anseo,
Aige tá na manaigh ar aimsir,
Eisean an tAb ar a ndeineann siad rud,
Ar a shon deinid troscadh is treadhanas.

'Buachaill mar sheanduine meirtneach ag siúl,
Masla ar choimirce Dé,
An té 'dhéanfadh éagóir dá leithéid ar gharsún
Do chuirfeadh sé cochall ar ghréin;

'Do scaipfeadh an oíche ar fud an mheán lae,
Do bhainfeadh an teanga den abhainn,
Do chuirfeadh coir drúise in intinn na n-éan
Is do líonfadh le náire an domhan.

'Tá an buachaill seo dall ar an aigne fhiáin
A thoirchíonn smaointe éagsúla
Gan bacadh le hAb ná le clog ná le riail
Ach luí síos le smaoineamh a dhúile.

'Ní bhlaisfidh sé choíche tréanmheisce mná
A chorraíonn mar chreideamh na sléibhte,
'Thug léargas do Dante ar Fhlaitheas Dé tráth,
Nuair a thuirling na haingil i riocht véarsaí,'

Perspiration on the beads gripped in my hands,
My trousers stuck to my knees,
A hooded procession of monks glided past;
Though it would have been vulgar to stare,

Stare at them I did, without pity or compassion
As the Jews stared long ago
At Lazarus shyly issuing from the tomb,
Their keen eyes all round burning him.

They filed past us one by one,
A cemetery in perpetual prayer,
And a thick cloud of sepulchral mildew
Settled like melancholy on the evening's cheek.

'Death casts a frost over life here,
The monks are his retinue,
He the Abbot they serve,
It's for him they endure fast and abstinence.

'A youth walking like an enfeebled old man
Is an insult to the mercy of God;
Whoever would inflict such wrong on a boy
Would pull a hood over the sun;

'Would spread night across midday,
Would rip the tongue from the river,
Plant lechery in the minds of birds
And fill the world with shame.

'This boy is blind to the wild imagination
That fertilises diversity of thought,
That cares nothing for Abbot or bell or rule
But lies down with its deepest desire.

'He will never be woman-drunk
With the longing that moves mountains,
The desire that once opened the heavens for Dante
When angels descended in the shape of verses.'

Sin é dúirt an ego bhí uaibhreach easumhal,
Is é dallta le feirg an tsaoil,
Ach do smaoiníos ar ball, is an ceol os ár gcionn,
Gur mó ná an duine an tréad.

D'fhéachas laistiar díom ar fhásach mo shaoil,
Is an paidrín brúite im dhóid,
Peaca, díomhaointeas is caiteachas claon,
Blianta urghránna neantóg.

D'fhéachas ar bheatha na manach anonn,
D'aithníos dán ar an dtoirt,
Meadaracht, glaine, doimhinbhrí is comhfhuaim,
Bhí m'aigne cromtha le ceist.

Do bhlaiseas mórfhuascailt na faoistine ar maidin,
Aiseag is ualach ar ceal,
Scaoileadh an t-ancaire, rinceas sa Laidin,
Ba dhóbair dom tuirling ar Neamh.

Ach do bhlaiseas, uair eile, iontaoibh asam féin,
Mo chuid fola ar fiuchadh le neart,
Do shamhlaíos gur lonnaigh im intinn Spiorad Naomh
Is gur thiteadar m'fhocail ó Neamh.

Buarach ar m'aigne Eaglais Dé,
Ar shagart do ghlaofainn coillteán,
Béalchráifeacht an Creideamh, ól gloine gan léan,
Mairfeam go dtiocfaidh an bás!

Manaigh mar bheachaibh ag fuaimint im cheann,
M'aigne cromtha le ceist,
Nótaí ag rothaíocht anonn is anall,
Deireadh le Complin de gheit.

Sranntarnach na stoirme i Mellerí aréir
Is laethanta an pheaca bhoig mar bhreoiteacht ar mo chuimhne
Is na laethanta a leanfaidh iad fá cheilt i ndorn Dé,
Ach greim fhir bháite ar Mhellerí an súgán seo filíochta.

So spoke the arrogant, insubordinate ego,
Blind with the world's fury;
But I thought later, as music pealed over us,
That the individual is less than the congregation.

I looked back at the waste of my life,
With the beads still tight in my fist,
Sin, idleness, bent prodigality
– A ghastly nettle-bed of years.

I looked at the life of the monks
And recognised there the form of a poem
– Measure, clarity, profundity and harmony –
My mind buckled under the weight of its questions.

This morning I savoured the release of Confession,
Restoration, a load laid aside,
The anchor was raised, I danced in Latin
And almost set foot in Heaven.

But I savoured too, once more, over-confidence:
My blood coursing with delight,
I imagined the Holy Spirit took up residence in me,
That my words had their origin in Heaven.

That God's church was a spancel on my mind,
The priest a eunuch, the Faith
Mere lip-service; drink up without anguish,
Let's live till we die!

The monks sounding through my head like bees,
My mind buckled from questioning,
Sung notes wheeling hither and thither:
Suddenly Compline was over.

The snoring of the storm in Melleray last night
And days of soft sin on my memory like sickness,
The days that will follow them lie hidden in God's fist,
But a drowning man's grip on Melleray is this twist of poetry.

translated by Patrick Crotty

SIOLLABADH

Bhí banaltra in otharlann
  I ngile an tráthnóna,
Is cuisleanna i leapachaibh
  Ag preabarnaigh go tomhaiste,
Do sheas sí os gach leaba
  Agus d'fhan sí seal ag comhaireamh
Is do bhreac sí síos an mheadaracht
  Bhí ag siollabadh ina meoraibh,
Is do shiollaib sí go rithimeach
  Fé dheireadh as an seomra,
Is d'fhág 'na diaidh mar chlaisceadal
  Na cuisleanna ag comhaireamh:
Ansin do leath an tAngelus
  Im-shiollabchrith ar bheolaibh,
Ach do tháinig éag ar Amenibh
  Mar chogarnach sa tseomra:
Do leanadh leis an gcantaireacht
  I mainistir na feola,
Na cuisleanna mar mhanachaibh
  Ag siollabadh na nónta.

CLAUSTROPHOBIA

  In aice an fhíona
  Tá coinneal is sceon,
  Tá dealbh mo Thiarna
  D'réir dealraimh gan chomhacht,
  Tá a dtiocfaidh den oíche
  Mar shluaite sa chlós,
  Tá rialtas na hoíche
  Lasmuigh den bhfuinneoig;
  Má mhúchann mo choinneal
  Ar ball de m'ainneoin
  Léimfidh an oíche
  Isteach im scamhóig,

SYLLABLING

A nurse was in a hospital
 In the afternoon brightness
And pulses there were throbbing
 Regularly in beds;
She stood before each bed-stead
 And stayed a short while counting,
Jotting down the measure
 Syllabling in each wrist;
She syllabled herself at length
 Rhythmically from the ward
And left behind a chorus
 Of pulses keeping time.
It was then the Angelus spread its
 Syllable-shake across lips there
Till Amens died away
 Like whispering in the ward:
But the murmuring continued
 In the monastery of flesh,
The pulses going like monks
 Syllabling their plain-chant.

translated by Patrick Crotty

CLAUSTROPHOBIA

Next to the wine
Stand a candle and terror,
The statue of my Lord
Bereft of its power;
What's left of the night
Is massing in the yard,
Night's empire
Is outside the window;
If my candle fails
Despite my efforts
The night will leap
Right into my lungs,

Sárófar m'intinn
Is ceapfar dom sceon,
Déanfar díom oíche,
Bead im dhoircheacht bheo:
    Ach má mhaireann mo choinneal
    Aon oíche amháin
    Bead im phoblacht solais
    Go dtiocfaidh an lá

REO

Maidin sheaca ghabhas amach
Is bhí seál póca romham ar sceach,
Rugas air le cur im phóca
Ach sciorr sé uaim mar bhí sé reoite:
Ní héadach beo a léim óm ghlaic
Ach rud fuair bás aréir ar sceach:
Is siúd ag taighde mé fé m'intinn
Go bhfuaireas macasamhail an ní seo –
    Lá dar phógas bean dem mhuintir
    Is í ina cónra reoite, sínte.

FIABHRAS

Tá sléibhte na leapa mós ard,
Tá breoiteacht 'na brothall 'na lár,
Is fada an t-aistear urlár,
    Is na mílte is na mílte i gcéin
    Tá suí agus seasamh sa saol.

Atáimid i gceantar bráillín,
Ar éigean más cuimhin linn cathaoir,
Ach bhí tráth sar ba mhachaire sinn,
    In aimsir choisíochta fadó,
    Go mbímis chomh hard le fuinneog.

My mind will collapse
And terror be made for me,
Taken over by night,
I'll be darkness alive:
    But if my candle lasts
    Just this one night
    I'll be a republic of light
    Until dawn.

translated by Patrick Crotty

FROZEN STIFF

As I went out one frosty morning
A handkerchief lay before me on a bush
I grasped it to put it in my pocket
But, frozen, it slithered away.
No living cloth leaped from my hand
But a thing that died last night on a bush:
Rummaging then the depths of my mind
I came up with this parallel –
    The day I kissed a woman of my people
    And she in her coffin, frozen, stretched.

translated by Patrick Crotty

FEVER

The mountains of the bed are high,
The sick-valley sultry with heat,
It's a long way down to the floor,
    And miles and miles further
    To a world of work and leisure.

We're in a land of sheets
Where chairs have no meaning,
But there was a time before this levelled time,
    A walking time long ago,
    When we were high as a window.

127

Tá pictiúir ar an bhfalla ag at,
Tá an fráma imithe ina lacht,
Ceal creidimh ní féidir é bhac,
   Tá nithe ag druidim fém dhéin,
   Is braithim ag titim an saol.

Tá ceantar ag taisteal ón spéir,
Tá comharsanacht suite ar mo mhéar,
Dob fhuirist dom breith ar shéipéal,
   Tá ba ar an mbóthar ó thuaidh,
   Is níl ba na síoraíochta chomh ciúin.

The picture on the wall is heaving,
The frame has liquefied,
Without faith I can't hold it at bay,
    Everything's driving at me
    And I feel the world falling away.

A whole district's arriving from the sky,
A neighbourhood's set up on my finger,
Easy now to grab a church –
    There are cows on the northern road
    And the cows of eternity are not so quiet.

translated by Patrick Crotty

VALENTIN IREMONGER

Born Dublin, 1918. Educated at Synge Street Christian Brothers'
School, Coláiste Mhuire and the Abbey Theatre School of Acting.
Actor and producer at Abbey and Gate theatres, 1940–6. Entered Irish
diplomatic service, 1946. Ambassador to Sweden, Norway and Finland
(1964–8), India (1968–73), Luxembourg (1973–9) and Portugal
(1979–83). Poetry editor of *Envoy*, 1949–51. Co-edited *Contemporary
Irish Poetry* (1949) with Robert Greacen. Translated Mící Mac Gabhann's
Rothaí Móra an tSaoil as *The Hard Road to Klondike* (1962) and Dónal
Mac Amhlaigh's *Dialann Deoraí* as *An Irish Navvy, the Diary
of an Exile* (1964). Died 1991.

Iremonger wrote a small number of impressive lyrics in his late twenties
and very little thereafter. 'This Houre Her Vigill' negotiates a debt to
John Crowe Ransom to vindicate itself as an authentic and memorable
elegy. 'Clear View in Summer' is perhaps the most spacious of half a
dozen or so meditations on the tyranny of time – a theme which
obsessed Iremonger and may have silenced him. The syncopated
rhythms and nonchalant pose of 'Icarus' provided a lead no Irish
poet would follow for decades.

THIS HOURE HER VIGILL

Elizabeth, frigidly stretched,
On a spring day surprised us
With her starched dignity and the quietness
Of her hands clasping a black cross.

With book and candle and holy water dish
She received us in the room with the blind down.
Her eyes were peculiarly closed and we knelt shyly
Noticing the blot of her hair on the white pillow.

We met that evening by the crumbling wall
In the field behind the house where I lived
And talked it over, but could find no reason
Why she had left us whom she had liked so much.

Death, yes, we understood: something to do
With age and decay, decrepit bodies;
But here was this vigorous one, aloof and prim,
Who would not answer our furtive whispers.

Next morning, hearing the priest call her name,
I fled outside, being full of certainty,
And cried my seven years against the church's stone wall.
For eighteen years I did not speak her name

Until this autumn day when, in a gale,
A sapling fell outside my window, its branches
Rebelliously blotting the lawn's green. Suddenly, I thought
Of Elizabeth, frigidly stretched.

CLEAR VIEW IN SUMMER

Heavy with leaves the garden bushes again
Sun, and the trees admire them, lazily.
Cabbages and carnations, drills and beds of them, droop tiredly
And far away the hills, like dry dogs, crouching, squeal for water.
Love, who is it whispers everything is in order
On this summer afternoon, when nothing moves, not even the
    flies, strangely,
As we relax by the lawn, here under the pear-tree, watching idly
The leaves declining, the shadows surely lengthen.

But it won't be always summer – not for us; there are bad times
    coming
When you and I will look with envy on old photographs,
Remembering how we stood, there in the sun, looking like gods,
While the days of our lives, like fruit, swelled and decayed,
And how, by the lake,
Its surface, one August evening, unchipped, walking, we laughed
As love slipped his arms through ours and we gladly followed
The path he showed us through life's valley running.

There'll be much to recall then, when, like wet late summer
    leaves,

131

The days under our tread don't rustle, no other summer waiting
Around the turn of a new year with rich clothes to grace us
Whose subtle beauty will have long since languished;
And Nature's flashing greenness will stitch up our hearts with
　anguish
Each day when August with sunlight riddles the branches, the
　leaves taking
Voluptuously the south west wind's caresses
Year after dying year.

And yet the declension of each following season, each day's
Defection, splits open our hope only and not our courage, safe
　and sound
In the deep shelter of our awareness; the bushes and tall trees
Flourish and go down unconsciously in defeat
While full-grown man, whose pride the angels weep,
Watches love itself gutter out some dull evening, nobody around,
Winter moving in, no fuel left, the lights not working, the lease
Unrenewable, summer a seldom-remembered scat-phrase.

ICARUS

As, even to-day, the airman, feeling the plane sweat
Suddenly, seeing the horizon tilt up gravely, the wings shiver,
Knows that, for once, Daedalus has slipped up badly,
Drunk on the job, perhaps, more likely dreaming, high-flier
　Icarus,
Head butting down, skidding along the light-shafts
Back, over the tones of the sea-waves and the slip-stream, heard
The gravel-voiced, stuttering trumpets of his heart

Sennet among the crumbling court-yards of his brain the mistake
Of trusting somebody else on an important affair like this;
And, while the flat sea, approaching, buckled into oh! avenues
Of acclamation, he saw the wrong story fan out into history,
Truth, undefined, lost in his own neglect. On the hills,
The summer-shackled hills, the sun spanged all day;
Love and the world were young and there was no ending:

But star-chaser, big-time-going, chancer Icarus
Like a dog on the sea lay and the girls forgot him,
And Daedalus, too busy hammering another job,
Remembered him only in pubs. No bugler at all
Sobbed taps for the young fool then, reported missing,
Presumed drowned, wing-bones and feathers on the tide
Drifting in casually, one by one.

FERGUS ALLEN

Born London, of Irish father, 1921. Moved to Dublin at six months. Educated at Newtown School, Waterford, and Trinity College Dublin. Long career in British civil service (as, *inter alia*, director of hydraulics research and First Civil Service Commissioner). Has lived in Berkshire since his retirement.

Allen was in his seventy-third year when his first collection of poems was published. He writes gracefully and with an almost hermetic self-possession in a variety of styles, many of his poems combining a taste for the exotic with a note of resignation. 'The Fall', an uncharacteristic foray into light verse, seems destined for immortality as a recitation piece.

ELEGY FOR FAUSTINA

Faustina, if that was your name, you are dead,
And your beauty, which sculptors hinted at in stone
And poets expanded their language to render in words,
Is less than a cobweb in a scholar's mind.
And now I (how foolish it sounds) feel for you something –
At all costs let us not call it love.

But there are nights when instead of sleeping I think of you
And lie feverishly awake on knives of roses,
And as it were through a crack in an embankment
Besieging sorrow enters, and ridiculous tears
Exude from my prosaic mud-coloured eyes.
Later I sleep, dreaming perhaps of streets and buses.

Or in the sunlight, walking through the streets,
My tie neatly knotted and my hair smoothed down,
To all appearances like someone in his senses,
There are days when it seems you are continually present
And I think of your cream-coloured body, your carmine lips
And your impossible pride (for that I blame your parents).

But each time, as though through depths of glass, I see you
Surrounded by netted birds and captured lovers,
I remember today's ruin which tourists yawn at
Was the temple where self-consuming candles flared,
That Venus was someone important when you were young
And the fixed stars were fixed in different places.

THE FALL

The Garden of Eden (described in the Bible)
Was Guinness's Brewery (mentioned by Joyce),
Where innocent Adam and Eve were created
And dwelt from necessity rather than choice;

For nothing existed but Guinness's Brewery,
Guinness's Brewery occupied all,
Guinness's Brewery everywhere, anywhere –
Woe that expulsion succeeded the Fall!

The ignorant pair were encouraged in drinking
Whatever they fancied whenever they could,
Except for the porter or stout which embodied
Delectable knowledge of Evil and Good.

In Guinness's Brewery, innocent, happy,
They tended the silos and coppers and vats,
They polished the engines and coopered the barrels
And even made pets of the Brewery rats.

One morning while Adam was brooding and brewing
It happened that Eve had gone off on her own,
When a serpent like ivy slid up to her softly
And murmured seductively, Are we alone?

O Eve, said the serpent, I beg you to sample
A bottle of Guinness's excellent stout,
Whose nutritive qualities no one can question
And stimulant properties no one can doubt;

It's tonic, enlivening, strengthening, heartening,
Loaded with vitamins, straight from the wood,
And further enriched with the not undesirable
Lucrative knowledge of Evil and Good.

So Eve was persuaded and Adam was tempted,
They fell and they drank and continued to drink
(Their singing and dancing and shouting and prancing
Prevented the serpent from sleeping a wink).

Alas, when the couple had finished a barrel
And swallowed the final informative drops,
They looked at each other and knew they were naked
And covered their intimate bodies with hops.

The anger and rage of the Lord were appalling,
He wrathfully cursed them for taking to drink
And hounded them out of the Brewery, followed
By beetles (magenta) and elephants (pink).

The crapulous couple emerged to discover
A universe full of diseases and crimes,
Where porter could only be purchased for money
In specified places at specified times.

And now in this world of confusion and error
Our only salvation and hope is to try
To threaten and bargain our way into Heaven
By drinking the heavenly Brewery dry.

MÁIRE MHAC AN TSAOI

Born into prominent republican family, Dublin, 1922. Learned Irish as a
child in west Kerry Gaeltacht. Educated at University College Dublin
and the Sorbonne. Abandoned Celtic studies for law degree and career
in Irish diplomatic service in Paris and Madrid. Lived in Ghana and
New York before settling in Dublin in late 1960s. Wrote *A Concise
History of Ireland* (1972) with her husband, Conor Cruise O'Brien.

Máire Mhac an tSaoi's poetry is notable for its vernacular purity and its
continuity with the idioms and motifs of traditional song. Her early
work, which unsentimentally portrays the sexuality of young
womanhood, has received most critical attention, though she has
produced poems of distinction in all phases of her career. 'Ceathrúintí
Mháire Ní Ogáin' explores an unhappy love affair in the persona
of Máire Ní Ógáin, mistress of the eighteenth-century poet
Donncha Rua Mac Conmara. 'Ná bí ag déanamh Máire Ní Ógáin
díot féin' – 'Don't be making a Mary Hogan [that is, a fool] of
yourself' – is a Munster proverb.

CAOINEADH

Glór goil ar an ngaoith
   Is brat síne liathaigh spéartha,
Ise dob áille fág ina luí
   Ina caoluaigh chúng ina haonar.

Tiocfaidh an leoithne bhog aniar
   Is an duilliúr úr ar lomaghéaga,
Líonfaidh ré is éireoidh grian,
   Ina gcúrsa síor triallfaidh réalta;

Is as an gcré tá os a cionn,
   As a hucht geal, as a caomhchorp,
Trí aoibh an lae is deora ón ndrúcht,
   Trí fhód aníos fásfaidh féara –

Ach choíche ní cúmfar ceol ceart,
   Feasta, ná caoinvéarsa;
Cailleann anois an croí a neart,
   Is an mheabhair ghlic, cailleann a héifeacht.

CEATHRÚINTÍ MHÁIRE NÍ ÓGÁIN

I

Ach a mbead gafa as an líon seo –
Is nár lige Dia gur fada san –
Béidir go bhfónfaidh cuimhneamh
Ar a bhfuaireas de shuaimhneas id bhaclainn.

Nuair a bheidh ar mo chumas guíochtaint,
Comaoine is éisteacht Aifrinn,
Cé déarfaidh ansan nach cuí dhom
Ar 'shonsa is ar mo shon féin achaine?

Ach comhairle idir dhá linn duit,
Ná téir ródhílis in achrann,

LAMENT

The sound of tears on the wind
   And storm-clouds darkening the skies;
She, the loveliest, let her lie
   In her little narrow grave on her own.

From the west the gentle breeze will come
   And the fresh leaf on boughs now bare,
Moon will wax and sun will rise,
   And the stars resume their courses;

And from the clay above her,
   From her bright breast, from her dear corpse,
Through the day's beauty and the dew's tears,
   Up through the sod will grow grasses

But never will appropriate music be composed,
   No never, nor delicate verses;
Now the heart loses it strength,
   And the quick mind, it loses its usefulness.

translated by Patrick Crotty

MARY HOGAN'S QUATRAINS

I

If I once got free of this net –
And God grant that won't be too long –
I could perhaps live on the memory
Of the ease I found in your arms.

When I learn again how to pray,
Hear Mass and go to Communion,
Who'll say then it's not right
To storm heaven for you and for me.

But a bit of advice in the meantime –
Don't get too fondly attached;

139

Mar go bhfuilimse meáite ar scaoileadh
Pé cuibhrinn é a snaidhmfear eadrainn.

II

Beagbhean ar amhras daoine,
Beagbhean ar chros na sagart,
Ar gach ní ach a bheith sínte
Idir tú agus falla –

Neamhshuím liom fuacht na hoíche,
Neamhshuím liom scríb is fearthainn,
Sa domhan cúng rúin teolaí seo
Ná téann thar fhaobhar na leapan –

Ar a bhfuil romhainn ní smaoinfeam,
Ar a bhfuil déanta cheana,
Linne an uain, a chroí istigh,
Is mairfidh sí go maidin.

III

Achar bliana atáim
Ag luí farat id chlúid,
Deacair anois a rá
Cad leis a raibh mo shúil!

Ghabhais de chosaibh i gcion
A tugadh chomh fial ar dtúis,
Gan aithint féin féd throigh
Fulag na feola a bhrúigh!

Is fós tá an creat umhal
Ar mhaithe le seanagheallúint,
Ach ó thost cantain an chroí
Tránn áthas na bpleisiúr.

IV

Tá naí an éada ag deol mo chí'se,
Is mé ag tál air de ló is d'oíche;
An gárlach gránna ag cur na bhfiacal,
Is de nimh a ghreama mo chuisle líonta.

For I am intent on breaking
Every bond there could ever be between us.

II

A fig for people's opinions,
A fig for the priest's interdictions,
For everything but lying stretched
Between you and the wall –

The freezing night is nothing,
And nothing the driving rain
To the secret world of warmth that spans
From one side of the bed to the other.

No need to think of the future
Nor of what has gone before –
Now is the hour, dear heart:
It will last until morning.

III

A whole year now I've spent
Stretched beneath your quilt,
It's difficult at this stage to say
What I was hoping to gain!

Your feet trod all over
What was given so freely at first,
While you had never a thought for
What trampled flesh must endure.

And still the body submits
For the sake of an ancient promise,
But now that the song has been stilled in my heart
Delight ebbs from our love-making.

IV

The child of jealousy is suckling my breast
– He demands it by day and by night –
He's an ugly whelp and he's cutting his teeth,
Their grip fills my veins with poison.

A ghrá, ná maireadh an trú beag eadrainn,
Is a fholláine, shláine a bhí ár n-aithne;
Barántas cnis a chloígh lem chneas airsin,
Is séala láimhe a raibh gach cead aici.

Féach nach meáite mé ar chion a shéanadh,
Cé gur sháigh an t-amhras go doimhin a phréa'cha;
Ar láir dhea-tharraic ná déan éigean,
Is díolfaidh sí an comhar leat ina séasúr féinig.

V

Is éachtach an rud í an phian,
Mar chaitheann an cliabh,
Is ná tugann faoiseamh ná spás
Ná sánas de ló ná d'oích '–

An té atá i bpéin mar táim
Ní raibh uaigneach ná ina aonar riamh,
Ach ag iompar cuileachtan de shíor
Mar bhean gin féna coim.

VI

'Ní chodlaím ist oíche' –
Beag an rá, ach an bhfionnfar choíche
Ar shúile oscailte
Ualach na hoíche?

VII

Fada liom anocht!
Do bhí ann oíche
Nárbh fhada faratsa –
Dá leomhfainn cuimhneamh.

Go deimhin níor dheacair san,
An ród a d'fhillfinn –
Dá mba cheadaithe
Tar éis aithrí ann.

Don't let the little wretch divide us, love,
So wholesome and healthy was our mating;
Skin to skin was our union's guarantee,
Its seal a hand granted every freedom.

Look, I've no wish to deny affection,
Even if doubt's roots have driven deep;
Don't force a reliable mare, and she'll
Serve you well in the future.

V

Pain is a wonderful thing!
How it wears out the rib-cage,
And gives no relief nor respite
By day or by night –

The person in pain like me
Can never be solitary,
Carrying an eternal companion
Like a mother carrying her unborn child.

VI

'I don't sleep at night' –
An easy boast, but who can measure
The weight of the night
On open eyes?

VII

How long tonight is!
There was once a night
We did not think long –
If I dare to remember.

The road I'd follow
Would be no hard road –
If return were permitted
After repentance.

Luí chun suilt
Is éirí chun aoibhnis
Siúd ba chleachtadh dhúinn –
Dá bhfaighinn dul siar air.

Lying down for pleasure
And rising with delight
Such was our practice –
If I could only resume it.

translated by Patrick Crotty

PEARSE HUTCHINSON

Born Glasgow, of Irish parents, 1927. Moved to Dublin, 1932. Educated
at Synge Street Christian Brothers' School and University College
Dublin. Translator with International Labour Organisation, Geneva,
1951–3. Drama critic, Radio Éireann, 1957–61. Lived in Spain for much
of the 1960s. Gregory Fellow in Poetry, University of Leeds, 1971–3.
Founder and co-editor of the literary magazine *Cyphers*.
Has translated extensively from Catalan and other Iberian languages.

Hutchinson writes in English and Irish. His work in both languages is
distinguished by its geniality and its concern for social justice. In English,
in particular, he is capable of an unusual lyric grace. These qualities
make any collection by Hutchinson highly readable, though some
readers may regret the informal, occasional quality of the greater
number of his poems.

MÁLAGA
for Sammy Sheridan

The scent of unseen jasmine on the warm night beach.

The tram along the sea road all the way from town
through its wide open sides drank unseen jasmine down.
Living was nothing all those nights but that strong flower,
whose hidden voice on darkness grew to such mad power
I could have sworn for once I travelled through full peace
and even love at last had perfect calm release
only by breathing in the unseen jasmine scent,
that ruled us and the summer every hour we went.

The tranquil unrushed wine drunk on the daytime beach.
Or from an open room all that our sight could reach
was heat, sea, light, unending images of peace;
and then at last the night brought jasmine's great release –
not images but calm uncovetous content,
the wide-eyed heart alert at rest in June's own scent.

146

In daytime's humdrum town from small child after child
we bought cluster on cluster of the star flower's wild
white widowed heads, re-wired on strong weed stalks they'd
    trimmed
to long green elegance; but still the whole month brimmed
at night along the beach with a strong voice like peace;
and each morning the mind stayed crisp in such release.

Some hint of certainty, still worth longing I could teach,
lies lost in a strength of jasmine down a summer beach.

GAELTACHT

Bartley Costello, eighty years old,
sat in his silver-grey tweeds on a kitchen chair,
at his door in Carraroe, the sea only yards away,
smoking a pipe, with a pint of porter beside his boot:
'For the past twenty years I've eaten nothing only
periwinkles, my own hands got them off those rocks.
You're a quarter my age, if you'd stick to winkles
you'd live as long as me, and keep as spry.'

In the Liverpool Bar, at the North Wall,
on his way to join his children over there,
an old man looked at me, then down at his pint
of rich Dublin stout. He pointed at the black glass:
'Is lú í an Ghaeilge ná an t-uisce sa ngloine sin.'

Beartla Confhaola, prime of his manhood,
driving between the redweed and the rock-fields,
driving through the sunny treeless quartz glory of Carna,
answered the foreigners' glib pity, pointing at the
small black cows: 'You won't get finer anywhere
than those black porry cattle.' In a pub near there,
one of the locals finally spoke to the townie:
'Labhraim le stráinséirí. Creidim gur chóir bheith
ag labhairt le stráinséirí.' Proud as a man who'd claim:
'I made an orchard of a rock-field,
bougainvillea clamber my turf-ricks.'

147

A Dublin tourist on a red-quarter strand
hunting firewood found the ruins of a boat,
started breaking the struts out – an old man came,
he shook his head, and said:
'Áá, a mhac: ná bí ag briseadh báid.'

The low walls of rock-fields in the west
are a beautiful clean whitegrey. There are chinks between
the neat stones to let the wind through safe,
you can see the blue sun through them.
But coming eastward in the same county,
the walls grow higher, darkgrey:
an ugly grey. And the chinks disappear:
through those walls you can see nothing.

Then at last you come to the city,
beautiful with salmon basking becalmed black below
a bridge over the pale-green Corrib; and ugly
with many shopkeepers looking down on men like
Bartley Costello and Beartla Confhaola because they
speak in Irish, eat periwinkles, keep
small black porry cattle, and on us
because we are strangers.

The Gaelic means, in verse 2: The Gaelic is less than the water in that glass; in
verse 3: I speak with strangers. I believe it's right to be speaking with strangers
(strangers, here, has the sense of outlanders, foreigners, runners-in); in verse 4:
Ah, son: don't be breaking a boat.

SOMETIMES FEEL

Like an old, wrecked sponge-diver leaking,
like a suit-of-armour leaking,
like a tree-stump leafing
after the shameful white has darkened over,
like an unwashed potato brutally cut,
the sickly off-white spattered
with dark patches of decay.

RICHARD MURPHY

Born Milford House, County Galway, 1927. First eight years spent in
Ceylon, where father (later governor of the Bahamas) was last British
mayor of Colombo. Educated at County Galway home, at Wellington
College, Magdalen College, Oxford, and the Sorbonne. English teacher
in Crete, 1953–4. Spent 1960s in Cleggan, County Galway, where he
restored a house and two Galway hookers (gaff-rigged work boats).
Visiting Professor of Poetry, Princeton University, 1974–5.
Lives Killiney, County Dublin, and regularly visits Sri Lanka.

'They were truly Irish,' wrote Richard Murphy of the boys who lived
outside the crumbling demesne wall of Milford House, 'and that is what
my brother and I wanted to be. They seemed sharper, freer, more
cunning than we were.' Murphy is perhaps the last Anglo-Irish poet,
fascinated by native modes of existence which appear more instinctive
than his own. 'Seals at High Island' evokes the romance and violence of
life beyond the pale of gentility; in 'Morning Call', celebration of the
wayward vitality of a pair of itinerant girls is tinged with an
unmistakably patrician benevolence. Much as he may admire it, the
speaker in these poems is excluded from the world of unselfconscious
intensity the seals and tinker girls share. Murphy's concern with
building, boat restoration and sailing – and indeed with poem
construction – might be said to embody a diminished, solitary version of
the colonist's 'civilising' imperative. The sea which confounds all
attempts at mastery may be identified, in one of its aspects at least, with
the Gaelic Irish to whom the poet feels bound by ties both of affection
and blood (as evinced by his surname and his insistence on his descent
from Patrick Sarsfield). Each of the first forty-nine sonnets in *The Price of
Stone* (1985) articulates a fragment of personal, familial or national
history through the 'character' of a building or man-made structure. In
the fiftieth, 'Natural Son', the poet's own voice breaks through in
response to the birth of his son as the living present emerges from the
debris of the past. Like the historical tableau *The Battle of Aughrim*
(1968), *The Price of Stone* demands to be read entire.

The boom above my knees lifts, and the boat
Drops, and the surge departs, departs, my cheek
Kissed and rejected, kissed, as the gaff sways
A tangent, cuts the infinite sky to red
Maps, and the mast draws eight and eight across
Measureless blue, the boatmen sing or sleep.

We point all day for our chosen island,
Clare, with its crags purpled by legend:
There under castles the hot O'Malleys,
Daughters of Granuaile, the pirate queen
Who boarded a Turk with a blunderbuss,
Comb red hair and assemble cattle.
Across the shelved Atlantic groundswell
Plumbed by the sun's kingfisher rod,
We sail to locate in sea, earth and stone
The myth of a shrewd and brutal swordswoman
Who piously endowed an abbey.
Seven hours we try against wind and tide,
Tack and return, making no headway.
The north wind sticks like a gag in our teeth.

Encased in a mirage, steam on the water,
Loosely we coast where hideous rocks jag,
An acropolis of cormorants, an extinct
Volcano where spiders spin, a purgatory
Guarded by hags and bristled with breakers.

The breeze as we plunge slowly stiffens:
There are hills of sea between us and land,
Between our hopes and the island harbour.
A child vomits. The boat veers and bucks.
There is no refuge on the gannet's cliff.
We are far, far out: the hull is rotten,
The spars are splitting, the rigging is frayed,
And our helmsman laughs uncautiously.
What of those who must earn their living
On the ribald face of a mad mistress?
We in holiday fashion know

150

This is the boat that belched its crew
Dead on the shingle in the Cleggan disaster.

Now she dips, and the sail hits the water.
She luffs to a squall; is struck; and shudders.
Someone is shouting. The boom, weak as scissors,
Has snapped. The boatman is praying.
Orders thunder and canvas cannonades.
She smothers in spray. We still have a mast;
The oar makes a boom. I am told to cut
Cords out of fishing-lines, fasten the jib.
Ropes lash my cheeks. Ease! Ease at last:
She swings to leeward, we can safely run.
Washed over rails our Clare Island dreams,
With storm behind us we straddle the wakeful
Waters that draw us headfast to Inishbofin

The bows rock as she overtakes the surge.
We neither sleep nor sing nor talk,
But look to the land where the men are mowing.
What will the islanders think of our folly?

The whispering spontaneous reception committee
Nods and smokes by the calm jetty.
Am I jealous of these courteous fishermen
Who hand us ashore, for knowing the sea
Intimately, for respecting the storm
That took nine of their men on one bad night
And five from Rossadillisk in this very boat?
Their harbour is sheltered. They are slow to tell
The story again. There is local pride
In their home-built ships.
We are advised to return next day by the mail.

But tonight we stay, drinking with people
Happy in the monotony of boats,
Bringing the catch to the Cleggan market,
Cultivating fields, or retiring from America
With enough to soak till morning or old age.

The bench below my knees lifts, and the floor
Drops, and the words depart, depart, with faces
Blurred by the smoke. An old man grips my arm,
His shot eyes twitch, quietly dissatisfied.
He has lost his watch, an American gold
From Boston gas-works. He treats the company
To the secretive surge, the sea of his sadness.
I slip outside, fall among stones and nettles,
Crackling dry twigs on an elder tree,
While an accordion drones above the hill.

Later, I reach a room, where the moon stares
Cobwebbed through the window. The tide has ebbed,
Boats are careened in the harbour. Here is a bed.

THE POET ON THE ISLAND
to Theodore Roethke

On a wet night, laden with books for luggage,
And stumbling under the burden of himself,
He reached the pier, looking for a refuge.

Darkly he crossed to the island six miles off:
The engine pulsed, the sails invented rhythm,
While the sea expanded and the rain drummed softly.

Safety on water, he rocked with a new theme:
And in the warmth of his mind's greenhouse bloomed
A poem nurtured like a chrysanthemum.

His forehead, a Prussian helmet, moody, domed,
Relaxed in the sun: a lyric was his lance.
To be loved by the people, he, a stranger, hummed

In the herring-store on Sunday crammed with drunks
Ballads of bawdry with a speakeasy stress.
Yet lonely they left him, 'one of the Yanks'.

The children understood. This was not madness.
How many orphans had he fathered in words
Robust and cunning, but never heartless.

He watched the harbour scouted by sea-birds:
His fate was like fish under poetry's beaks:
Words began weirdly to take off inwards.

Time that they calendar in seasons not in clocks,
In gardens dug over and houses roofed,
Was to him a see-saw of joys and shocks,

Where his body withered but his style improved.
A storm shot up, his glass cracked in a gale:
An abstract thunder of darkness deafened

The listeners he'd once given roses, now hail.
He'd burst the lyric barrier: logic ended.
Doctors were called, and he agreed to sail.

from THE BATTLE OF AUGHRIM

CASEMENT'S FUNERAL

After the noose, and the black diary deeds
Gossiped, his fame roots in prison lime:
The hanged bones burn, a revolution seeds.
Now Casement's skeleton is flying home.

A gun salutes, the troops slow-march, our new
Nation atones for her shawled motherland
Whose welcome gaoled him when a U-boat threw
This rebel quixote soaked on Banna Strand.

Soldiers in green guard the draped catafalque
With chalk remains of once ambiguous bone
Which fathered nothing till the traitor's dock
Hurt him to tower in legend like Wolfe Tone.

From gaol yard to the Liberator's tomb
Pillared in frost, they carry the freed ash,
Transmuted relic of a death-cell flame
Which purged for martyrdom the diarist's flesh.

On the small screen I watch the packed cortège
Pace from High Mass. Rebels in silk hats now
Exploit the grave with an old comrade's speech:
White hair tossed, a black cape flecked with snow.

SEALS AT HIGH ISLAND

The calamity of seals begins with jaws.
Born in caverns that reverberate
With endless malice of the sea's tongue
Clacking on shingle, they learn to bark back
In fear and sadness and celebration.
The ocean's mouth opens forty feet wide
And closes on a morsel of their rock.

Swayed by the thrust and backfall of the tide,
A dappled grey bull and a brindled cow
Copulate in the green water of a cove.
I watch from a cliff-top, trying not to move.
Sometimes they sink and merge into black shoals;
Then rise for air, his muzzle on her neck,
Their winged feet intertwined as a fishtail.

She opens her fierce mouth like a scarlet flower
Full of white seeds; she holds it open long
At the sunburst in the music of their loving;
And cries a little. But I must remember
How far their feelings are from mine marooned.
If there are tears at this holy ceremony
Theirs are caused by brine and mine by breeze.

When the great bull withdraws his rod, it glows
Like a carnelian candle set in jade.
The cow ripples ashore to feed her calf;

While an old rival, eyeing the deed with hate,
Swims to attack the tired triumphant god.
They rear their heads above the boiling surf,
Their terrible jaws open, jetting blood.

At nightfall they haul out, and mourn the drowned,
Playing to the sea sadly their last quartet,
An improvised requiem that ravishes
Reason, while ripping scale up like a net:
Brings pity trembling down the rocky spine
Of headlands, till the bitter ocean's tongue
Swells in their cove, and smothers their sweet song.

STORMPETREL

Gipsy of the sea
In winter wambling over scurvy whaleroads,
Jooking in the wake of ships,
A sailor hooks you
And carves his girl's name on your beak.

Guest of the storm
Who sweeps you off to party after party,
You flit in a sooty grey coat
Smelling of must
Barefoot across a sea of broken glass.

Waif of the afterglow
On summer nights to meet your mate you jink
Over sea-cliff and graveyard,
Creeping underground
To hatch an egg in a hermit's skull.

Pulse of the rock
You throb till daybreak on your cryptic nest
A song older than fossils,
Ephemeral as thrift.
It ends with a gasp.

MORNING CALL

Up from the trawlers in the fishdock they walk to my house
On high-soled clogs, stepping like fillies back from a forge
Newly shod, to wake me at sunrise from a single bed
With laughter peeling skin from a dream ripening on the mossy
Branches of my head – 'Let us in! Let us in! – and half-naked
I stumble over a floor of heaped paper to open my door of glass
To a flood that crosses the threshold, little blue waves

Nudging each other, dodging rocks they've got to leap over,
Freshening my brackish pools, to tell me of 'O such a night
Below in the boats!' 'We can't go home! What *will* they say?'
Can I think of a lie to protect them from God only knows
What trouble this will cause, what rows? 'We'll run away
And never come back!' – till they flop into black armchairs,
Two beautiful teenage girls from a tribe of tinkers,

Lovely as seals wet from fishing, hauled out on a rock
To dry their dark brown fur glinting with scales of salmon
When the spring tide ebbs. This is their everlasting day
Of being young. They bring to my room the sea's iodine odour
On a breeze of voices ruffling my calm as they comb their long
Hair tangled as weed in a rockpool beginning to settle clear.
Give me the sea-breath from your mouths to breathe a while!

from THE PRICE OF STONE

ROOF-TREE

After you brought her home with your first child
How did you celebrate? Not with a poem
She might have loved, but orders to rebuild
The house. Men tore me open, room by room.

Your daughter's cries were answered by loud cracks
Of hammers stripping slates; the clawing down
Of dozed rafters; dull, stupefying knocks
On walls. Proudly your hackwork made me groan.

Your greed for kiln-dried oak that could outlast
Seven generations broke her heart. My mind
You filled with rot-proof hemlock at a cost
That killed her love. The dust spread unrefined.

To renovate my structure, which survives,
You flawed the tenderest movement of three lives.

CONVENIENCE

The public servant of men's private parts,
Plain clothed in the underground below Eros,
With white glazed stalls, and see-through mirror arts,
I plumb our language empire's omphalos.

Your profane oracle I speak through a crack
In a mental block, going far back to the year
You stood here, epicentred on the shock
Of gross accusation, quaking at words like queer.

I watched you face an absurd firing squad
Unbuttoning uniforms. I, too, had lost
My primal sense in the promiscuous crowd.
Detected, blackmailed, judged, you paid the cost.

A life sentence, ambiguously imposed,
Props you behind all kinds of bars, exposed.

KYLEMORE CASTLE

Built for a cotton king, who loved the view
Unspoilt by mills, improved by famine's hand
That cleared away people, petrified I grew
Grotesquely rich on mountainous, poor land.

To last for ever, I had to be faced in stone
Dressed by wage-skeletons; a spindly pile
Of storm-grey turrets that defended no one,
And broke my maker, with his fabricated style.

Coming from church to hold her usual place
On Christmas nights, wheeled to the dining-room,

His wife's corpse embalmed in a sealed glass case
Obeyed his command in the brandy-lit gloom.

Now, my linenfold panelled halls retain
In mortmain his dark airs, which nuns maintain.

NATURAL SON

Before the spectacled professor snipped
The cord, I heard your birth-cry flood the ward,
And lowered your mother's tortured head, and wept.
The house you'd left would need to be restored.

No worse pain could be borne, to bear the joy
Of seeing you come in a slow dive from the womb,
Pushed from your fluid home, pronounced 'a boy'.
You'll never find so well equipped a room.

No house we build could hope to satisfy
Every small need, now that you've made this move
To share our loneliness, much as we try
Our vocal skill to wall you round with love.

This day you crave so little, we so much
For you to live, who need our merest touch.

THOMAS KINSELLA

Born Dublin, 1928. Educated at University College Dublin. Worked as
civil servant from 1948 until retiring from senior position in Department
of Finance, 1965. Taught at University of Southern Illinois, 1965–70,
and at Temple University, Philadelphia, for more than twenty years
from 1970. Now lives in County Wicklow. A process of sombre
retrieval from the past can be seen at work alike in Kinsella's poetry
and in his extensive translation from the Irish – *The Táin* (1969),
An Duanaire, 1600–1900: Poems of the Dispossessed (1981) and
The New Oxford Book of Irish Verse (1986). *The Dual Tradition:
An Essay on Poetry and Politics in Ireland* appeared in 1995.

Kinsella's early verse paid homage both to the agility of Auden and the
grandiloquence of Yeats, qualities he came to distrust in his later
practice. All but the opening piece in the selection derive from the
series of longer poems or sequences to which the second half of his
career has been devoted. In these interconnecting works of echoing
phrases and motifs, fragments of reminiscence from the poet's individual
struggle towards awareness are apprehended against a background of the
impersonal processes of history and prehistory. Voracity is a key trope
of this writing, whether in relation to the devouring of weaker
biological or political organisms by stronger, or to the poetic
imagination's forced consumption of the mess of the actual. The will
towards survival in the organic sphere provides a figure for the aesthetic
urge towards structure, and the recapitulations, blind alleys and
adaptations of evolutionary development are replicated in the gradually
unfolding poem series itself. It is impossible to reflect the scope and
movement of such a poetry in an anthology. I have preferred some of
the most nearly freestanding or lyrical individual poems or passages, but
all nine extracts yield their full significance only in the light of the more
abstract, metaphysical material which surrounds them. *One Fond
Embrace*, represented here by its introductory section, plays a
cannibalistic variation on the voracity metaphor to indict the materialism
of Dublin's ruling class. This late poem reintroduces a satirical, social
dimension more or less absent from Kinsella's work since
the *Nightwalker* sequence of 1967.

CHRYSALIDES

Our last free summer we mooned about at odd hours
Pedalling slowly through country towns, stopping to eat
Chocolate and fruit, tracing our vagaries on the map.

At night we watched in the barn, to the lurch of melodeon
    music,
The crunching boots of countrymen – huge and weightless
As their shadows – twirling and leaping over the yellow concrete.

Sleeping too little or too much, we awoke at noon
And were received with womanly mockery into the kitchen,
Like calves poking our faces in with enormous hunger.

Daily we strapped our saddlebags and went to experience
A tolerance we shall never know again, confusing
For the last time, for example, the licit and the familiar.

Our instincts blurred with change; a strange wakefulness
Sapped our energies and dulled our slow-beating hearts
To the extremes of feeling – insensitive alike

To the unique succession of our youthful midnights,
When by a window ablaze softly with the virgin moon
Dry scones and jugs of milk awaited us in the dark,

Or to lasting horror: a wedding flight of ants
Spawning to its death, a mute perspiration
Glistening like drops of copper in our path.

from NOTES FROM THE LAND OF THE DEAD

HEN WOMAN

The noon heat in the yard
smelled of stillness and coming thunder.
A hen scratched and picked at the shore.

It stopped, its body crouched and puffed out.
The brooding silence seemed to say 'Hush...'

The cottage door opened,
a black hole
in a whitewashed wall so bright
the eyes narrowed.
Inside, a clock murmured 'Gong...'

(I had felt all this before...)

She hurried out in her slippers
muttering, her face dark with anger,
and gathered the hen up jerking
languidly. Her hand fumbled.
Too late. Too late.

It fixed me with its pebble eyes
(seeing what mad blur?).
A white egg showed in the sphincter;
mouth and beak opened together;
and time stood still.

Nothing moved: bird or woman,
fumbled or fumbling – locked there
(as I must have been) gaping.

*

There was a tiny movement at my feet,
tiny and mechanical; I looked down.
A beetle like a bronze leaf
was inching across the cement,
clasping with small tarsi
a ball of dung bigger than its body.
The serrated brow pressed the ground humbly,
lifted in a short stare, bowed again;
the dung-ball advanced minutely,
losing a few fragments,
specks of staleness and freshness.

*

A mutter of thunder far off
– time not quite stopped.
I saw the egg had moved a fraction:
a tender blank brain
under torsion, a clean new world.

As I watched, the mystery completed.
The black zero of the orifice
closed to a point
and the white zero of the egg hung free,
flecked with greenish brown oils.

It slowly turned and fell.
Dreamlike, fussed by her splayed fingers,
it floated outward, moon–white,
leaving no trace in the air,
and began its drop to the shore.

★

I feed upon it still, as you see;
there is no end to that which,
not understood, may yet be noted
and hoarded in the imagination,
in the yolk of one's being, so to speak,
there to undergo its (quite animal) growth,
dividing blindly,
twitching, packed with will,
searching in its own tissue
for the structure
in which it may wake.
Something that had – clenched
in its cave – not been
now was: an egg of being.
Through what seemed a whole year it fell
– as it still falls, for me,
solid and light, the red gold beating
in its silvery womb,
alive as the yolk and white
of my eye; as it will continue
to fall, probably, until I die,

through the vast indifferent spaces
with which I am empty.

★

It smashed against the grating
and slipped down quickly out of sight.
It was over in a comical flash.
The soft mucous shell clung a little longer,
then drained down.
She stood staring, in blank anger.
Then her eyes came to life, and she laughed
and let the bird flap away.
'It's all the one
There's plenty more where that came from!'

Hen to pan!
It was a simple world.

ANCESTOR

I was going up to say something,
and stopped. Her profile against the curtains
was old, and dark like a hunting bird's.

It was the way she perched on the high stool,
staring into herself, with one fist
gripping the side of the barrier around her desk
– or her head held by something, from inside.
And not caring for anything around her
or anyone there by the shelves.
I caught a faint smell, musky and queer.

I may have made some sound – she stopped rocking
and pressed her fist in her lap; then she stood up
and shut down the lid of the desk, and turned the key.
She shoved a small bottle under her aprons
and came toward me, darkening the passageway.

Ancestor . . . among sweet- and fruit-boxes.
Her black heart . . .
                    Was that a sigh?

– brushing by me in the shadows,
with her heaped aprons, through the red hangings
to the scullery, and down to the back room.

TEAR

I was sent in to see her.
A fringe of jet drops
chattered at my ear
as I went in through the hangings.

I was swallowed in chambery dusk.
My heart shrank
at the smell of disused
organs and sour kidney.

The black aprons I used to
bury my face in
were folded at the foot of the bed
in the last watery light from the window

(Go in and say goodbye to her)
and I was carried off
to unfathomable depths.
I turned to look at her.

She stared at the ceiling
and puffed her cheek, distracted,
propped high in the bed
resting for the next attack.

The covers were gathered close
up to her mouth,
that the lines of ill-temper still
marked. Her grey hair

was loosened out like
a young woman's all over
the pillow, mixed with the shadows
criss-crossing her forehead

and at her mouth and eyes,
like a web of strands tying down her head
and tangling down toward the shadow
eating away the floor at my feet.

I couldn't stir at first, nor wished to,
for fear she might turn and tempt me
(my own father's mother)
with open mouth

– with some fierce wheedling whisper –
to hide myself one last time
against her, and bury my
self in her drying mud.

Was I to kiss her? As soon
kiss the damp that crept
in the flowered walls
of this pit.

Yet I had to kiss.
I knelt by the bulk of the death bed
and sank my face in the chill
and smell of her black aprons.

Snuff and musk, the folds against my eyelids,
carried me into a derelict place
smelling of ash: unseen walls and roofs
rustled like breathing.

I found myself disturbing
dead ashes for any trace
of warmth, when far off
in the vaults a single drop

splashed. And I found
what I was looking for
– not heat nor fire,
not any comfort,

but her voice, soft, talking to someone
about my father: 'God help him, he cried
big tears over there by the machine
for the poor little thing.' Bright

drops on the wooden lid for
my infant sister. My own
wail of child-animal grief
was soon done, with any early guess

at sad dullness and tedious pain
and lives bitter with hard bondage.
How I tasted it now –
her heart beating in my mouth!

She drew an uncertain breath
and pushed at the clothes
and shuddered tiredly.
I broke free

and left the room
promising myself
when she was really dead
I would really kiss.

My grandfather half looked up
from the fireplace as I came out,
and shrugged and turned back
with a deaf stare to the heat.

I fidgeted beside him for a minute
and went out to the shop.
It was still bright there
and I felt better able to breathe.

Old age can digest
anything: the commotion
at Heaven's gate – the struggle
in store for you all your life.

How long and hard it is
before you get to Heaven,
unless like little Agnes
you vanish with early tears.

from ONE

38 PHOENIX STREET

Look.
          I was lifted up
past rotten bricks weeds
to look over the wall.
A mammy lifted up a baby on the other side
Dusty smells. Cat. Flower bells
hanging down purple red.

Look.
          The other. Looking.
My finger picked at a bit of dirt
on top of the wall and a quick
wiry redgolden thing
ran back down a little hole.

★

We knelt up on our chairs in the lamplight
and leaned on the brown plush, watching the gramophone.
The turning record shone and hissed
under the needle, liftfalling, liftfalling.
John McCormack chattered in his box.

Two little tongues of flame burned
in the lamp chimney, wavering
their tips. On the glassy belly
little drawnout images quivered.
Jimmy's mammy was drying the delph in the shadows.

★

Mister Cummins always hunched down
sad and still beside the stove,
with his face turned away toward the bars.
His mouth so calm, and always set so sadly.
A black rubbery scar stuck on his white forehead.

Sealed in his sad cave. Hisshorror erecting
slowly out of its rock nests, nosing the air.
He was buried for three days under a hill of dead,
the faces congested down all round him,
grinning *Dardanelles!* in the dark.

They noticed him by a thread of blood
glistening among the black crusts on his forehead.
His heart gathered all its weakness, to beat.

A worm hanging down, its little round
black mouth open. Sad father.

★

I spent the night there once
in a strange room, tucked in against the wallpaper
on the other side of our own bedroom wall.

Up in a corner of the darkness the Sacred Heart
leaned down in his long clothes over a red oil lamp
with his women's black hair and his eyes lit up in red,
hurt and blaming. He held out the Heart
with his women's fingers, like a toy.

The lamp-wick, with a tiny head
of red fire, wriggled in its pool.
The shadows flickered: the Heart beat!

HIS FATHER'S HANDS

I drank firmly
and set the glass down between us firmly.
You were saying.

My father.
Was saying.

His finger prodded and prodded,
marring his point. Emphas-
emphasemphasis.

I have watched
his father's hands before him

    cupped, and tightening the black Plug
between knife and thumb,
carving off little curlicues
to rub them in the dark of his palms,

or cutting into new leather at his bench,
levering a groove open with his thumb,
insinuating wet sprigs for the hammer.

He kept the sprigs in mouthfuls
and brought them out in silvery
units between his lips.

I took a pinch out of their hole
and knocked them one by one into the wood,
bright points among hundreds gone black,
other children's – cousins and others, grown up.

    Or his bow hand scarcely moving,
scraping in the dark corner near the fire,
his plump fingers shifting on the strings.

To his deaf, inclined head
he hugged the fiddle's body,
whispering with the tune

with breaking heart
when'er I hear
in privacy, across a blocked void,

the wind that shakes the barley.
The wind. . .
round her grave. . .

on my breast in blood she died. . .
But blood for blood without remorse
I've ta'en. . .

Beyond that.

★

Your family, Thomas, met with and helped
many of the Croppies in hiding from the Yeos
or on their way home after the defeat
in south Wexford. They sheltered the Laceys
who were later hanged on the Bridge in Ballinglen
between Tinahely and Anacorra.

From hearsay, as far as I can tell
the Men Folk were either Stone Cutters
or masons or probably both.
                              In the 18
and late 1700s even the farmers
had some other trade to make a living.

They lived in Farnese among a Colony
of North of Ireland or Scotch settlers left there
in some of the dispersals or migrations
which occurred in this Area of Wicklow and Wexford
and Carlow. And some years before that time
the Family came from somewhere around Tullow.

Beyond that.

★

Littered uplands. Dense grass. Rocks everywhere,
wet underneath, retaining memory of the long cold.

First, a prow of land
chosen, and webbed with tracks;

then boulders chosen
and sloped together, stabilized in menace.

I do not like this place.
I do not think the people who lived here
were ever happy. It feels evil.
Terrible things happened.
I feel afraid here when I am on my own.

★

Dispersals or migrations.
Through what evolutions or accidents
toward that peace and patience
by the fireside, that blocked gentleness. . .

That serene pause, with the slashing knife,
in kindly mockery,
as I busy myself with my little nails
at the rude block, his bench.

The blood advancing
– gorging vessel after vessel –
and altering in them
one by one.

Behold, that gentleness already
modulated twice, in others:
to earnestness and iteration;
to an offhandedness, repressing various impulses.

★

Extraordinary. . . The big block – I found it
years afterward in a corner of the yard
in sunlight after rain
and stood it up, wet and black:
it turned under my hands, an axis
of light flashing down its length,
and the wood's soft flesh broke open,
countless little nails
squirming and dropping out of it.

171

1956

Fifteen minutes or thereabouts
of Prelude and Liebestod
– elephant into orgasm –
and I was about ready.

I crooked my foot
around the chair-leg
and my fingers around
the pen, and set

the star-dome
creaking with music
at absolute zero
across the bankrupt night.

A couple of hundred yards around the corner
in a moon-flooded office in Merrion Street
my Finance files dreamed,
propped at the ledge,

my desk moved
                    infinitesimally.
Over the entire country,
over market and harbour, in silvery light,

emanations of government
materialised and embraced
downward and began
metaphysically to bite.

A small herd of friends
stared back from the Mailboat rail.
A mongrel dog lapped
in a deserted town square.

A book came
fluttering out of the dark
and flapped
at the window.

from THE MESSENGER

It is an August evening, in Wicklow.
It is getting late. They have tussled in love.
They are hidden, near the river bank.
            They lie face up in the grass, not touching,
head close to head, a woman and her secret husband.
A gossamer ghost arrows and hesitates

out of the reeds, and stands in the air above them
insect-shimmering, and settles on a bright
inner upturn of her dress. The wings

close up like palms. The body, a glass worm,
is pulsing. The tail-tip winces and quivers:

I *think* this is where I come in . . .

Trailing a sunless instinct,
a saw-jawed multiple past,
an edible (almost liquid)
vulnerability,
and winged! – weightless and wondrous! –
up from the bloodied slime
through the arms of a black rainbow
scooping down in beauty
he has come, he has arisen
out of the pool of night!

It is! It is!
            Hurry!
says the great womb-whisper.
Quick!
            I am all egg!

from OUT OF IRELAND

HARMONIES

Seamus of the Smart Suit, box player, made
signals to us across the grass tussocks and graves
the day we all came down from Cork
to commemorate our musical friend.

By Gobnait's sculpted lump
– a slab of a woman on a frieze
of stone buds and the locked bodies of bees –
he struggled in his nose with English,

showing the Holy Stations and instructing
with rigid finger and embarrassed snorts,
his box squeezed shut back in the house
with Máirtín's pipes and the pair of fiddles,

the same instruments, ranging together
in natural sweetness, with a many-sounded
and single voice, that gave Iohannes Scotus
– Eriugena, and instructing the known world –

his harmonious certainty: that the world's parts,
ill-fitted in their stresses and their pains,
will combine at last in polyphonic sweet-breathing union
and all created Nature ascend like joined angels,

limbs and bodies departing the touch of Earth
static in a dance of return, all Mankind gathered
stunned at the world's edge
silent in a choir of understanding.

from ONE FOND EMBRACE

Enough
is enough:
poring over that organic pot.

174

I knuckled my eyes.
Their drying jellies
answered with speckles and images.

Time spurted in the narrows of my wrists
channelled, for the moment, where I choose.
I leaned back and stretched

and embraced all
this hearth and home
echoing with the ghosts

of prides and joys,
bicycles and holy terrors,
our grown and scattered loves.

And all this place
where (it occurs to me)
I never want to be anywhere else.

Where the particulars conspire.
Which is not to say
serenity and the interplay of friends

but the brick walls
of this sagging district, against which
it alerts me to knock my head.

With a scruffy Nineteenth Century
history of half-finished
colonials and upstarts. Still with us.

With a half charm,
half gracious, spacious,
and a miscellaneous vigour.

Sniffed at. Our neighbourhood developer
thinking big in his soiled crombie.
The rodent element bidding out

– and who will deny them
a desirable nest, semi-detached,
and a pound in the pocket?

Catholic Action next door:
the double look over the half curtain;
social workers herding their problems

in off the street
with snooker cues and rosary beads;
Knights of Mercedes and the naked bulb

parked at large along both paths
in witness that the poor
are being given a party.

Invisible speculators, urinal architects
and the Corporation hand in hand
in potent compliant dance

flourishing their Compulsory Purchase Orders
– a sovereign tool contrived
for digging out our Alien Beauties

in their metaphysical prime
(dug in though absentee)
employed in easement of our own native beauties,

planners of the wiped slate
bent painstaking over a bungled city
to turn it into a zoo:

Southward from Fatima Mansions
into the foothills
to where the transplanted can trudge

from Cherryfield Heights via Woodbine Crescent
through Bridget's Terrace and Kennedy's Villas
by Ard na Gréine and Cúl na Gaoithe

to Shangri-La for a bottle of milk;
Northward past our twinned experimental
concrete piss-towers for the underprivileged;

and at the heart, where the river runs
through Viking ghosts at every tide
past a set of shadow structures

that our city fathers, fumbling in their shadow budget,
beheld in vision for a while,
pulverising until the cash failed,

laying flat an enduring monument to themselves,
an office car park sunk deep in history.
May their sewers blast under them!

A sluggish creature
and difficult to house-train,
it spatters its own nest.

Dirty money gives dirty access.
And we were the generation
of positive disgrace.

And I want to throw my pen down.
And I want to throw my self down
and hang loose over some vault of peace.

JOHN MONTAGUE

Born Brooklyn, 1929. Raised in County Tyrone by his aunts from 1933. Educated St Patrick's College, Armagh, and University College Dublin. Attended postgraduate and writers' courses at a series of American universities, 1953–6. Publicity officer for Bord Fáilte, 1956–9. Settled in Paris, 1961, with periods teaching in Berkeley, California (1964, 1965), and University College Dublin, 1967–71. Lecturer in University College Cork, 1972–88. D.Litt. from State University of New York, 1987. Visiting professor at University of Albany, 1989–. Editor of *The Faber Book of Irish Verse* (1974) and *Bitter Harvest* (1989). Montague has published two works of fiction, *Death of a Chieftain and Other Stories* (1964) and *The Lost Notebook* (1987). *The Figure in the Cave and Other Essays* appeared in 1989.

The aesthetic at once recommended and embodied in '11 rue Daguerre' serves the tactfully symbolic art of 'A Drink of Milk', 'The Trout' and other early poems by John Montague. As his career evolved, however, Montague became less interested in a poetry of implication than in an imaginative engagement with history and politics. Conscious of his status as the first northern Catholic poet of international stature since the settlement of 1922, he evinces in his work an almost bardic sense of responsibility towards the North's minority community and the dispossessed Gaelic world from which it derives. Two book-length sequences, *The Rough Field* (1972) and *The Dead Kingdom* (1984), measure the broken history of the poet's family against the disruptions of centuries of conflict in Tyrone and Ireland generally. (The second of these is perhaps the more successful, and certainly the more integrated work: its dominant seven-syllable line, subtly interstitched with phrases of popular song, marks a considerable technical achievement. As the power of this poetry is cumulative, however, *The Dead Kingdom* is not represented here.) Montague has seemed to many to be at his best in the short lyric of personal experience – frequently the love poem – in which he displays the steady empirical fidelity promoted by '11 rue Daguerre'. An art of underemphasis and curtailment, his poetry can raise reticence to the status of eloquence.

178

Like dolmens round my childhood, the old people.

Jamie MacCrystal sang to himself,
A broken song without tune, without words;
He tipped me a penny every pension day,
Fed kindly crusts to winter birds.
When he died, his cottage was robbed,
Mattress and money box torn and searched.
Only the corpse they didn't disturb.

Maggie Owens was surrounded by animals,
A mongrel bitch and shivering pups,
Even in her bedroom a she-goat cried.
She was a well of gossip defiled,
Fanged chronicler of a whole countryside:
Reputed a witch, all I could find
Was her lonely need to deride.

The Nialls lived along a mountain lane
Where heather bells bloomed, clumps of foxglove.
All were blind, with Blind Pension and Wireless,
Dead eyes serpent-flicked as one entered
To shelter from a downpour of mountain rain.
Crickets chirped under the rocking hearthstone
Until the muddy sun shone out again.

Mary Moore lived in a crumbling gatehouse,
Famous as Pisa for its leaning gable.
Bag-apron and boots, she tramped the fields
Driving lean cattle from a miry stable.
A by-word for fierceness, she fell asleep
Over love stories, Red Star and Red Circle,
Dreamed of gypsy love rites, by firelight sealed.

Wild Billy Eagleson married a Catholic servant girl
When all his Loyal family passed on:
We danced round him shouting 'To Hell with King Billy',
And dodged from the arc of his flailing blackthorn.
Forsaken by both creeds, he showed little concern

Until the Orange drums banged past in the summer
And bowler and sash aggressively shone.

Curate and doctor trudged to attend them,
Through knee-deep snow, through summer heat,
From main road to lane to broken path,
Gulping the mountain air with painful breath.
Sometimes they were found by neighbours,
Silent keepers of a smokeless hearth,
Suddenly cast in the mould of death.

Ancient Ireland, indeed! I was reared by her bedside,
The rune and the chant, evil eye and averted head,
Fomorian fierceness of family and local feud.
Gaunt figures of fear and of friendliness,
For years they trespassed on my dreams,
Until once, in a standing circle of stones,
I felt their shadows pass

Into that dark permanence of ancient forms.

THE TROUT

Flat on the bank I parted
Rushes to ease my hands
In the water without a ripple
And tilt them slowly downstream
To where he lay, tendril light,
In his fluid sensual dream.

Bodiless lord of creation
I hung briefly above him
Savouring my own absence
Senses expanding in the slow
Motion, the photographic calm
That grows before action.

As the curve of my hands
Swung under his body

180

He surged, with visible pleasure.
I was so preternaturally close
I could count every stipple
But still cast no shadow, until

The two palms crossed in a cage
Under the lightly pulsing gills.
Then (entering my own enlarged
Shape, which rode on the water)
I gripped. To this day I can
Taste his terror on my hands.

A DRINK OF MILK

In the girdered dark
of the byre, cattle move;
warm engines hushed
to a siding groove

before the switch flicks
down for milking.
In concrete partitions
they rattle their chains

while the farmhand eases
rubber tentacles to tug
lightly but rhythmically
on their swollen dugs

and up the pale cylinders
of the milking machine
mounts an untouched
steadily pulsing stream.

Only the tabby steals
to dip its radar whiskers
with old fashioned relish
in a chipped saucer

and before Seán lurches
to kick his boots off
in the night-silent kitchen
he draws a mug of froth

to settle on the sideboard
under the hoard of delft.
A pounding transistor shakes
the Virgin on her shelf

as he dreams towards bed.
A last glance at a magazine,
he puts the mug to his head,
grunts, and drains it clean.

from A CHOSEN LIGHT

I 11 RUE DAGUERRE

At night, sometimes, when I cannot sleep
I go to the *atelier* door
And smell the earth of the garden.

It exhales softly,
Especially now, approaching springtime,
When tendrils of green are plaited

Across the humus, desperately frail
In their passage against
The dark, unredeemed parcels of earth.

There is white light on the cobblestones
And in the apartment house opposite –
All four floors – silence.

In that stillness – soft but luminously exact,
A chosen light – I notice that
The tips of the lately grafted cherry-tree

Are a firm and lacquered black.

FAMILY CONFERENCE

When the wall between her and ghost
Wears thin, then snuff, spittoon,
Soothing drink cannot restrain:
She ransacks the empty house.
The latch creaks with the voice
Of a husband, the crab of death
Set in his bowels, even the soft moon
Caught in the bathroom window
Is a grieving woman, her mother
Searching for home in the Asylum.
What awaits, she no longer fears
As dawn paints in the few trees
Of her landscape, a rusty shed
And garden. Today grandchildren
Call, but what has she to say
To the buoyant living, who may
Raise family secrets with the dead?

THE SAME GESTURE

There is a secret room
of golden light where
everything – love, violence,
hatred is possible;
and, again love.

Such intimacy of hand
and mind is achieved
under its healing light
that the shifting of
hands is a rite

like court music.
We barely know our
selves there though
it is what we always were
– most nakedly are –

and must remember
when we leave, re-
suming our habits
with our clothes:
work, phone, drive

through late traffic
changing gears with
the same gesture as
eased your snowbound
heart and flesh.

LAST JOURNEY
I.M. *James Montague*

We stand together
on the windy platform;
how crisp the rails
running out of sight
through the wet fields!

Carney, the station master,
is peering over
his frosted window:
the hand of the signal
points down.

Crowned with churns
a cart creaks up the
incline of Main Street
to the sliding doors
of the Co-Op.

A smell of coal,
the train is coming . . .
you climb slowly in,
propped by my hand to
a seat, back to the engine,

and we leave, waving
a plume of black smoke
over the rushy meadows,
small hills & hidden villages –
Beragh, Carrickmore,

Pomeroy, Fintona –
placenames that sigh
like a pressed melodeon
across this forgotten
Northern landscape.

SMALL SECRETS

Where I work
out of doors
children come
to present me
with an acorn
a pine cone –
small secrets –

and a fat
grass snail
who uncoils
to carry his
whorled house
over the top
of my table.

With a pencil
I nudge him
back into
himself, but
fluid horns
unfurl, damp
tentacles, to

probe, test
space before
he drags his
habitation
forward again
on his single
muscular foot

rippling along
its liquid self–
creating path.
With absorbed,
animal faces
the children
watch us both

but he will
have none of
me, the static
angular world
of books, papers –
which is neither
green nor moist –

only to climb
around, over
as with rest-
less glistening
energy, he races
at full tilt
over the ledge

onto the grass.
All I am left
with is, between
pine cone & acorn
the silver smear
of his progress
which will soon

wear off, like
the silvery galaxies,
mother of pearl
motorways, woven
across the grass
each morning by
the tireless snails

of the world,
minute as grains
of rice, gross
as conch or
triton, bequeath-
ing their shells
to the earth.

DOWAGER

I dwell in this leaky Western castle.
American matrons weave across the carpet,
Sorefooted as camels, and less useful.

Smooth Ionic columns hold up a roof.
A chandelier shines on a foxhound's coat:
The grandson of a grandmother I reared.

In the old days I read or embroidered,
But now it is enough to see the sky change,
Clouds extend or smother a mountain's shape.

Wet afternoons I ride in the Rolls;
Windshield wipers flail helpless against the rain:
I thrash through pools like smashing panes of glass.

And the light afterwards! Hedges steam,
I ride through a damp tunnel of sweetness,
The bonnet strewn with bridal hawthorn

From which a silver lady leaps, always young.
Alone, I hum with satisfaction in the sun,
An old bitch, with a warm mouthful of game.

from THE CAVE OF NIGHT

III CAVE

The rifled honeycomb
of the high-rise hotel
where a wind tunnel moans.
While jungleclad troops
ransack the Falls, race
through huddled streets,
we lie awake, the wide
window washed with rain,
your oval face, and tide
of yellow hair luminous
as you turn to me again
seeking refuge as the
cave of night blooms
with fresh explosions.

HERBERT STREET REVISITED
for Madeleine

I

A light is burning late
in this Georgian Dublin street:
someone is leading our old lives!

And our black cat scampers again
through the wet grass of the convent garden
upon his masculine errands.

The pubs shut: a released bull,
Behan shoulders up the street,
topples into our basement, roaring 'John!'

A pony and donkey cropped flank
by flank under the trees opposite;
short neck up, long neck down,

as Nurse Mullen knelt by her bedside
to pray for her lost Mayo hills,
the bruised bodies of Easter Volunteers.

Animals, neighbours, treading the pattern
of one time and place into history,
like our early marriage, while

tall windows looked down upon us
from walls flushed light pink or salmon
watching and enduring succession.

II

As I leave, you whisper,
'don't betray our truth'
and like a ghost dancer,
invoking a lost tribal strength
I halt in tree-fed darkness

to summon back our past,
and celebrate a love that eased
so kindly, the dying bone,
enabling the spirit to sing
of old happiness, when alone.

III

So put the leaves back on the tree,
put the tree back in the ground,
let Brendan trundle his corpse down
the street singing, like Molly Malone.

Let the black cat, tiny emissary
of our happiness, streak again
through the darkness, to fall soft
clawed into a landlord's dustbin.

Let Nurse Mullen take the last
train to Westport, and die upright
in her chair, facing a window
warm with the blue slopes of Nephin.

And let the pony and donkey come –
look, someone has left the gate open –
like hobbyhorses linked in
the slow motion of a dream

parading side by side, down
the length of Herbert Street,
rising and falling, lifting
their hooves through the moonlight.

JAMES SIMMONS

Born Derry, 1933. Educated at Foyle College, Derry, Campbell
College, Belfast, and University of Leeds. Taught at Friends' School,
Lisburn, 1958–63, and Ahmadu Bello University, Nigeria, 1963–6.
Founded the *Honest Ulsterman*, 1968. Lecturer in English and drama at
New University of Ulster, Coleraine, 1968–86. Presently co-director of
the Poets' House, a creative writing school in Portmuck, County
Antrim. A singer–songwriter as well as a poet, Simmons has
published a critical study, *Sean O'Casey* (1983).

Wary of rhetoric and of what he sees as the élitist assumptions of much
modern verse, Simmons adheres to traditional forms and a tough,
colloquially based poetic language. His characteristic idiom offers a
street-wise counterpart to John Hewitt's Calvinistic neatness. The note
of wry melancholy in the selected pieces is typical.

ONE OF THE BOYS

Our youth was gay but rough,
much drink and copulation.
If that seems not enough
blame our miseducation.
In shabby boarding houses
lips covered lips,
and in our wild carouses
there were companionships.
Cheap and mundane the setting
of all that we remember:
in August, dance-hall petting,
cinemas in December.
Now middle-aged I know,
and do not hide the truth,
used or misused years go
and take all kinds of youth.
We test the foreign scene
or grow too fat in banks,

salesmen for margarine,
soldiers in tanks,
the great careers all tricks,
the fine arts all my arse,
business and politics
a cruel farce.
Though fear of getting fired
may ease, and work is hated
less, we are tired, tired
and incapacitated.
On golf courses, in bars,
crutched by the cash we earn,
we think of nights in cars
with energy to burn.

WEST STRAND VISIONS

The man alone at the third floor window
is the man alone at the cliff's edge.
Below him gulls are cutting each other's
invisible paths of flight. Bent sideways
in his cockpit above the dog-fight
alone he observes engaging bi-planes
locked in each other's sights and strategies,
diving, swerving and climbing heavily,
and droning earthward in flames.

The man watching the pony-girl waving
on the West Strand to her three assistants
and suddenly rearing her horse and wheeling
off at a canter, followed by donkeys
into the grey curtain of rain,
is the man watching barbarians gather,
Tamburlaine, was it, or Genghis Khan,
shaggy in robes strange to the watcher,
returned from reconnoitring,
deciding and acting on God's plan.

The man who watches neglected children
leaping in yellow light of sunset
by waters whipped by wind, majestic
ten yards out and fierce,
but gentle in the shallows,
is me, estranged from mystery,
trying to hear what they say,
envying no one in the world but they
who never use words like 'beauty',
shouting in apparent ecstasy
a pane of glass and fifty yards away.

FROM THE IRISH

Most terrible was our hero in battle blows:
hands without fingers, shorn heads and toes
were scattered. That day there flew and fell
from astonished victims eyebrow, bone and entrail,
like stars in the sky, like snowflakes, like nuts in May,
like a meadow of daisies, like butts from an ashtray.

Familiar things, you might brush against or tread
upon in the daily round, were glistening red
with the slaughter the hero caused, though he had gone.
By proxy his bomb exploded, his valour shone.

BRENDAN KENNELLY

Born Ballylongford, County Kerry, 1936. Educated at St Ita's College,
Tarbert, Trinity College Dublin, and the University of Leeds.
Has taught for three decades at TCD, where he is professor of
modern literature.

Kennelly is a prolific poet whose verse shares something of the
conversational fluency for which he is celebrated as a media personality.
A more bracing, driven and antithetical quality enters his work in
Cromwell (1983), a sequence of 254 narrative and dramatic poems and
mock sonnets. Here Kennelly addresses the bloody imperatives of Irish
history by way of a series of fantastic confrontations between such
archetypal figures as Edmund Spenser, the Belly, the Butcher,
Oliver Cromwell and his complicitous victim, Buffún.

from CROMWELL

THREE TIDES

In our very own little civil war
The sea, as employed by some, is an exemplary weapon
Combining an ability to finish a job
With a reliable style of humiliation.
Proper use of such elemental efficiency, however,
Is available only to those who know
The sea's judicial character
In its constitutional ebb and flow.
As it approaches the shore
It nudges, first, a shy, frothful poison
Reminiscent of the slime on dying lips
Prior to that rattle that can still
Shred even the most knitted family
And cause fretful speculation about a will.
This is a slow poison, rhythmically, sensually slow.
Perhaps the stimulating moon
Quickens the pace because our law-abiding sea
Accelerates like a well-executed plan

Of dependable drowning waves, inexorable as generations
Of a fertile Catholic family true to God's
Randy laws, coming, going, coming, going, like sons
And daughters to work or hell or money or England or spawning
    beds.
Properly judged, a man buried up to his neck in the shore
Will take three tides to die. His brothers (mine too) say
This gives him time to meditate on his mistake
In taking the wrong side in that most uncivil war.
Unlike our manly land, our sea has never lied.
My father drowns to the moon's laws, head to one side.

VINTAGE

Jimeen Connor, the butcher, is coming round
The corner of the garage where his cabin
Stands, cosy enough there on sheltered ground.
Passing the spuds and cabbage in his garden
He rams the meathook into Oliver's belly,
Lifts him holus-bolus, hangs him from the iron
Ring. Soon enough, the ground is bloody.
Oliver protests, gurgling. Jimeen is gone
For his hacksaw, he's back, he's cutting
Oliver up, he's catching the blood in a plastic
Bucket, he smiles stretching it towards me:
'I'll have to salt and barrel Olly before eating.
Try this old Puritan wine. Vintage. Knock it back.'

If this is a dream, I dream it scares me
Because the blood of that honest Huntingdon farmer
Turned soldier turned statesman, albeit not wine
As rashly announced by the butcher Connor,
Seemed much the same as yours or mine.
I could have sworn as I stood there watching
It pour into the plastic bucket
I saw and heard the lips murmuring
Religiously, 'Fuck it. Fuck it.'

Next, the butcher – or was it myself? – tipped
The bucket on its side, the blood
Splashed the grass in a red unruly sprawl.

I remember thinking, as the blood escaped
Into the earth, that Oliver did what Oliver did.
So did the butcher. So do I. So do we all.

SEAMUS HEANEY

Born Mossbawn, Tamniarn, County Derry, 1939. Educated at St
Columb's College, Derry, and Queen's University Belfast. Worked as a
secondary school teacher, 1962–3. Lecturer at St Joseph's College,
Belfast, 1963–6 and at Queen's University, 1966–70. Guest lecturer at
University of California, Berkeley, 1970–1. Lived as a freelance writer at
Glanmore, County Wicklow, 1971–5. Lecturer at Carysfort College,
Dublin, 1975. Head of English department, Carysfort, 1976–81.
Founder member and director of Field Day Theatre Company, 1980.
Lecturer at University of Harvard, 1982–4. Boylston Professor of
Rhetoric and Oratory at Harvard since 1984. Professor of Poetry,
Oxford University, 1989–94. Has published two influential collections
of critical essays, *Preoccupations* (1980) and *The Government of the Tongue*
(1988). *The Cure at Troy*, a version of Sophocles' *Philoctetes*, was staged
by Field Day at Derry's Guildhall in 1990.

From the subtly emblematic rural naturalism of 'Churning Day' through
the mythopoeic grandeur of 'North' (represented here by 'Funeral
Rites') to the adroit cerebration of 'From the Canton of Expectation'
and 'Lightenings', Heaney has been the most protean, as well as the
most internationally visible, Irish poet since Yeats. His career in some
respects shadows that of the earlier writer: his Bloody Sunday poem
'Casualty' can be read at once as a critique of 'The Fisherman' and as an
attempt to define the lyric imagination's responsibilities to its troubled
times in a more ethically alert and egalitarian way than Yeats did. A
concern with loss and its potential retrieval in art persists through
Heaney's many changes of style and direction. The early work finds in
lyric accomplishment itself a consoling analogue for the vanishing skills
and crafts of the countryside. The poems of the early 1970s seek to
disinter lost historical possibilities embedded in Hiberno-English – as
'Broagh', for example, does by meditating on a County Derry place
name. An increasingly intimate concern for the victims of the northern
violence leaves Heaney's art tentative and equivocal with regard to its
restorative powers in 'Casualty' and the other elegies of *Field Work*
(1979), a pivotal volume. The later books bring a variety of mood and
mode to their exploration of the relationship between artistic autonomy
and commitment, memory and invention, inheritance and personal
identity. Taken as a whole, Heaney's work orchestrates a debate
between what is earthy, rooted, dumb or instinctive, on the one hand,
and ethereal, unconstrained, articulate or rational, on the other. In
formal resource – its success in *keeping going* – it has few parallels
in contemporary poetry.

A thick crust, coarse-grained as limestone rough-cast,
hardened gradually on top of the four crocks
that stood, large pottery bombs, in the small pantry.
After the hot brewery of gland, cud and udder
cool porous earthenware fermented the buttermilk
for churning day, when the hooped churn was scoured
with plumping kettles and the busy scrubber
echoed daintily on the seasoned wood.
It stood then, purified, on the flagged kitchen floor.

Out came the four crocks, spilled their heavy lip
of cream, their white insides, into the sterile churn.
The staff, like a great whisky muddler fashioned
in deal wood, was plunged in, the lid fitted.
My mother took first turn, set up rhythms
that slugged and thumped for hours. Arms ached.
Hands blistered. Cheeks and clothes were spattered
with flabby milk.

                    Where finally gold flecks
began to dance. They poured hot water then,
sterilized a birchwood-bowl
and little corrugated butter-spades.
Their short stroke quickened, suddenly
a yellow curd was weighting the churned up white,
heavy and rich, coagulated sunlight
that they fished, dripping, in a wide tin strainer,
heaped up like gilded gravel in the bowl.

The house would stink long after churning day,
acrid as a sulphur mine. The empty crocks
were ranged along the wall again, the butter
in soft printed slabs was piled on pantry shelves.
And in the house we moved with gravid ease,
our brains turned crystals full of clean deal churns,
the plash and gurgle of the sour-breathed milk,
the pat and slap of small spades on wet lumps.

BROAGH

Riverbank, the long rigs
ending in broad docken
and a canopied pad
down to the ford.

The garden mould
bruised easily, the shower
gathering in your heelmark
was the black O

in *Broagh*,
its low tattoo
among the windy boortrees
and rhubarb-blades

ended almost
suddenly, like that last
gh the strangers found
difficult to manage.

THE TOLLUND MAN

I

Some day I will go to Aarhus
To see his peat-brown head,
The mild pods of his eye-lids,
His pointed skin cap.

In the flat country near by
Where they dug him out,
His last gruel of winter seeds
Caked in his stomach,

Naked except for
The cap, noose and girdle,
I will stand a long time.
Bridegroom to the goddess,

She tightened her torc on him
And opened her fen,
Those dark juices working
Him to a saint's kept body,

Trove of the turfcutters'
Honeycombed workings.
Now his stained face
Reposes at Aarhus.

II

I could risk blasphemy,
Consecrate the cauldron bog
Our holy ground and pray
Him to make germinate

The scattered, ambushed
Flesh of labourers,
Stockinged corpses
Laid out in the farmyards,

Tell-tale skin and teeth
Flecking the sleepers
Of four young brothers, trailed
For miles along the lines.

III

Something of his sad freedom
As he rode the tumbril
Should come to me, driving,
Saying the names

Tollund, Grabaulle, Nebelgard,
Watching the pointing hands
Of country people,
Not knowing their tongue.

Out there in Jutland
In the old man-killing parishes
I will feel lost,
Unhappy and at home.

from MOSSBAWN: TWO POEMS IN DEDICATION
for Mary Heaney

I SUNLIGHT

There was a sunlit absence.
The helmeted pump in the yard
heated its iron,
water honeyed

in the slung bucket
and the sun stood
like a griddle cooling
against the wall

of each long afternoon.
So, her hands scuffled
over the bakeboard,
the reddening stove

sent its plaque of heat
against her where she stood
in a floury apron
by the window.

Now she dusts the board
with a goose's wing,
now sits, broad-lapped,
with whitened nails

and measling shins:
here is a space
again, the scone rising
to the tick of two clocks.

And here is love
like a tinsmith's scoop
sunk past its gleam
in the meal-bin.

FUNERAL RITES

I

I shouldered a kind of manhood
stepping in to lift the coffins
of dead relations.
They had been laid out

in tainted rooms,
their eyelids glistening,
their dough-white hands
shackled in rosary beads.

Their puffed knuckles
had unwrinkled, the nails
were darkened, the wrists
obediently sloped.

The dulse-brown shroud,
the quilted satin cribs:
I knelt courteously
admiring it all

as wax melted down
and veined the candles,
the flames hovering
to the women hovering

behind me.
And always, in a corner,
the coffin lid,
its nail-heads dressed

with little gleaming crosses.
Dear soapstone masks,
kissing their igloo brows
had to suffice

before the nails were sunk
and the black glacier
of each funeral
pushed away.

II

Now as news comes in
of each neighbourly murder
we pine for ceremony,
customary rhythms:

the temperate footsteps
of a cortège, winding past
each blinded home.
I would restore

the great chambers of Boyne,
prepare a sepulchre
under the cupmarked stones.
Out of side-streets and by-roads

purring family cars
nose into line,
the whole country tunes
to the muffled drumming

of ten thousand engines.
Somnambulant women,
left behind, move
through emptied kitchens

imagining our slow triumph
towards the mounds.
Quiet as a serpent
in its grassy boulevard

the procession drags its tail
out of the Gap of the North
as its head already enters
the megalithic doorway.

III

When they have put the stone
back in its mouth
we will drive north again
past Strang and Carling fjords,

the cud of memory
allayed for once, arbitration
of the feud placated,
imagining those under the hill

disposed like Gunnar
who lay beautiful
inside his burial mound,
though dead by violence

and unavenged.
Men said that he was chanting
verses about honour
and that four lights burned

in corners of the chamber:
which opened then, as he turned
with a joyful face
to look at the moon.

CASUALTY

I

He would drink by himself
And raise a weathered thumb
Towards the high shelf,
Calling another rum
And blackcurrant, without
Having to raise his voice,
Or order a quick stout
By a lifting of the eyes
And a discreet dumb-show
Of pulling off the top,
At closing time would go
In waders and peaked cap
Into the showery dark,
A dole-kept breadwinner
But a natural for work.
I loved his whole manner,
Sure-footed but too sly,
His deadpan sidling tact,
His fisherman's quick eye
And turned observant back.

Incomprehensible
To him, my other life.
Sometimes, on his high stool,
Too busy with his knife
At a tobacco plug
And not meeting my eye,
In the pause after a slug
He mentioned poetry.
We would be on our own
And, always politic
And shy of condescension,
I would manage by some trick
To switch the talk to eels
Or lore of the horse and cart
Or the Provisionals.

But my tentative art
His turned back watches too:
He was blown to bits
Out drinking in a curfew
Others obeyed, three nights
After they shot dead
The thirteen men in Derry.
PARAS THIRTEEN, the walls said,
BOGSIDE NIL. That Wednesday
Everybody held
His breath and trembled.

II

It was a day of cold
Raw silence, wind-blown
Surplice and soutane:
Rained-on, flower-laden
Coffin after coffin
Seemed to float from the door
Of the packed cathedral
Like blossoms on slow water.
The common funeral
Unrolled its swaddling band,
Lapping, tightening
Till we were braced and bound
Like brothers in a ring.

But he would not be held
At home by his own crowd
Whatever threats were phoned,
Whatever black flags waved.
I see him as he turned
In that bombed offending place,
Remorse fused with terror
In his still knowable face,
His cornered outfaced stare
Blinding in the flash.

He had gone miles away
For he drank like a fish

Nightly, naturally
Swimming towards the lure
Of warm lit-up places,
The blurred mesh and murmur
Drifting among glasses
In the gregarious smoke.
How culpable was he
That last night when he broke
Our tribe's complicity?
'Now you're supposed to be
An educated man,'
I hear him say. 'Puzzle me
The right answer to that one.'

III

I missed his funeral,
Those quiet walkers
And sideways talkers
Shoaling out of his lane
To the respectable
Purring of the hearse . . .
They move in equal pace
With the habitual
Slow consolation
Of a dawdling engine,
The line lifted, hand
Over fist, cold sunshine
On the water, the land
Banked under fog: that morning
When he took me in his boat,
The screw purling, turning
Indolent fathoms white,
I tasted freedom with him.
To get out early, haul
Steadily off the bottom,
Dispraise the catch, and smile
As you find a rhythm
Working you, slow mile by mile,
Into your proper haunt
Somewhere, well out, beyond . . .

Dawn-sniffing revenant,
Plodder through midnight rain,
Question me again.

BADGERS

When the badger glimmered away
into another garden
you stood, half-lit with whiskey,
sensing you had disturbed
some soft returning.

The murdered dead,
you thought.
But could it not have been
some violent shattered boy
nosing out what got mislaid
between the cradle and the explosion,
evenings when windows stood open
and the compost smoked down the backs?

Visitations are taken for signs.
At a second house I listened
for duntings under the laurels
and heard intimations whispered
about being vaguely honoured.

And to read even by carcasses
the badgers have come back.
One that grew notorious
lay untouched in the roadside.
Last night one had me braking
but more in fear than in honour.

Cool from the sett and redolent
of his runs under the night,
the bogey of fern country
broke cover in me
for what he is:

pig family
and not at all what he's painted.

How perilous is it to choose
not to love the life we're shown?
His sturdy dirty body
and interloping grovel.
The intelligence in his bone.
The unquestionable houseboy's shoulders
that could have been my own.

THE HARVEST BOW

As you plaited the harvest bow
You implicated the mellowed silence in you
In wheat that does not rust
But brightens as it tightens twist by twist
Into a knowable corona,
A throwaway love-knot of straw.

Hands that aged round ashplants and cane sticks
And lapped the spurs on a lifetime of game cocks
Harked to their gift and worked with fine intent
Until your fingers moved somnambulant:
I tell and finger it like braille,
Gleaning the unsaid off the palpable.

And if I spy into its golden loops
I see us walk between the railway slopes
Into an evening of long grass and midges,
Blue smoke straight up, old beds and ploughs in hedges,
An auction notice on an outhouse wall –
You with a harvest bow in your lapel,

Me with the fishing rod, already homesick
For the big lift of these evenings, as your stick
Whacking the tips off weeds and bushes
Beats out of time, and beats, but flushes

Nothing: that original townland
Still tongue-tied in the straw tied by your hand.

The end of art is peace
Could be the motto of this frail device
That I have pinned up on our deal dresser –
Like a drawn snare
Slipped lately by the spirit of the corn
Yet burnished by its passage, and still warm.

THE BIRTHPLACE

I

The deal table where he wrote, so small and plain,
the single bed a dream of discipline.
And a flagged kitchen downstairs, its mote-slants

of thick light: the unperturbed, reliable
ghost life he carried, with no need to invent.
And high trees round the house, breathed upon

day and night by winds as slow as a cart
coming late from market, or the stir
a fiddle could make in his reluctant heart.

II

That day, we were like one
of his troubled pairs, speechless
until he spoke for them,

haunters of silence at noon
in a deep lane that was sexual
with ferns and butterflies,

scared at our hurt,
throat-sick, heat-struck, driven
into the damp-floored wood

where we made an episode
of ourselves, unforgettable,
unmentionable,

and broke out again like cattle
through bushes, wet and raised,
only yards from the house.

III

Everywhere being nowhere,
who can prove
one place more than another?

We come back emptied,
to nourish and resist
the words of coming to rest:

birthplace, roofbeam, whitewash,
flagstone, hearth,
like unstacked iron weights

afloat among galaxies.
Still, was it thirty years ago
I read until first light

for the first time, to finish
The Return of the Native?
The corncrake in the aftergrass

verified himself, and I heard
roosters and dogs, the very same
as if he had written them.

from SWEENEY REDIVIVUS

THE CLERIC

I heard new words prayed at cows
in the byre, found his sign
on the crock and the hidden still,

211

smelled fumes from his censer
in the first smokes of morning.
Next thing he was making a progress

through gaps, stepping out sites,
sinking his crozier deep
in the fort-hearth.

If he had stuck to his own
cramp-jawed abbesses and intoners
dibbling round the enclosure,

his Latin and blather of love,
his parchments and scheming
in letters shipped over water –

but no, he overbore
with his unctions and orders,
he had to get in on the ground.

History that planted its standards
on his gables and spires
ousted me to the marches

of skulking and whingeing.
Or did I desert?
Give him his due, in the end

he opened my path to a kingdom
of such scope and neuter allegiance
my emptiness reigns at its whim.

FROM THE FRONTIER OF WRITING

The tightness and the nilness round that space
when the car stops in the road, the troops inspect
its make and number and, as one bends his face

towards your window, you catch sight of more
on a hill beyond, eyeing with intent
down cradled guns that hold you under cover

and everything is pure interrogation
until a rifle motions and you move
with guarded unconcerned acceleration –

a little emptier, a little spent
as always by that quiver in the self,
subjugated, yes, and obedient.

So you drive on to the frontier of writing
where it happens again. The guns on tripods;
the sergeant with his on-off mike repeating

data about you, waiting for the squawk
of clearance; the marksman training down
out of the sun upon you like a hawk.

And suddenly you're through, arraigned yet freed,
as if you'd passed from behind a waterfall
on the black current of a tarmac road

past armour-plated vehicles, out between
the posted soldiers flowing and receding
like tree shadows into the polished windscreen.

FROM THE CANTON OF EXPECTATION

I

We lived deep in a land of optative moods,
under high, banked clouds of resignation.
A rustle of loss in the phrase *Not in our lifetime*,
the broken nerve when we prayed *Vouchsafe* or *Deign*,
were creditable, sufficient to the day.

Once a year we gathered in a field
of dance platforms and tents where children sang

songs they had learned by rote in the old language.
An auctioneer who had fought in the brotherhood
enumerated the humiliations
we always took for granted, but not even he
considered this, I think, a call to action.
Iron-mouthed loudspeakers shook the air
yet nobody felt blamed. He had confirmed us.
When our rebel anthem played the meeting shut
we turned for home and the usual harassment
by militiamen on overtime at roadblocks.

II

And next thing, suddenly, this change of mood.
Books open in the newly wired kitchens.
Young heads that might have dozed a life away
against the flanks of milking cows were busy
paving and pencilling their first causeways
across the prescribed texts. The paving stones
of quadrangles came next and a grammar
of imperatives, the new age of demands.
They would banish the conditional for ever,
this generation born impervious to
the triumph in our cries of *de profundis*.
Our faith in winning by enduring most
they made anathema, intelligences
brightened and unmannerly as crowbars.

III

What looks the strongest has outlived its term.
The future lies with what's affirmed from under.
These things that corroborated us when we dwelt
under the aegis of our stealthy patron,
the guardian angel of passivity,
now sink a fang of menace in my shoulder.
I repeat the word 'stricken' to myself
and stand bareheaded under the banked clouds
edged more and more with brassy thunderlight.
I yearn for hammerblows on clinkered planks,
the uncompromised report of driven thole-pins,
to know there is one among us who never swerved

214

from all his instincts told him was right action,
who stood his ground in the indicative,
whose boat will lift when the cloudburst happens.

WHEELS WITHIN WHEELS

I

The first real grip I ever got on things
Was when I learned the art of pedalling
(By hand) a bike turned upside down, and drove
Its back wheel preternaturally fast.
I loved the disappearance of the spokes,
The way the space between the hub and rim
Hummed with transparency. If you threw
A potato into it, the hooped air
Spun mush and drizzle back into your face;
If you touched it with a straw, the straw frittered.
Something about the way those pedal treads
Worked very palpably at first against you
And then began to sweep your hand ahead
Into a new momentum – that all entered me
Like an access of free power, as if belief
Caught up and spun the objects of belief
In an orbit coterminous with longing.

II

But enough was not enough. Who ever saw
The limit in the given anyhow?
In fields beyond our house there was a well
('The well' we called it. It was more a hole
With water in it, with small hawthorn trees
On one side, and a muddy, dungy ooze
On the other, all tramped through by cattle).
I loved that too. I loved the turbid smell,
The sump-life of the place like old chain oil.
And there, next thing, I brought my bicycle.
I stood its saddle and its handlebars
Into the soft bottom, I touched the tyres

215

To the water's surface, then turned the pedals
Until like a mill-wheel pouring at the treadles
(But here reversed and lashing a mare's tail)
The world-refreshing and immersed back wheel
Spun lace and dirt-suds there before my eyes
And showered me in my own regenerate clays.
For weeks I made a nimbus of old glit.
Then the hub jammed, rims rusted, the chain snapped.

III

Nothing rose to the occasion after that
Until, in a circus ring, drumrolled and spotlit,
Cowgirls wheeled in, each one immaculate
At the still centre of a lariat.
Perpetuum mobile. Sheer pirouette.
Tumblers. Jongleurs. Ring-a-rosies. *Stet!*

from LIGHTENINGS

VIII

The annals say: when the monks of Clonmacnoise
Were all at prayers inside the oratory
A ship appeared above them in the air.

The anchor dragged along behind so deep
It hooked itself into the altar rails
And then, as the big hull rocked to a standstill,

A crewman shinned and grappled down the rope
And struggled to release it. But in vain.
'This man can't bear our life here and will drown,'

The abbot said, 'unless we help him.' So
They did, the freed ship sailed, and the man climbed back
Out of the marvellous as he had known it.

IX

A boat that did not rock or wobble once
Sat in long grass one Sunday afternoon
In nineteen forty-one or two. The heat

Out on Lough Neagh and in where cattle stood
Jostling and skittering near the hedge
Grew redolent of the tweed skirt and tweed sleeve

I nursed on. I remember little treble
Timber-notes their smart heels struck from planks,
Me cradled in an elbow like a secret

Open now as the eye of heaven was then
Above three sisters talking, talking steady
In a boat the ground still falls and falls from under.

KEEPING GOING
for H. H.

1

The piper coming from far away is you
With a whitewash brush for a sporran
Wobbling round you, a kitchen chair
Upside down on your shoulder, your right arm
Pretending to tuck the bag beneath your elbow,
Your pop-eyes and big cheeks nearly bursting
With laughter, but keeping up the drone
Inside your nose, between catches of breath.

2

The whitewash brush. An old blanched skirted thing
On the back of the byre door, biding its time
Until spring airs spelled lime in a work-bucket
And a potstick to mix it in with water.
Those smells brought tears to the eyes, we inhaled
A kind of greeny burning and thought of brimstone.

But the slop of the actual job
Of brushing walls, the watery grey
Being lashed on in broad swatches, then drying out
Whiter and whiter, all that worked like magic.
Where had we come from, what was this kingdom
We knew we'd been restored to? Our shadows
Moved on the wall and a tar border glittered
The full length of the house, a black divide
Like a freshly-opened, pungent, reeking trench.

3

Piss at the gable, the dead will congregate.
But separately. The women after dark,
Hunkering there a moment before bedtime,
The only time the soul was let alone.
The only time that face and body calmed
In the eye of heaven.
                        Buttermilk and urine,
The pantry, the housed beasts, the listening bedroom.
We were all together there in a foretime,
In a knowledge that might not translate beyond
Those wind-heaved midnights we still cannot be sure
Happened or not. It smelled of hill-fort clay
And cattle dung. When the thorn tree was cut down
You broke your arm. I shared the dread
When a strange bird perched for days on the byre roof.

4

That scene, with Macbeth helpless and desperate
In his nightmare – when he meets the hags again
And sees the apparitions in the pot –
I felt at home with that one all right. Hearth,
Steam and ululation, the smoky hair
Curtaining a cheek. 'Don't go near bad boys
In that college you're bound for. Do you hear me?
Do you hear me speaking to you? Don't forget.'
And then the potstick quickening the gruel,
The steam crown swirled, everything intimate
And fear-swathed brightening for a moment,
Then going dull and fatal and away.

5

Grey matter like gruel flecked with blood
In spatters on the whitewash. A clean spot
Where his head had been, other stains subsumed
In the parched wall he leant his back against
That morning just like any other morning,
Part-time reservist, toting his lunch-box.
A car came slow down Castle Street, made the halt,
Crossed the Diamond, slowed again and stopped
Level with him, although it was not his lift.
And then he saw an ordinary face
For what it was and a gun in his own face.
His right leg was hooked back, his sole and heel
Against the wall, his right knee propped up steady,
So he never moved, just pushed with all his might
Against himself, then fell past the tarred strip,
Feeding the gutter with his copious blood.

6

My dear brother, you have good stamina.
You stay on where it happens. Your big tractor
Pulls up at the Diamond, you wave at people,
You shout and laugh above the revs, you keep
Old roads open by driving on the new ones.
You called the pipers' sporrans whitewash brushes
And then dressed up and marched us through the kitchen.
But you cannot make the dead walk or right wrong.
I see you at the end of your tether sometimes,
In the milking parlour, holding yourself up
Between two cows until your turn goes past,
Then coming to to the smell of dung again
And wondering, is this all? As it was
In the beginning, is now and shall be?
Then rubbing your eyes and seeing our old brush
Up on the byre door, and keeping going.

219

MICHAEL LONGLEY

Born Belfast, of English parents, 1939. Educated at the Royal Belfast
Academical Institution and Trinity College Dublin, where he studied
classics. Secondary school teacher in Dublin, London and Belfast,
1963–70. Worked for many years with the Arts Council of Northern
Ireland before retiring from post of Combined Arts Director in 1991.
Longley has edited *Causeway: The Arts in Ulster* (1971) and an anthology
of Northern Irish children's poetry, *Over the Moon and Under the Stars*
(1971), as well as selections of the poetry of Louis MacNeice and
W.R. Rodgers and a volume of reminiscences of the painter
Paul Henry. *Tuppenny Stung: Autobiographical Chapters*,
appeared in 1994.

Longley's formalism acts as a bulwark against a chaos his poems evoke
with varying degrees of grotesquery, exuberance and terror. Home
serves as his characteristic trope for a hard-won, fragile civility – a
choice of figure which may reflect an Ulsterman's problematic sense of
belonging. Wry equivocation about domesticity in early pieces like
'Caravan' paves the way for the subsequent poetry's concern with
despoliations of household order by political violence. There is a
despairing irony in Longley's recognition of the domesticating
imperative behind Odysseus's slaughter of the suitors and faithless
housemaids in 'The Butchers' (a title which glancingly acknowledges
Belfast's most notorious sectarian killers, the Shankill Butchers). Many of
Longley's poems, like MacNeice's, are set in the west of Ireland,
particularly in Mayo, where he has a second home. (His reading of
Ireland through Scapa Flow in 'Ghost Town' recalls the earlier poet's
use of Icelandic and Scottish landscapes.) 'River & Fountain', written to
mark the quatercentenery of Trinity College, embodies an ingeniously
personal, typically delicate response to the demands of public poetry.

IN MEMORIAM

My father, let no similes eclipse
Where crosses like some forest simplified
Sink roots into my mind; the slow sands
Of your history delay till through your eyes

I read you like a book. Before you died,
Re-enlisting with all the broken soldiers
You bent beneath your rucksack, near collapse,
In anecdote rehearsed and summarised
These words I write in memory. Let yours
And other heartbreaks play into my hands.

Now I see in close-up, in my mind's eye,
The cracked and splintered dead for pity's sake
Each dismal evening predecease the sun,
You, looking death and nightmare in the face
With your kilt, harmonica and gun,
Grow older in a flash, but none the wiser
(Who, following the wrong queue at The Palace,
Have joined the London Scottish by mistake),
Your nineteen years uncertain if and why
Belgium put the kibosh on the Kaiser.

Between the corpses and the soup canteens
You swooned away, watching your future spill.
But, as it was, your proper funeral urn
Had mercifully smashed to smithereens,
To shrapnel shards that sliced your testicle.
That instant I, your most unlikely son,
In No Man's Land was surely left for dead,
Blotted out from your far horizon.
As your voice now is locked inside my head,
I yet was held secure, waiting my turn.

Finally, that lousy war was over.
Stranded in France and in need of proof
You hunted down experimental lovers,
Persuading chorus girls and countesses:
This, father, the last confidence you spoke.
In my twentieth year your old wounds woke
As cancer. Lodging under the same roof
Death was a visitor who hung about,
Strewing the house with pills and bandages,
Till he chose to put your spirit out.

Though they overslept the sequence of events
Which ended with the ambulance outside,
You lingering in the hall, your bowels on fire,
Tears in your eyes, and all your medals spent,
I summon girls who packed at last and went
Underground with you. Their souls again on hire,
Now those lost wives as re-created brides
Take shape before me, materialise.
On the verge of light and happy legend
They lift their skirts like blinds across your eyes.

CARAVAN

A rickety chimney suggests
The diminutive stove,
Children perhaps, the pots
And pans adding up to love –

So much concentrated under
The low roof, the windows
Shuttered against snow and wind,
That you would be magnified

(If you were there) by the dark,
Wearing it like an apron
And revolving in your hands
As weather in a glass dome,

The blizzard, the day beyond
And – tiny, barely in focus –
Me disappearing out of view
On probably the only horse,

Cantering off to the right
To collect the week's groceries,
Or to be gone for good
Having drawn across my eyes

Like a curtain all that light
And the snow, my history
Stiffening with the tea towels
Hung outside the door to dry.

WOUNDS

Here are two pictures from my father's head –
I have kept them like secrets until now:
First, the Ulster Division at the Somme
Going over the top with 'Fuck the Pope!'
'No Surrender!': a boy about to die,
Screaming 'Give 'em one for the Shankill!'
'Wilder than Gurkhas' were my father's words
Of admiration and bewilderment.
Next comes the London-Scottish padre
Resettling kilts with his swagger-stick,
With a stylish backhand and a prayer.
Over a landscape of dead buttocks
My father followed him for fifty years.
At last, a belated casualty,
He said – lead traces flaring till they hurt –
'I am dying for King and Country, slowly.'
I touched his hand, his thin head I touched.

Now, with military honours of a kind,
With his badges, his medals like rainbows,
His spinning compass, I bury beside him
Three teenage soldiers, bellies full of
Bullets and Irish beer, their flies undone.
A packet of Woodbines I throw in,
A lucifer, the Sacred Heart of Jesus
Paralysed as heavy guns put out
The night-light in a nursery for ever;
Also a bus-conductor's uniform –
He collapsed beside his carpet-slippers
Without a murmur, shot through the head
By a shivering boy who wandered in
Before they could turn the television down

Or tidy away the supper dishes.
To the children, to a bewildered wife,
I think 'Sorry Missus' was what he said.

GHOST TOWN

I have located it, my ghost town –
A place of interminable afternoons,
Sad cottages, scythes rusting in the thatch;
Of so many hesitant surrenders to
Enfolding bog, the scuts of bog cotton.

The few residents include one hermit
Persisting with a goat and two kettles
Among the bracken, a nervous spinster
In charge of the post office, a lighthouse-keeper
Who emerges to collect his groceries.

Since no one has got around to it yet
I shall restore the sign which reads CINEMA,
Rescue from the verge of invisibility
The faded stills of the last silent feature –
I shall become the local eccentric:

Already I have retired there to fill
Several gaps in my education –
The weather's ways, a handful of neglected
Pentatonic melodies and, after a while,
Dialect words for the parts of the body.

Indeed, with so much on my hands, family
And friends are definitely not welcome –
Although by the time I am accepted there
(A reputation and my own half-acre)
I shall have written another letter home.

MAN LYING ON A WALL
Homage to L.S. Lowry

You could draw a straight line from the heels,
Through calves, buttocks and shoulderblades
To the back of the head: pressure points
That bear the enormous weight of the sky.
Should you take away the supporting structure
The result would be a miracle or
An extremely clever conjuring trick.
As it is, the man lying on the wall
Is wearing the serious expression
Of popes and kings in their final slumber,
His deportment not dissimilar to
Their stiff, reluctant exits from this world
Above the shoulders of the multitude.

It is difficult to judge whether or not
He is sleeping or merely disinclined
To arrive punctually at the office
Or to return home in time for his tea.
He is wearing a pinstripe suit, black shoes
And a bowler hat: on the pavement
Below him, like a relic or something
He is trying to forget, his briefcase
With everybody's initials on it.

WREATHS

THE CIVIL SERVANT

He was preparing an Ulster fry for breakfast
When someone walked into the kitchen and shot him:
A bullet entered his mouth and pierced his skull,
The books he had read, the music he could play.

He lay in his dressing gown and pyjamas
While they dusted the dresser for fingerprints
And then shuffled backwards across the garden
With notebooks, cameras and measuring tapes.

225

They rolled him up like a red carpet and left
Only a bullet hole in the cutlery drawer;
Later his widow took a hammer and chisel
And removed the black keys from his piano.

THE GREENGROCER

He ran a good shop, and he died
Serving even the death-dealers
Who found him busy as usual
Behind the counter, organised
With holly wreaths for Christmas,
Fir trees on the pavement outside.

Astrologers or three wise men
Who may shortly be setting out
For a small house up the Shankill
Or the Falls, should pause on their way
To buy gifts at Jim Gibson's shop,
Dates and chestnuts and tangerines.

THE LINEN WORKERS

Christ's teeth ascended with him into heaven:
Through a cavity in one of his molars
The wind whistles: he is fastened for ever
By his exposed canines to a wintry sky.

I am blinded by the blaze of that smile
And by the memory of my father's false teeth
Brimming in their tumbler: they wore bubbles
And, outside of his body, a deadly grin.

When they massacred the ten linen workers
There fell on the road beside them spectacles,
Wallets, small change, and a set of dentures:
Blood, food particles, the bread, the wine.

Before I can bury my father once again
I must polish the spectacles, balance them
Upon his nose, fill his pockets with money
And into his dead mouth slip the set of teeth.

from MAYO MONOLOGUES

SELF-HEAL

I wanted to teach him the names of flowers,
Self-heal and centaury; on the long acre
Where cattle never graze, bog asphodel.
Could I love someone so gone in the head
And, as they say, was I leading him on?
He'd slept in the cot until he was twelve
Because of his babyish ways, I suppose,
Or the lack of a bed: hadn't his father
Gambled away all but rushy pasture?
His skull seemed to be hammered like a wedge
Into his shoulders, and his back was hunched,
Which gave him an almost scholarly air,
But he couldn't remember the things I taught:
Each name would hover above its flower
Like a butterfly unable to alight.
That day I pulled a cuckoo-pint apart
To release the giddy insects from their cell.
Gently he slipped his hand between my thighs.
I wasn't frightened; and still I don't know why,
But I ran from him in tears to tell them.
I heard how every day for one whole week
He was flogged with a blackthorn, then tethered
In the hayfield. I might have been the cow
Whose tail he would later dock with shears,
And he the ram tangled in barbed wire
That he stoned to death when they set him free.

THE LINEN INDUSTRY

Pulling up flax after the blue flowers have fallen
And laying our handfuls in the peaty water
To rot those grasses to the bone, or building stooks
That recall the skirts of an invisible dancer,

We become a part of the linen industry
And follow its processes to the grubby town

227

Where fields are compacted into window-boxes
And there is little room among the big machines.

But even in our attic under the skylight
We make love on a bleach green, the whole meadow
Draped with material turning white in the sun
As though snow reluctant to melt were our attire.

What's passion but a battering of stubborn stalks,
Then a gentle combing out of fibres like hair
And a weaving of these into christening robes,
Into garments for a marriage or funeral?

Since it's like a bereavement once the labour's done
To find ourselves last workers in a dying trade,
Let flax be our matchmaker, our undertaker,
The provider of sheets for whatever the bed –

And be shy of your breasts in the presence of death,
Say that you look more beautiful in linen
Wearing white petticoats, the bow on your bodice
A butterfly attending the embroidered flowers.

BETWEEN HOVERS
in memory of Joe O'Toole

And not even when we ran over the badger
Did he tell me he had cancer, Joe O'Toole
Who was psychic about carburettor and clutch
And knew a folk cure for the starter-engine.
Backing into the dark we floodlit each hair
Like a filament of light our lights had put out
Somewhere between Kinnadoohy and Thallabaun.
I dragged it by two gritty paws into the ditch.
Joe spotted a ruby where the canines touched.
His way of seeing me safely across the duach
Was to leave his porch light burning, its sparkle
Shifting from widgeon to teal on Corragaun Lake.
I missed his funeral. Close to the stony roads

He lies in Killeen Churchyard over the hill.
This morning on the burial mound at Templedoomore
Encircled by a spring tide and taking in
Cloonaghmanagh and Claggan and Carrigskeewaun,
The townlands he'd wandered tending cows and sheep,
I watched a dying otter gaze right through me
At the islands in Clew Bay, as though it were only
Between hovers and not too far from the holt.

HOMERIC POEMS

LAERTES

When he found Laertes alone on the tidy terrace, hoeing
Around a vine, disreputable in his gardening duds,
Patched and grubby, leather gaiters protecting his shins
Against brambles, gloves as well, and, to cap it all,
Sure sign of his deep depression, a goatskin duncher,
Odysseus sobbed in the shade of a pear-tree for his father
So old and pathetic that all he wanted then and there
Was to kiss him and hug him and blurt out the whole story,
But the whole story is one catalogue and then another,
So he waited for images from that formal garden,
Evidence of a childhood spent traipsing after his father
And asking for everything he saw, the thirteen pear-trees,
Ten apple-trees, forty fig-trees, the fifty rows of vines
Ripening at different times for a continuous supply,
Until Laertes recognised his son and, weak at the knees,
Dizzy, flung his arms around the neck of great Odysseus
Who drew the old man fainting to his breast and held him there
And cradled like driftwood the bones of his dwindling father.

ARGOS

There were other separations, and so many of them
That Argos the dog who waited twenty years for Odysseus
Has gone on waiting, still neglected on the manure-heap
At our front door, flea-ridden, more dead than alive
Who chased wild goats once, and roe-deer; the favourite,
A real thoroughbred, a marvel at picking up the scent,

229

Who even now is wagging his tail and drooping his ears
And struggling to get nearer to the voice he recognises
And dying in the attempt; until like Odysseus
We weep for Argos the dog, and for all those other dogs,
For the rounding-up of hamsters, the panic of white mice
And the deportation of one canary called Pepiček.

THE BUTCHERS

When he had made sure there were no survivors in his house
And that all the suitors were dead, heaped in blood and dust
Like fish that fishermen with fine-meshed nets have hauled
Up gasping for salt water, evaporating in the sunshine,
Odysseus, spattered with muck and like a lion dripping blood
From his chest and cheeks after devouring a farmer's bullock,
Ordered the disloyal housemaids to sponge down the armchairs
And tables, while Telemachos, the oxherd and the swineherd
Scraped the floor with shovels, and then between the portico
And the roundhouse stretched a hawser and hanged the women
So none touched the ground with her toes, like long-winged
    thrushes
Or doves trapped in a mist-net across the thicket where they
    roost,
Their heads bobbing in a row, their feet twitching but not for
    long,
And when they had dragged Melanthios's corpse into the
    haggard
And cut off his nose and ears and cock and balls, a dog's dinner,
Odysseus, seeing the need for whitewash and disinfectant,
Fumigated the house and the outhouses, so that Hermes
Like a clergyman might wave the supernatural baton
With which he resurrects or hypnotises those he chooses,
And waken and round up the suitors' souls, and the housemaids',
Like bats gibbering in the nooks of their mysterious cave
When out of the clusters that dangle from the rocky ceiling
One of them drops and squeaks, so their souls were bat-squeaks
As they flittered after Hermes, their deliverer, who led them
Along the clammy sheughs, then past the oceanic streams
And the white rock, the sun's gatepost in that dreamy region,
Until they came to a bog-meadow full of bog-asphodels
Where the residents are ghosts or images of the dead.

Still looking for a scoot-hole, Phemios the poet
In swithers, fiddling with his harp, jukes to the hatch,
Lays the bruckle yoke between porringer and armchair,
Makes a ram-stam for Odysseus, grammels his knees,
Then bannies and bams wi this highfalutin blether:
'I ask for pity and respect. How could you condemn
A poet who writes for his people and Parnassus,
Autodidact, his repertoire god-given? I beg you
Not to be precipitate and cut off my head. Spare me
And I'll immortalise you in an ode. Telemachos
Your own dear son will vouch that I was no party-hack
At the suitors' dinner-parties. Overwhelmed and out-
Numbered, I gave poetry readings against my will.'
I gulder to me da: 'Dinnae gut him wi yer gully,
He's only a harmless crayter. And how's about Medon
The toast-master whose ashy-pet I was? Did ye ding him
When the oxherd and the swineherd stormed the steading?'
Thon oul gabble-blooter's a canny huer and hears me
From his fox's-slumber in cow-hides under a chair –
Out he spalters, flaffing his hands, blirting to my knees:
'Here I am, dear boy! Put in a word for me before
Your hot-blooded pater slaughters me as one of them –
The suitors I mean, bread-snappers, belly-bachelors.'
Long-headed Odysseus smiles at him and says: 'Wheesht!
You may thank Telemachos for this chance to wise up
And pass on the message of oul dacency. Go out
And sit in the haggard away from this massacre,
You and the well-spoken poet, while I redd the house.'
They hook it and hunker fornenst the altar of Zeus,
Afeard and skelly-eyed, keeking everywhere for death.

RIVER & FOUNTAIN

I

I am walking backwards into the future like a Greek.
I have nothing to say. There is nothing I would describe.

231

It was always thus: as if snow has fallen on Front
Square, and, feeling the downy silence of the snowflakes
That cover cobbles and each other, white erasing white,
I read shadow and snow-drift under the Campanile.

II

'It fits on to the back of a postage stamp,' Robert said
As he scribbled out in tiny symbols the equation,
His silhouette a frost-flower on the window of my last
Year, his page the sky between chimney-stacks, his head
And my head at the city's centre aching for giddy
Limits, mathematics, poetry, squeaky nibs at all hours.

III

Top of the staircase, Number Sixteen in Botany Bay,
Slum-dwellers, we survived gas-rings that popped, slop-
Buckets in the bedrooms, changeable 'wives', and toasted
Doughy doorsteps, Freshmen turning into Sophisters
In front of the higgledy flames: our still-life, crusts
And buttery books, the half-empty marmalade jar.

IV

My Dansette record player bottled up like genies
Sibelius, Shostakovich, Bruckner, dusty sleeves
Accumulating next to Liddel and Scott's *Greek–English
Lexicon* voices the fluffy needle set almost free.
I was the culture vulture from Ulster, Vincent's joke
Who heard *The Rite of Spring* and contemplated suicide.

V

Adam was first to read the maroon-covered notebooks
I filled with innocent outpourings, Adam the scholar
Whose stammer could stop him christening this and that,
Whose Eden was annotation and vocabulary lists
In a precise classicist's hand, the love of words as words.
My first and best review was Adam's 'I like these–I–I–'

VI

'College poet? Village idiot you mean!' (Vincent again).
In neither profession could I settle comfortably
Once Derek arrived reciting Rimbaud, giving names
To the constellations over the Examination Hall.
'Are you Longley? Can I borrow your typewriter? Soon?'
His was the first snow party I attended. I felt the cold.

VII

We were from the North, hitch-hikers on the Newry Road,
Faces that vanished from a hundred driving-mirrors
Down that warren of reflections – O'Neill's Bar, Nesbitt's –
And through Front Gate to Connemara and Inishere,
The raw experience of market towns and clachans, then
Back to Rooms, village of minds, poetry's townland.

VIII

Though College Square in Belfast and the Linen Hall
Had been our patch, nobody mentioned William Drennan.
In Dublin what dreams of liberty, the Index, the Ban:
Etonians on Commons cut our accents with a knife.
When Brendan from Ballylongford defied the Bishop, we
Flapped our wings together and were melted in the sun.

IX

A bath-house lotus-eater – fags, sodden *Irish Times* –
I tagged along with the Fabians, to embarrass Church
And State our grand design. Would-be class-warriors
We raised, for a moment, the Red Flag at the Rubrics,
Then joined the Civil Service and talked of Civil Rights.
Was Trinity a Trojan Horse? Were we Greeks at all?

X

'The Golden Mean is a tension, Ladies, Gentlemen,
And not a dead level': the Homeric head of Stanford
Who would nearly sing the first lines of the *Odyssey*.
That year I should have failed, but, teaching the *Poetics*,

He asked us for definitions, and accepted mine:
'Sir, if prose is a river, then poetry's a fountain.'

XI

Someone has skipped the seminar. Imagine his face,
The children's faces, my wife's: she sat beside me then
And they were waiting to be born, ghosts from a future
Without Tom: he fell in love just once and died of it.
Oh, to have turned away from everything to one face,
Eros and Thanatos your gods, icicle and dew.

XII

Walking forwards into the past with more of an idea
I want to say to my friends of thirty years ago
And to daughters and a son that Belfast is our home,
Prose a river still – the Liffey, the Lagan – and poetry
A fountain that plays in an imaginary Front Square.
When snow falls it is feathers from the wings of Icarus.

MICHAEL HARTNETT

Born Newcastle West, County Limerick, 1941. Educated at University
College Dublin. Lived in London and Madrid in the 1960s before
returning to Ireland to work variously as a telephonist, house painter and
lecturer in creative writing. Now lives in Dublin. A prolific translator,
Hartnett has published versions of Lorca, Dáibhí Ó Bruadair, Pádraigín
Haicéad and Nuala Ní Dhomhnaill in book form. Currently working on
a volume of translations from Aodhagán Ó Rathaille.

The vehement, unironical tonalities of Hartnett's poetry place it further
from the orthodoxies of twentieth century taste than the work of any
comparably gifted contemporary Irish writer. Distrustful of a modernity
which threatens communality and its supporting context in the natural
world, Hartnett seeks continuity with the eighteenth-century poets of
his native Munster – mouthpieces of a dying Gaelic culture – rather than
with the individualist traditions of nineteenth- and twentieth-century
European verse. From 1975 to 1985 he asserted that continuity by
writing only in Irish. Though vigorous and various, his Irish verse
generally lacks the hard clarity of his best work in English. The first
three pieces in the selection represent the spare lyricism of his early
manner. 'Sneachta Gealaí '77' bewails the impotence of the poet in the
modern world, a theme Hartnett would address with rage in 'An
Phurghóid' ('The Purge') and with bleak melancholy in 'An Mánlia
Nocht' ('The Naked Surgeon'), two long poems in Irish. Like much of
his prolific output since his return to English, 'The Man who Wrote
Yeats, the Man who Wrote Mozart' probes the mystery – and the
morality – of the creative act.

BREAD

Her iron beats
the smell of bread
from damp linen,
silver, crystal
and warm white things.
Whatever bird
I used to be,
hawk or lapwing,
tern, or something
wild, fierce or shy,
these birds are dead
and I come here
on tiring wings.
Odours of bread . . .

I HAVE EXHAUSTED THE DELIGHTED RANGE . . .

I have exhausted the delighted range
of small birds, and now, a new end to pain
makes a mirage of what I wished my life.
Torture, immediate to me, is strange;
all that is left of the organs remain
in an anaesthetic of unbelief.

Coerced by trivia, nothing to gain
but now, or to be pleased through one long night

and forsake instead something immortal?
And the graceless heron is killed in flight
and falls like a lopped flower into the stalks.

Small birds, small poems, are not immortal:
nor, however passed, is one intense night:
there is no time now for my dream of hawks.

FOR MY GRANDMOTHER, BRIDGET HALPIN

Maybe morning lightens over
the coldest time in all the day,
but not for you. A bird's hover,
seabird, blackbird, or bird of prey,
was rain, or death, or lost cattle.
The day's warning, the red plovers
so etched and small in clouded sky
was book to you, and true bible.
You died in utter loneliness,
your acres left to the childless.
You never saw the animals
of God, and the flower under
your feet; and the trees change a leaf;
and the red fur of a fox on
a quiet evening; and the long
birches falling down the hillside.

from A FAREWELL TO ENGLISH
for Brendan Kennelly

1

Her eyes were coins of porter and her West
Limerick voice talked velvet in the house:
her hair was black as the glossy fireplace
wearing with grace her Sunday-night-dance best.
She cut the froth from glasses with a knife
and hammered golden whiskies on the bar
and her mountainy body tripped the gentle
mechanism of verse: the minute interlock
of word and word began, the rhythm formed.
I sunk my hands into tradition
sifting the centuries for words. This quiet
excitement was not new: emotion challenged me
to make it sayable. The clichés came

at first, like matchsticks snapping from the world
of work: mánla, séimh, dubhfholtach, álainn, caoin:
they came like grey slabs of slate breaking from
an ancient quarry, mánla, séimh, dubhfholtach,
álainn, caoin, slowly vaulting down the dark
unused escarpments, mánla, séimh, dubhfholtach,
álainn, caoin, crashing on the cogs, splinters
like axeheads damaged the wheels, clogging
the intricate machine, mánla, séimh,
dubhfholtach, álainn, caoin. Then Pegasus
pulled up, the girth broke and I was flung back
on the gravel of Anglo-Saxon.
What was I doing with these foreign words?
I, the polisher of the complex clause,
wizard of grasses and warlock of birds
midnight-oiled in the metric laws?

dubhfholtach: blacklocked
álainn: beautiful
mánla, séimh and *caoin*: words whose meanings hover about the English
    adjectives 'graceful', 'gentle'.

LAMENT FOR TADHG CRONIN'S CHILDREN

That day the sails of the ship were torn
and a fog obscured the lawns.
In the whitewashed house the music stopped.
A spark jumped up at the gables
and the silk quilts on the bed caught fire.
They cry without tears –
their hearts cry –
for the three dead children.

Christ God neglect them not
nor leave them in the ground!

They were ears of corn!
They were apples!
They were three harpstrings!
And now their limbs lie underground
and the black beetle walks across their faces.
I, too, cry without tears –
my heart cries –
for the three dead children.

based on a poem by Aodhagán Ó Rathaille

THE MAN WHO WROTE YEATS,
THE MAN WHO WROTE MOZART
for John B. Keane

In crisp italic, meticulous and signed,
the manuscripts arrived by every post.
From somewhere in the North.
From someone not quite right.
From someone with a perfect hand who wrote,
'"What then?" sang Plato's ghost,
"What does it shadow forth?"'
with one word changed in every other line.

I was confronted once again
by a mind which lives by that
intangible, subordinating rule,
the mental scaffolding of which
rests on shifting ground:
the compulsion to believe
what is provably untrue;
and seems to us to be
something not quite right,
something not quite sound.

239

I could have, very easily, undermined
the props that gave such makebelieve support;
but not so long before I wrote
a piece based on a line
I'd read in Alexander Pope –
so could I now afford
to call his work a fraud
and give the benefit of truth to mine?
If he believed that he had written Yeats
as I believed my poem was mine
he was no sham but simply lacked the art
to make his source opaque
with a flourish of technique.
Or maybe he was mad
and was dancing to a lie,
a dance so furious
that it does not stop when its music does.

And I knew this lie: it is a brake
that holds a frantic flywheel back
which, if it's loosened,
spins the cogs inside the head
at such a frightening rate
it cuts to fragile tangles
and to quivering springs
the fine machinery of the brain;
for I have seen a wounded mind retreat
away from windows that could see the street
when its lie has been exposed
and move to the dead corners of a house
and hide in the remotest room
to where no contradictions come
and an endless talking flows
between it and its cherished lie,
a broken doll in tawdry clothes.
And if anyone intrudes
and tries to comfort and confront
there will be silence in the rooms –
for after contradiction silence comes.

Perhaps he sat there in his northern glen,
in some pub or kitchen, and convinced
an audience and himself
that a poet had arrived;
and so enchanted with the praise,
the adulation that the Irish give
to one they think a scribe,
he brought, with manic, altering pen,
astonished poems of Yeats
before the eyes of equally astonished men.

And in Austria, 1791,
real rustics, in an evening light,
trudge and murmur up a hill
towards the entrance of a gaudy *Schloss*
to stand about a statued yard all night,
obedient, at a total loss,
to suffer music that they cannot grasp
from Franz, the Graf von Walsegg's quill.

'My latest Opus, a quartet
for 'cello, flute, viola, violin,
has got a suave *adagio*, based
(with some refinements)
on a peasant air.
It floats about and *interlaces*, as it were,
all the fabric of the piece,
with its silver thread
above the labour of the strings
that try to reach a semblance of its grace
without ever getting there.'
Thus, in his baroque domain
(Stoppach, Pottschach, Ziegersberg and Klam)
the kindly Count von Walsegg rambles on,
gracious in a gilded chair,
to family and friends;
with all the servants there
admiring in its plush

the German flute he had especially made
and his 'cello, chestnut in its curves,
and the music, glittering on an ornate shelf
in vellum bindings commissioned by the Graf,
immaculately scripted by himself
(black notes like beads of jet,
treble clefs like heads of fern):
Sonata, Trio, and Quartet
by Franz Anton Hoffmeister and François Devienne –
with some notes changed in every other staff.

And yet the Count loved music
(as my fellow-poet loved
every line he ever cribbed).
An adept on the 'cello and the flute,
he kept his court musicians,
copied out whole works by hand,
and paid out gulden by the score;
but like my fellow-poet
the pages that he turned,
the alchemy of quill and nib,
the structures of another man,
the very perfume of the ink
transformed a striving to adore
to a more cunning thing.
Von Walsegg had an audience in thrall
and was not bothered that beyond
the limits of his county and estate
his name was never heard;
he in fact preferred
(to possible exposure and disdain)
the smug comfort of a local fame.
But Death which disregards
all claims and provenance
came into his *ersatz* life
and took his twenty-year-old
Countess off his hands;
and only finest marble,

marble cut like music,
and music that was marble-like
would do to mark his mourning for his wife:
so Johann Martin Fischer,
finest sculptor of his day,
was commissioned – to design
a fitting monument
to guard her bones and honour them,
and to see her soul
safely placed among the saints –
Mozart, to write a requiem.

Till now von Walsegg was content
to re-embroider any trifling cloth
his monies could so easily procure;
but soon, a *Mozart* would present
a great and glittering robe
to wrap in definite remembrance here
his dead wife's soul;
and so at last the Count had found
a work to match his mania
and went on to claim (his alibi a smile)
the magnificent *pastiche*
as his last and greatest tribute to his wife
and took the plaudits as his due
and bowed into the candelabra's glow.
But the snickering musicians knew.
The snickering musicians always know.
Oh the wardrobes we have gone through
to dress our naked minds!
What goods we've cheapened and what suits
we've tried to cover up our tattered clothes,
to patch up every threadbare place
through which sharp wind continually blows
from the cold halls of space.
As Aristotle crippled logic
for two thousand years
and Plato and his minions
cluttered up the sky

with their humming spheres
the convolvuli
of things already done
keep us trapped, like any moon
bound to its sun like a tethered goat
whose grass must finally run out;
and though not at all at ease
in this treadmill heaven,
as we argue from the given to the given
we see as we spin past
other systems, other stars
that we can never visit;
and though taught there's nothing new
underneath the sun,
that there's a limit to the roses
we can breed and cull,
we are not at all at ease
with the insistent notion
of something new underneath the skull.

I, I think, have not succumbed
(not all the time, at any rate)
to von Walsegg's and my fellow-poet's
more cunning and more artless ways
but if others' work had so bedazed their minds,
so made the base of all they wrote –
how much am I bedazed?
How much mine is what I write?
Does the superimposition of a poem
naturalise another's thought
or bend his stray reflections
to the poet's will
as some composers build
partitas on the squeak that's made
as hands slide up guitars?
It is like pouring milk into a stream
high up a hill:
though down it comes some hundred feet
(effervescent over rocks

or lulled to tarns
behind some elbow of grassed turf,
falls, tumbles, run or slows as smooth
as a dark honey ooze)
and may be called
a rivulet, a runnel or a rill,
it still comes out a stream
that someone poured some milk into
high up a hill.

So, repeatedly seduced and repeatedly annoyed
at being seduced and led
by the odder machinations of the heart,
I try to move outside the human rote
but find myself instead
in landscapes where the plants,
the beasts, are strictly catalogued;
where frightening hybrids melt into the dark
and where language that lacks echoes
strikes discords in the head.
So, fearing a descent
to syntax that ignores
the grammar of our kind,
I try to hew out parables
from the broken torsos that I find.

But I am not contented in my mind.

Mé féin faoin aer san oíche,
ag speachadh seoda sneachta i bpáirc,
gach teach reoite, gach nead préacháin
mar ghealach dhubh ag snámh le hais na fíor-ré.
Mé féin ag damhsa faoin ngealach,
seanrince gan cheol leis ach ceol cuisle:
is mé féin go huaigneach – an seanuaigneas.

Thar imeall na spéire tá céasadh is goin
is an bás go fonóideach
a lámha ina phóca
ag feadaíl sa tsráid;
mé féin sa sneachta gealaí
ag moladh nead préacháin –
an file go sotalach, foclach, slán.

Myself outside at night,
kicking snow-jewels in a field,
each house frozen, each rook's nest
a black moon swimming by the real moon.
Myself dancing under the moon,
an old dance with no music
but pulse-music:
and myself lonely – the ancient loneliness.

Over the border, torture and wounds
and death sneers
hands in pockets
whistles at street corners:
and myself in the moonsnow
praising a rook's nest –
the poet, arrogant, verbose, safe.

translated by the author

EAMON GRENNAN

Born Dublin, 1941. Educated at University College Dublin and Harvard
University. Lectures in English at Vassar College, New York State.
Spends part of each year in Ireland.

Grennan's years in the United States are reflected in the intonations and
at times in the settings of his poems. He writes in a flexible, discursive
idiom which allows scope alike for meditation and for a sensuous
rendition of concrete particulars.

TOTEM

All Souls' over, the roast seeds eaten, I set
on a backporch post our sculpted pumpkin under the weather,
warm still for November. Night and day it gapes
in at us through the kitchen window, going soft
in the head. Sleepwalker-slow, a black rash of ants
harrows this hollowed globe, munching the pale peach
flesh, sucking its seasoned last juices dry. In a
week, when the ants and humming flies are done, only
a hard remorseless light drills and tenants it
through and through. Within, it turns mould-black
in patches, stays days like this while the weather
takes it in its shifty arms: wide eye-spaces shine,
the disapproving mouth holds firm. Another week,
a sad leap forward: sunk to one side so an eye-socket's
almost blocked, it becomes a monster of its former
self. Human, it would have rotted beyond unhappiness and
horror to some unspeakable subject state – its nose
no more than a vertical hole, the thin bridge of amber
between nose and mouth in ruins. The other socket opens
wider than ever: disbelief. It's all downhill
from here: knuckles of sun, peremptory steady fingers
of frost, strain all day and night at it, cracking
the rind, kneading the knotted fibres free. The crown
with its top-knot mockery of stalk caves in; the skull

buckles; the whole head drips tallowy tears: the end
is in sight. In a day or two it topples on itself
like ruined thatch, pus-white drool spidering
from the corner of the mouth and worming its way
down the body-post. All dignity to the winds, it bows its
bogeyman face of dread to the inevitable. And now, November
almost out, it is in the bright unseasonable sunshine
a simmer of pulp, a slow bake, amber shell speckled
chalk-grey with lichen. Light strikes and strikes
its burst surfaces: it sags, stays at the end of its
brief tether – a helmet of dark circles, death caul. Here
is the last umbilical gasp, everybody's nightmare parent,
the pitiless system rubbing our noses in it. But
pity poor lantern-head with his lights out, glob
by greasy glob going back where he came from. As each
seed-shaped drop falls free, it catches and clutches
for one split second the light. When the pumpkin
lapses to our common ground at last – where a white
swaddle of snow will fold it in no time from sight –
I try to take in the empty space it's left
on top of the wooden post: it is that empty space.

FOUR DEER

Four deer lift up their lovely heads to me
in the dusk of the golf course I plod across
towards home. They're browsing the wet grass
the snow has left and, statued, stare at me
in deep silence and I see whatever light there is
gather to glossy pools in their eight mild,
barely curious but wary eyes. When one at a time
they bend again to feed, I can hear the crisp
moist crunch of the surviving grass
between their teeth, imagine the slow lick of a tongue
over whickering lips. They've come from the unlit
winter corners of their fright to find
a fresh season, this early gift, and stand
almost easy at the edge of white snow islands and
lap the grey-green sweet depleted grass. About them

hangs an air of such domestic sense, the comfortable
hush of folk at home with one another, a familiar
something I sense in spite of the great gulf of strangeness
we must look over at each other. Tails flicker
white in thickening dusk and I feel their relief at
the touch of cold snow underfoot while their faces
nuzzle grass, as if, like birds, they had crossed
unspeakable vacant wastes with nothing but hunger
shaping their brains and driving them from leaf to
dry leaf, sour strips of bark, under a thunder of guns
and into the cold comfort of early dark. I've seen
their straight despairing lines cloven in snowfields
under storm, an Indian file of famished natives, poor
unprayed-for wanderers through blinding chill, seasoned
castaways in search of home ports, which they've found
at last, here on winter's verge between our houses and
their trees. All of a sudden, I've come too close. Moving
as one mind they spring in silent waves
over the grass, then crack snow with sharp hard
snaps, lightfooting it into the sanctuary of a pine grove
where they stand looking back at me, a deer-shaped
family of shadows against the darker arch of trees and
this rusting dusk. When silence settles over us again
and they bow down to browse, the sound of grass being
lipped, bitten, meets me across the space between us. Close
enough for comfort, they see we keep, instinctively, our
distance, sharing this air where a few last shards of
daylight still glitter in little meltpools or spread a skin
of brightness on the ice, the ice stiffening towards midnight
under the clean magnesium burn of a first star.

BREAKING POINTS
for Joe Butwin

They all want to break at some point,
if you can only find it, he says, hoisting
the wedgeheaded heavy axe and coming down with it
in one swift glittering arc: a single *chunk,*
then the gleam of two half moons of maple

250

rolling over in the driveway. He finds
his proper rhythm, my strong friend from the west,
standing each half straight up,
then levelling swinging striking
dead centre: two quarters
fall apart from one another
and lie, off-white flesh shining,
on the cracked tarmac. I stand back
and watch him bend and bring to the chopping-place
a solid sawn-off wheel of the maple bough
the unexpected early snow brought down
in a clamorous rush of stricken leafage, a great weight
he walks gingerly under
and gently sets down. When he tests it with his eye

I remember a builder of drystone walls
saying the same thing about rocks and big stones,
turning one over and over, hunting its line
of least resistance, then offering it a little
dull tap with his mallet: the stone, as if he'd
slipped the knot holding it together, opened
– cloned – and showed its bright
inner life to the world. Joe goes on logging
for a furious hour, laying around him
the split quarters, littering the tar-black driveway
with their matte vanilla glitter. Seeing him
lean on the axe-shaft
for a minute's headbent silence
in the thick of his handiwork,

I remember standing in silence at the centre
of the living-room I was leaving for the last time
after ten years of marriage, the polished pine floor
scattered with the bits and pieces
I was taking with me,
the last battle still singing
in my head, the crossed limbs of the children
sofa-sprawled in sleep. And as soon as he finishes
and comes in, steam
sprouting from his red wet neck
and matted hair, dark maps of sweat

staining his navyblue T-shirt, I want to say
as he drains his second glass of lemonade

that this is the way it is
in the world we make and break
for ourselves: first the long green growing, then
the storm, the heavy axe, those shining remnants
that'll season for a year
before the fire gets them; this is the way
it is, this violent concentrated action
asserting ourselves to ourselves, the way we stand
and flail our way to freedom of a sort,
and after the heat and blistering deed of it
how the heart beats in its birdcage of bone
and you're alone
with your own staggered, sufficient body, its
toll taken, on the nervous verge
of exaltation. But I say nothing, pour more
lemonade, open a beer, listen to the tale he tells

of breakage back home – the rending-place
we reach when the labouring heart
fails us and we say, *What
now? What else? What?* In the dusk
assembling against the window,
I can see the big gouged maple
radiant where the bough stormed off,
and the split logs
scattered and bright over the driveway – in what
from this Babylonian distance looks like
a pattern of solid purposes or the end of joy.

DEREK MAHON

Born Belfast, 1941. Educated at the Royal Belfast Academical Institution
and Trinity College Dublin. From 1970 to 1985 he worked in London
as a journalist (including stints as features editor of *Vogue* and literary
editor of the *New Statesman*) and scriptwriter. After two years in Kinsale,
County Cork, he moved in 1988 to Dublin. Now lives in New York as
a freelance writer and lecturer. A distinguished translator from the
French, he has published versions of Molière, de Nerval and Philippe
Jaccottet in book form. Mahon has edited *The Sphere Book of Modern
Irish Poetry* (1972) and (with Peter Fallon) *The Penguin Book of
Contemporary Irish Poetry* (1990).

Mahon's stylish and even sprightly melancholy has reminded critics of
Louis MacNeice, as has his liking for formal strategies which at once
endorse and subvert classicism. His sensibility is more purely speculative
than the earlier poet's, however, and his irony more desolating. The
apocalyptic perspectives of 'Lives' and 'An Image from Beckett' derive
from late-twentieth-century conditions beyond the reach of MacNeice's
humanism. Though Mahon recoils from commitment, the northern crisis
is deeply implicated in his mature poetry. The oblique commentaries of
'The Snow Party' and 'A Disused Shed in Co. Wexford' lend a
macrocosmic frame of reference and a near metaphysical significance to
Irish troubles past and present. The latter poem gives voice by proxy to
those relicts and victims to whom history, *pace* Auden, can only say
'Alas'. 'Courtyards in Delft' draws connections between British and
Dutch imperialism, and between Ulster and South Africa, while
'Tractatus' typifies the apparent ease with which Mahon can
shade from whimsy into vision.

A DYING ART

'That day would skin a fairy –
A dying art,' she said.
Not many left of the old trade.
Redundant and remote, they age
Gracefully in dark corners
With lamp-lighters, sail-makers
And native Manx speakers.

And the bone-handled knives with which
They earned their bread? My granny grinds
Her plug tobacco with one to this day.

ECCLESIASTES

God, you could grow to love it, God-fearing, God-
    chosen purist little puritan that,
for all your wiles and smiles, you are (the
    dank churches, the empty streets,
the shipyard silence, the tied-up swings) and
    shelter your cold heart from the heat
of the world, from woman-inquisition, from the
    bright eyes of children. Yes you could
wear black, drink water, nourish a fierce zeal
    with locusts and wild honey, and not
feel called upon to understand and forgive
    but only to speak with a bleak
afflatus, and love the January rains when they
    darken the dark doors and sink hard
into the Antrim hills, the bog meadows, the heaped
    graves of your fathers. Bury that red
bandana, stick and guitar; this is your
    country, close one eye and be king.
Your people await you, their heavy washing
    flaps for you in the housing estates –
a credulous people. God, you could do it, God
    help you, stand on a corner stiff
with rhetoric, promising nothing under the sun.

AN IMAGE FROM BECKETT
for Doreen

In that instant
There was a sea, far off,
As bright as lettuce,

254

A northern landscape
And a huddle
Of houses along the shore.

Also, I think, a white
Flicker of gulls
And washing hung to dry –

The poignancy of those
Back yards – and the gravedigger
Putting aside his forceps.

Then the hard boards
And darkness once again.
But in that instant

I was struck by the
Sweetness and light,
The sweetness and light,

Imagining what grave
Cities, what lasting monuments,
Given the time.

They will have buried
My great-grandchildren, and theirs,
Beside me by now

With a subliminal batsqueak
Of reflex lamentation.
Our knuckle bones

Litter the rich earth
Changing, second by second,
To civilizations.

It was good while it lasted,
And if it only lasted
The Biblical span

Required to drop six feet
Through a glitter of wintry light,
There is No-One to blame.

Still, I am haunted
By that landscape,
The soft rush of its winds,

The uprightness of its
Utilities and schoolchildren –
To whom in my will,

This, I have left my will.
I hope they have time,
And light enough, to read it.

LIVES

for Seamus Heaney

First time out
I was a torc of gold
And wept tears of the sun.

That was fun
But they buried me
In the earth two thousand years

Till a labourer
Turned me up with a pick
In eighteen fifty-four

And sold me
For tea and sugar
In Newmarket-on-Fergus.

Once I was an oar
But stuck in the shore
To mark the place of a grave

When the lost ship
Sailed away. I thought
Of Ithaca, but soon decayed.

The time that I liked
Best was when
I was a bump of clay

In a Navaho rug,
Put there to mitigate
The too god-like

Perfection of that
Merely human artifact.
I served my maker well –

He lived long
To be struck down in
Tucson by an electric shock

The night the lights
Went out in Europe
Never to shine again.

So many lives,
So many things to remember!
I was a stone in Tibet,

A tongue of bark
At the heart of Africa
Growing darker and darker . . .

It all seems
A little unreal now,
Now that I am

An anthropologist
With my own
Credit card, dictaphone,

Army-surplus boots
And a whole boatload
Of photographic equipment.

I know too much
To be anything any more;
And if in the distant

Future someone
Thinks he has once been me
As I am today,

Let him revise
His insolent ontology
Or teach himself to pray.

THE SNOW PARTY
for Louis Asekoff

Bashō, coming
To the city of Nagoya,
Is asked to a snow party.

There is a tinkling of china
And tea into china;
There are introductions.

Then everyone
Crowds to the window
To watch the falling snow.

Snow is falling on Nagoya
And farther south
On the tiles of Kyōto.

Eastward, beyond Irago,
It is falling
Like leaves on the cold sea.

Elsewhere they are burning
Witches and heretics
In the boiling squares,

Thousands have died since dawn
In the service
Of barbarous kings;

But there is silence
In the houses of Nagoya
And the hills of Ise.

A REFUSAL TO MOURN

He lived in a small farm-house
At the edge of a new estate.
The trim gardens crept
To his door, and car engines
Woke him before dawn
On dark winter mornings.

All day there was silence
In the bright house. The clock
Ticked on the kitchen shelf,
Cinders moved in the grate,
And a warm briar gurgled
When the old man talked to himself;

But the door-bell seldom rang
After the milkman went,
And if a shirt-hanger
Knocked in an open wardrobe
That was a strange event
To be pondered on for hours

While the wind thrashed about
In the back garden, raking
The roof of the hen-house,
And swept clouds and gulls

Eastwards over the lough
With its flap of tiny sails.

Once a week he would visit
An old shipyard crony,
Inching down to the road
And the blue country bus
To sit and watch sun–dappled
Branches whacking the windows

While the long evening shed
Weak light in his empty house,
On the photographs of his dead
Wife and their six children
And the Missions to Seamen angel
In flight above the bed.

'I'm not long for this world,'
Said he on our last evening,
'I'll not last the winter,'
And grinned, straining to hear
Whatever reply I made;
And died the following year.

In time the astringent rain
Of those parts will clean
The words from his gravestone
In the crowded cemetery
That overlooks the sea
And his name be mud once again

And his boilers lie like tombs
In the mud of the sea bed
Till the next ice age comes
And the earth he inherited
Is gone like Neanderthal Man
And no records remain.

But the secret bred in the bone
On the dawn strand survives
In other times and lives,

Persisting for the unborn
Like a claw-print in concrete
After the bird has flown.

A DISUSED SHED IN CO. WEXFORD
Let them not forget us, the weak souls among the asphodels.
Seferis, Mythistorema, tr. Keeley and Sherrard

for J.G. Farrell

Even now there are places where a thought might grow –
Peruvian mines, worked out and abandoned
To a slow clock of condensation,
An echo trapped for ever, and a flutter
Of wild-flowers in the lift-shaft,
Indian compounds where the wind dances
And a door bangs with diminished confidence,
Lime crevices behind rippling rain-barrels,
Dog corners for bone burials;
And in a disused shed in Co. Wexford,

Deep in the grounds of a burnt-out hotel,
Among the bathtubs and the washbasins
A thousand mushrooms crowd to a keyhole.
This is the one star in their firmament
Or frames a star within a star.
What should they do there but desire?
So many days beyond the rhododendrons
With the world waltzing in its bowl of cloud,
They have learnt patience and silence
Listening to the rooks querulous in the high wood.

They have been waiting for us in a foetor
Of vegetable sweat since civil war days,
Since the gravel-crunching, interminable departure
Of the expropriated mycologist.
He never came back, and light since then
Is a keyhole rusting gently after rain.
Spiders have spun, flies dusted to mildew

And once a day, perhaps, they have heard something –
A trickle of masonry, a shout from the blue
Or a lorry changing gear at the end of the lane.

There have been deaths, the pale flesh flaking
Into the earth that nourished it;
And nightmares, born of these and the grim
Dominion of stale air and rank moisture.
Those nearest the door grow strong –
'Elbow room! Elbow room!'
The rest, dim in a twilight of crumbling
Utensils and broken pitchers, groaning
For their deliverance, have been so long
Expectant that there is left only the posture.

A half century, without visitors, in the dark –
Poor preparation for the cracking lock
And creak of hinges. Magi, moonmen,
Powdery prisoners of the old regime,
Web-throated, stalked like triffids, racked by drought
And insomnia, only the ghost of a scream
At the flash-bulb firing-squad we wake them with
Shows there is life yet in their feverish forms.
Grown beyond nature now, soft food for worms,
They lift frail heads in gravity and good faith.

They are begging us, you see, in their wordless way,
To do something, to speak on their behalf
Or at least not to close the door again.
Lost people of Treblinka and Pompeii!
'Save us, save us,' they seem to say,
'Let the god not abandon us
Who have come so far in darkness and in pain.
We too had our lives to live.
You with your light meter and relaxed itinerary,
Let not our naive labours have been in vain!'

COURTYARDS IN DELFT
Pieter de Hooch, 1659

for Gordon Woods

Oblique light on the trite, on brick and tile –
Immaculate masonry, and everywhere that
Water tap, that broom and wooden pail
To keep it so. House-proud, the wives
Of artisans pursue their thrifty lives
Among scrubbed yards, modest but adequate.
Foliage is sparse, and clings. No breeze
Ruffles the trim composure of those trees.

No spinet-playing emblematic of
The harmonies and disharmonies of love;
No lewd fish, no fruit, no wide-eyed bird
About to fly its cage while a virgin
Listens to her seducer, mars the chaste
Perfection of the thing and the thing made.
Nothing is random, nothing goes to waste.
We miss the dirty dog, the fiery gin.

That girl with her back to us who waits
For her man to come home for his tea
Will wait till the paint disintegrates
And ruined dikes admit the esurient sea;
Yet this is life too, and the cracked
Out-house door a verifiable fact
As vividly mnemonic as the sunlit
Railings that front the houses opposite.

I lived there as a boy and know the coal
Glittering in its shed, late-afternoon
Lambency informing the deal table,
The ceiling cradled in a radiant spoon.
I must be lying low in a room there,
A strange child with a taste for verse,
While my hard-nosed companions dream of fire
And sword upon parched veldt and fields of rain-swept gorse.

RATHLIN

A long time since the last scream cut short –
Then an unnatural silence; and then
A natural silence, slowly broken
By the shearwater, by the sporadic
Conversation of crickets, the bleak
Reminder of a metaphysical wind.
Ages of this, till the report
Of an outboard motor at the pier
Shatters the dream-time, and we land
As if we were the first visitors here.

The whole island a sanctuary where amazed
Oneiric species whistle and chatter,
Evacuating rock-face and cliff-top.
Cerulean distance, an oceanic haze –
Nothing but sea-smoke to the ice-cap
And the odd somnolent freighter.
Bombs doze in the housing estates
But here they are through with history –
Custodians of a lone light which repeats
One simple statement to the turbulent sea.

A long time since the unspeakable violence –
Since Somhairle Buidh, powerless on the mainland,
Heard the screams of the Rathlin women
Borne to him, seconds later, upon the wind.
Only the cry of the shearwater
And the roar of the outboard motor
Disturb the singular peace. Spray-blind,
We leave here the infancy of the race,
Unsure among the pitching surfaces
Whether the future lies before us or behind.

TRACTATUS

for Aidan Higgins

'The world is everything that is the case'
From the fly giving up in the coal-shed
To the Winged Victory of Samothrace.
Give blame, praise, to the fumbling God
Who hides, shame-facèdly, His agèd face;
Whose light retires behind its veil of cloud.

The world, though, is also so much more –
Everything that is the case imaginatively.
Tacitus believed mariners could *hear*
The sun sinking into the western sea;
And who would question that titanic roar,
The steam rising wherever the edge may be?

EILÉAN NÍ CHUILLEANÁIN

Born 1942 in Cork, daughter of Cormac Ó Cuilleanáin, professor of
Irish at University College Cork, and the novelist Eilís Dillon. Educated
at UCC and Oxford. Lecturer in Medieval and Renaissance English at
Trinity College Dublin since 1966. A founder and co-editor of *Cyphers*,
she has edited *Irish Women: Image and Achievement – Women in Irish
Culture from Earliest Times* (1985).

Ní Chuilleanáin emerges in her best work as a poet of powerful
intelligence who can sustain vivid, complex metaphors over numbers of
lines – a capacity some commentators have related to her interest in the
poetry of the English Renaissance. A subtle, elaborate exploration of
the historical experience of women is developed in many of
her more recent poems.

THE SECOND VOYAGE

Odysseus rested on his oar and saw
The ruffled foreheads of the waves
Crocodiling and mincing past: he rammed
The oar between their jaws and looked down
In the simmering sea where scribbles of weed defined
Uncertain depth, and the slim fishes progressed
In fatal formation, and thought
                  If there was a single
Streak of decency in these waves now, they'd be ridged
Pocked and dented with the battering they've had,
And we could name them as Adam named the beasts,
Saluting a new one with dismay, or a notorious one
With admiration; they'd notice us passing
And rejoice at our shipwreck, but these
Have less character than sheep and need more patience.

I know what I'll do he said;
I'll park my ship in the crook of a long pier
(And I'll take you with me he said to the oar)

I'll face the rising ground and walk away
From tidal waters, up riverbeds
Where herons parcel out the miles of stream,
Over gaps in the hills, through warm
Silent valleys, and when I meet a farmer
Bold enough to look me in the eye
With 'where are you off to with that long
Winnowing fan over your shoulder?'
There I will stand still
And I'll plant you for a gatepost or a hitching-post
And leave you as a tidemark. I can go back
And organise my house then.
                              But the profound
Unfenced valleys of the ocean still held him;
He had only the oar to make them keep their distance;
The sea was still trying under the ship's side.
He considered the water-lilies, and thought about fountains
Spraying as wide as willows in empty squares,
The sugarstick of water clattering into the kettle,
The flat lakes bisecting the rushes. He remembered spiders and
    frogs
Housekeeping at the roadside in brown trickles floored with
    mud,
Horsetroughs, the black canal, pale swans at dark:
His face grew damp with tears that tasted
Like his own sweat or the insults of the sea.

DEATHS AND ENGINES

    We came down above the houses
    In a stiff curve, and
    At the edge of Paris airport
    Saw an empty tunnel
    – The back half of a plane, black
    On the snow, nobody near it,
    Tubular, burnt-out and frozen.

    When we faced again
    The snow-white runways in the dark

267

No sound came over
The loudspeakers, except the sighs
Of the lonely pilot.

The cold of metal wings is contagious:
Soon you will need wings of your own,
Cornered in the angle where
Time and life like a knife and fork
Cross, and the lifeline in your palm
Breaks, and the curve of an aeroplane's track
Meets the straight skyline.

The images of relief:
Hospital pyjamas, screens round a bed
A man with a bloody face
Sitting up in bed, conversing cheerfully
Through cut lips:
These will fail you some time.

You will find yourself alone
Accelerating down a blind
Alley, too late to stop
And know how light your death is;
You will be scattered like wreckage,
The pieces every one a different shape
Will spin and lodge in the hearts
Of all who love you.

THE INFORMANT

Underneath the photograph
Of the old woman at her kitchen table
With a window beyond (fuchsias, a henhouse, the sea)
Are entered: her name and age, her late husband's occupation
(A gauger), her birthplace, not here
But in another parish, near the main road.
She is sitting with tea at her elbow
And her own fairy-cakes, baked that morning
For the young man who listens now to the tape

268

Of her voice changing, telling the story,
And hears himself asking,
Did you ever see it yourself?
                              Once, I saw it.

Can you describe it? But the sound
Takes off like a jet engine, the machine
Gone haywire, a tearing, an electric
Tempest. Then a stitch of silence.
Something has been lost, the voice resumes
Quietly now,
                    'The locks
Forced upward, a shift of air
Pulled over the head. The face bent
And the eyes winced, like craning
To look in the core of a furnace.
The man unravelled
Back to a snag, a dark thread'.

Then what happens?
                        The person disappears.
For a time he stays close by and speaks
In a child's voice. He is not seen, and
You must leave food out for him, and be careful
Where you throw water after you wash your feet.

And then he is gone?
                        He's gone, after a while.

*You find this more strange than the yearly miracle
Of the loaf turning into a child?*
Well, that's natural, she says,
I often baked the bread for that myself.

THE REAL THING

The Book of Exits, miraculously copied
Here in this convent by an angel's hand,
Stands open on a lectern, grooved
Like the breast of a martyred deacon.

269

The bishop has ordered the windows bricked up on this side
Facing the fields beyond the city.
Lit by the glow from the cloister yard at noon
On Palm Sunday, Sister Custos
Exposes her major relic, the longest
Known fragment of the Brazen Serpent.

True stories wind and hang like this
Shuddering loop wreathed on a lapis lazuli
Frame. She says, this is the real thing.
She veils it again and locks up.
On the shelves behind her the treasures are lined.
The episcopal seal repeats every coil,
Stamped on all closures of each reliquary
Where the labels read: *Bones
Of Different Saints. Unknown.*

Her history is a blank sheet,
Her vows a folded paper locked like a well.
The torn end of the serpent
Tilts the lace edge of the veil.
The real thing, the one free foot kicking
Under the white sheet of history.

SAINT MARGARET OF CORTONA
patroness of the Lock Hospital, Townsend Street, Dublin

She had become, the preacher hollows his voice,
A name not to be spoken, the answer
To the witty man's loose riddle, what's she
That's neither maiden, widow nor wife?

A pause opens its jaws
In the annual panegyric,
The word *whore* prowling silent
Up and down the long aisle.

Under the flourishing canopy
Where trios of angels mime the last trombone,

270

Behind the silver commas of the shrine,
In the mine of the altar her teeth listen and smile.

She is still here, she refuses
To be consumed. The weight of her bones
Burns down through the mountain.
Her death did not make her like this;

Her eyes were hollowed
By the bloody scene: the wounds
In the body of her child's father
Tumbled in a ditch. The door was locked,
The names flew and multiplied; she turned
Her back but the names clustered and hung
Out of her shoulderbones
Like children swinging from a father's arm,
Their tucked-up feet skimming over the ground.

EAVAN BOLAND

Born Dublin, 1944. Brought up in London, where her father was Irish ambassador, and New York, where he represented Ireland at the United Nations. Educated at Trinity College Dublin. Taught English at Trinity from 1966 to 1968. Has worked as a freelance lecturer in Ireland and the United States. A founder of Arlen House, a pioneering women's press, she has come to be regarded by a younger and vocal generation of Irish women writers as a crucial exemplar. Boland is a prolific literary journalist and poetry reviewer, mainly for the *Irish Times* and *PN Review* (Manchester). *Object Lessons: The Life of the Woman and the Poet in Our time* appeared in 1995.

Boland's earlier work is alert to crosscurrents in international poetry, which it accommodates somewhat dutifully to an Irish context. The situation of women emerges as a dominant concern in *In Her Own Image* (1975) and *Night Feed* (1982). An increasingly politicised approach to this theme is accompanied from the mid-1980s by a growing complexity of lyric form and a striking new authority in Boland's handling of the poetic line. Combining autobiography and history with a celebration of the more creative aspects of domesticity, the mature poetry meditates on the consolations and deceits of art. 'Anna Liffey' explicitly rehearses Boland's feminist aesthetic: the poem challenges the male-centred priorities of two key modernist texts by reappropriating the figure of Anna Liffey/Anna Livia from *Finnegans Wake* and by adapting to its own purposes both the idiom and the river motif of William Carlos Williams's *Paterson*.

LISTEN. THIS IS THE NOISE OF MYTH

This is the story of a man and woman
under a willow and beside a weir
near a river in a wooded clearing.
They are fugitives. Intimates of myth.

Fictions of my purpose. I suppose
I shouldn't say that yet or at least

before I break their hearts or save their lives
I ought to tell their story and I will.

When they went first it was winter; cold,
cold through the Midlands and as far West
as they could go. They knew they had to go –
through Meath, Westmeath, Longford,

their lives unravelling like the hours of light –
and then there were lambs under the snow
and it was January, aconite and jasmine
and the hazel yellowing and puce berries on the ivy.

They could not eat where they had cooked,
nor sleep where they had eaten
nor at dawn rest where they had slept.
They shunned the densities

of trees with one trunk and of caves
with one dark and the dangerous embrace
of islands with a single landing place.
And all the time it was cold, cold:

the fields still gardened by their ice,
the trees stitched with snow overnight,
the ditches full; frost toughening lichen,
darning lace into rock crevices.

And then the woods flooded and buds
blunted from the chestnut and the foxglove
put its big leaves out and chaffinches
chinked and flirted in the branches of the ash.

And here we are where we started from –
under a willow and beside a weir
near a river in a wooded clearing.
The woman and the man have come to rest.

Look how light is coming through the ash.
The weir sluices kingfisher blues.

The woman and the willow tree lean forward, forward.
Something is near; something is about to happen;

something more than Spring
and less than history. Will we see
hungers eased after months of hiding?
Is there a touch of heat in that light?

If they stay here soon it will be summer; things
returning, sunlight fingering minnowy deeps,
seedy greens, reeds, electing lights
and edges from the river. Consider

legend, self-deception, sin, the sum
of human purpose and its end; remember
how our poetry depends on distance,
aspect: gravity will bend starlight.

Forgive me if I set the truth to rights.
Bear with me if I put an end to this:
she never turned to him; she never leaned
under the sallow-willow over to him.

They never made love; not there; not here;
not anywhere; there was no winter journey;
no aconite, no birdsong and no jasmine,
no woodland and no river and no weir.

Listen. This is the noise of myth. It makes
the same sound as shadow. Can you hear it?
Daylight greys in the preceptories.
Her head begins to shine

pivoting the planets of a harsh nativity.
They were never mine. This is mine.
This sequence of evicted possibilities.
Displaced facts. Tricks of light. Reflections.

Invention. Legend. Myth. What you will.
The shifts and fluencies are infinite.

The moving parts are marvellous. Consider
how the bereavements of the definite

are easily lifted from our heroine.
She may or she may not. She was or wasn't
by the water at his side as dark
waited above the Western countryside.

O consolations of the craft.
How we put
the old poultices on the old sores,
the same mirrors to the old magic. Look.

The scene returns. The willow sees itself
drowning in the weir and the woman
gives the kiss of myth her human heat.
Reflections. Reflections. He becomes her lover.

The old romances make no bones about it.
The long and short of it. The end and the beginning.
The glories and the ornaments are muted.
And when the story ends the song is over.

FOND MEMORY

It was a school where all the children wore darned worsted;
where they cried – or almost all – when the Reverend Mother
announced at lunch-time that the King had died

peacefully in his sleep. I dressed in wool as well,
ate rationed food, played English games and learned
how wise the Magna Carta was, how hard the Hanoverians

had tried, the measure and complexity of verse,
the hum and score of the whole orchestra.
At three-o-clock I caught two buses home

where sometimes in the late afternoon
at a piano pushed into a corner of the playroom
my father would sit down and play the slow

lilts of Tom Moore while I stood there trying
not to weep at the cigarette smoke stinging up
from between his fingers and – as much as I could think –

I thought this is my country, was, will be again,
this upward-straining song made to be
our safe inventory of pain. And I was wrong.

THE BLACK LACE FAN MY MOTHER GAVE ME

It was the first gift he ever gave her,
buying it for five francs in the Galeries
in pre-war Paris. It was stifling.
A starless drought made the nights stormy.

They stayed in the city for the summer.
They met in cafés. She was always early.
He was late. That evening he was later.
They wrapped the fan. He looked at his watch.

She looked down the Boulevard des Capucines.
She ordered more coffee. She stood up.
The streets were emptying. The heat was killing.
She thought the distance smelled of rain and lightning.

These are wild roses, appliqued on silk by hand,
darkly picked, stitched boldly, quickly.
The rest is tortoiseshell and has the reticent,
clear patience of its element. It is

a worn-out, underwater bullion and it keeps,
even now, an inference of its violation.
The lace is overcast as if the weather
it opened for and offset had entered it.

The past is an empty café terrace.
An airless dusk before thunder. A man running.
And no way now to know what happened then –
none at all – unless, of course, you improvise:

The blackbird on this first sultry morning,
in summer, finding buds, worms, fruit,
feels the heat. Suddenly she puts out her wing –
the whole, full, flirtatious span of it.

THE LATIN LESSON

Easter light in the convent garden.
The eucalyptus tree glitters in it.
    A bell rings for
    the first class.

Today the Sixth Book of the Aeneid.
An old nun calls down the corridor.
    Manners, girls. Where
    are your manners?

Last night in his Lenten talk
the local priest asked us to remember
    everything is put here
    for a purpose:

even eucalyptus leaves are suitable
for making oil from to steep wool in,
    to sweeten our blankets
    and gaberdines.

My forefinger crawls on the lines.
A storm light comes in from the bay.
    How beautiful the words
    look, how

vagrant and strange on the page
before we crush them for their fragrance
    and crush them again
    to discover

the pathway to hell and that these
shadows in their shadow-bodies,

chittering and mobbing
on the far

shore, signalling their hunger for
the small usefulness of a life, are
the dead. And how
before the bell

will I hail the black keel and flatter the dark
boatman and cross the river and still
keep a civil tongue
in my head?

MIDNIGHT FLOWERS

I go down step by step.
The house is quiet, full of trapped heat and sleep.
In the kitchen everything is still.
Nothing is distinct; there is no moon to speak of.

I could be undone every single day by
paradox or what they call in the countryside
blackthorn winter,
when hailstones come with the first apple blossom.

I turn a switch and the garden grows.
A whole summer's work in one instant!
I press my face to the glass. I can see
shadows of lilac, of fuchsia; a dark likeness of blackcurrant:

little clients of suddenness, how sullen they are at
the margins of the light.
They need no rain, they have no roots.
I reach out a hand; they are gone.

When I was a child a snapdragon was
held an inch from my face. Look, a voice said, this
is the colour of your hair. And there it was, my head,
a pliant jewel in the hands of someone else.

ANNA LIFFEY

Life, the story goes,
Was the daughter of Cannan,
And came to the plain of Kildare.
She loved the flat-lands and the ditches
And the unreachable horizon.
She asked that it be named for her.
The river took its name from the land.
The land took its name from a woman.

A woman in the doorway of a house,
A river in the city of her birth.

There, in the hills above my house,
The river Liffey rises, is a source.
It rises in rush and ling heather and
Black peat and bracken and strengthens
To claim the city it narrated.
Swans. Steep falls. Small towns.
The smudged air and bridges of Dublin.

Dusk is coming.
Rain is moving east from the hills.

If I could see myself
I would see
A woman in a doorway
Wearing the colours that go with red hair.
Although my hair is no longer red.

I praise
The gifts of the river.
Its shiftless and glittering
Re-telling of a city,
Its clarity as it flows,
In the company of runt flowers and herons,
Around a bend at Islandbridge
And under thirteen bridges to the sea.
Its patience at twilight –
Swans nesting by it,
Neon wincing into it.

Maker of
Places, remembrances,
Narrate such fragments for me:

One body. One spirit
One place. One name.
The city where I was born.
The river that runs through it.
The nation which eludes me.

Fractions of a life
It has taken me a lifetime
To claim.

I came here in a cold winter.

I had no children. No country.
I did not know the name for my own life.

My country took hold of me.
My children were born.

I walked out in a summer dusk
To call them in.

One name. Then the other one.
The beautiful vowels sounding out home.

Make of a nation what you will
Make of the past
What you can –

There is now
A woman in a doorway.

It has taken me
All my strength to do this.

Becoming a figure in a poem.

Usurping a name and a theme.

A river is not a woman.
   Although the names it finds,
     The history it makes
And suffers –
   The Viking blades beside it,
     The muskets of the Redcoats,
       The flames of the Four Courts
Blazing into it
   Are a sign.
     Any more than
A woman is a river,
   Although the course it takes,
    Through swans courting and distraught willows,
Its patience
   Which is also its powerlessness,
    From Callary to Islandbridge,
     And from source to mouth,
Is another one.
      And in my late forties

Past believing
    Love will heal
        What language fails to know
And needs to say –
    What the body means –
        I take this sign
And I make this mark:
    A woman in the doorway of her house.
        A river in the city of her birth.
The truth of a suffered life.
    The mouth of it.

The seabirds come in from the coast
The city wisdom is they bring rain.
I watch them from my doorway.
I see them as arguments of origin –
Leaving a harsh force on the horizon
Only to find it
Slanting and falling elsewhere.

Which water –
The one they leave or the one they pronounce –
Remembers the other?

I am sure
The body of an ageing woman
Is a memory
And to find a language for it
Is as hard
As weeping and requiring
These birds to cry out as if they could
Recognize their element
Remembered and diminished in
A single tear.

An ageing woman
Finds no shelter in language.
She finds instead
Single words she once loved
Such as 'summer' and 'yellow'
And 'sexual' and 'ready'
Have suddenly become dwellings
For someone else –
Rooms and a roof under which someone else
Is welcome, not her. Tell me,
Anna Liffey,
Spirit of water,
Spirit of place,
How is it on this
Rainy Autumn night
As the Irish sea takes
The names you made, the names
You bestowed, and gives you back
Only wordlessness?

Autumn rain is
Scattering and dripping
From car-ports
And clipped hedges.
The gutters are full.

When I came here
I had neither
Children nor country.
The trees were arms.
The hills were dreams.

I was free
To imagine a spirit
In the blues and greens,
The hills and fogs
Of a small city.

My children were born.
My country took hold of me.
A vision in a brick house.
Is it only love
That makes a place?

I feel it change.
My children are
Growing up, getting older.
My country holds on
To its own pain.

I turn off
The harsh yellow
Porch light and
Stand in the hall.
Where is home now?

Follow the rain
Out to the Dublin hills.
Let it become the river.
Let the spirit of place be
A lost soul again.

In the end
It will not matter
That I was a woman. I am sure of it.
The body is a source. Nothing more.
There is a time for it. There is a certainty
About the way it seeks its own dissolution.
Consider rivers.
They are always en route to
Their own nothingness. From the first moment
They are going home. And so
When language cannot do it for us,
Cannot make us know love will not diminish us,
There are these phrases
Of the ocean

To console us.
Particular and unafraid of their completion.
In the end
Everything that burdened and distinguished me
Will be lost in this:
I was a voice.

PAUL DURCAN

Born Dublin, of County Mayo parents, 1944. Educated at Gonzaga
College and University College Cork. A full-time poet and a gifted
reader, he has performed his work for audiences in many countries.
Has collaborated with other Irish artists, notably the rock singer
Van Morrison and the traditional musician and composer
Mícheál Ó Súilleabháin. *Crazy About Women* (1991) and *Give Me
Your Hand* (1994), two books of poems with facing pictorial
reproductions, were written in response to paintings in the
National Galleries of Ireland and England respectively.

The twin and perhaps contradictory assumptions that poetry is a sacred
calling and that it should be accessible to everybody lie at the heart of
Durcan's work. His assiduous populism denied him serious critical
attention until the appearance in 1985 of *The Berlin Wall Café*. The
comic pathos of the title sequence's anatomy of the poet's dying
marriage revealed an imagination as exultantly responsive to personal
disorder as Sylvia Plath's or John Berryman's. Like those American
poets, Durcan is at his most inventive when his materials threaten to
overwhelm him. (*Daddy, Daddy* [1990] has an even more powerful and
much longer title sequence, but its narrative of the poet's relationship
with his father does not lend itself to selection.) The delight in
incongruity which enlivens the cartoon-like political satire of the earlier
work is perhaps shown to best advantage in the recent poems about
paintings, such as 'The Levite and His Concubine at Gibeah' (based on
the work of that name by Jan Victors). His ear for colloquial speech
vindicates Durcan's belief that poetry must grow out of ordinary life. A
distrust of systems and a concern for their victims gives an unabashedly
Romantic, antinomian character to his writing. Many of Durcan's most
vivid characterisations are women, like the protagonist of 'The Haulier's
Wife Meets Jesus on the Road Near Moone', arguably the strongest
feminist poem yet written in Ireland.

THE HAT FACTORY

Eleven o'clock and the bar is empty
Except for myself and an old man;

We sit with our backs to the street-window,
The sun in the east streaming through it;
And I think of childhood and swimming
Underwater by a famine pier;
The ashlar coursing of the stonework
Like the bar-room shelves
Seen through tidal amber seaweed
In the antique mirror;
Now myself and the old man floating
In the glow of the early morning sun
Twined round each other and our newspapers;
And our pint glasses like capstans on the pier.
We do not read our daily charters –
Charters of liberty to know what's going on –
But hold them as capes before reality's bull
And with grace of ease we make our passes,
El Cordobes might envy this old small man
For the sweet veronicas he makes in daily life.
He is the recipient of an old-age pension
While I am that low in society's scale
I do not rate the dole
But I am at peace with myself and so is he;
Although I do not know what he is thinking
His small round fragile noble mouth
Has the look of the door of Aladdin's cave
Quivering in expectation of the magic words;
Open sesame;
I suspect that like me he is thinking
Of the nothing-in-particular;
Myself, I am thinking of the local hat factory,
Of its history and the eerie fact
That in my small town I have never known
Anyone who worked in it
Or had to do with it at all;
As a child I used look through a hole in the hedge
At the hat factory down below in the valley;
I used lie flat on my face in the long grass
And put out my head through the hole;
Had the hatters looked out through their porthole windows
They would have seen high up in the hillside
A long wild hedgerow broken only

By the head of the child looking out through the hole;
I speculate;
And as to what kind of hats they make;
And do they have a range in black birettas;
And do they have a conveyor belt of toppers;
And do the workers get free hats?
And I recall the Pope's skull-cap
Placed on my head when as a boy-child
In a city hospital I lay near to death
And the black homburg of the red-nosed undertaker
And the balaclavas of assassins
And the pixies of the lost children of the murdered earth
And the multicoloured yamulka of the wandering Jew
And the black kippa of my American friend
In Jerusalem in the snow
And the portly Egyptian's tiny fez
And the tragic Bedouin's kefia in the sands of sun
And the monk's cowl and the nun's wimple
And the funereal mortarboards of airborn puritans
And the megalithic coifs of the pancake women of Brittany
And the sleek fedoras of well-to-do thugs
And sadistic squires' Napoleonic tricorns
And prancing horse-cavalry in their cruel shakos
And the heroic lifeboatman's black sou'wester
And the nicotine-stained wig of the curly-haired barrister
And the black busby used as a handbag by my laughing brother
And the silken turban of the highbrow widow
And foreign legionaries in nullah kepis
And May Day presidiums in astrakhans
And bonnets and boaters and sombreros and stetsons
And stove-pipes and steeples and mantillas and berets
And topis and sunhats and deerstalkers and pill-boxes
And naughty grandmothers in toques
And bishops' mitres and soldiers' helmets;
And in Languedoc and in Aran – cloth caps.
And what if you were a hatter
And you married a hatter
And all your sons and daughters worked as hatters
And you inhabited a hat-house all full of hats:
Hats, hats, hats, hats.
Hats: the apotheosis of an ancient craft;

And I think of all the nationalities of Israel
And of how each always clings to his native hat,
His priceless and moveable roof,
His hat which is the last and first symbol
Of a man's slender foothold on this earth.
Women and girls also work in the factory
But not many of them wear hats;
Some wear scarves, but rarely hats;
Now there'll be no more courting of maidens
In schooner hats on dangerous cliffs;
It seems part of the slavery of liberation
To empty relationships of all courtship
Of which hats were an exciting part.
Probably, I shall never wear a hat:
So thus I ask the old man
If I may look at his trilby
Old honesty –
And graciously he hands it to me
And with surprise
I note that it was manufactured
In the local hat factory
And I hand it back to him –
A crown to its king –
And like a king he blesses me when he goes,
Wishing me a good day before he starts
His frail progress home along the streets,
Along the lanes and terraces of the hillside,
To his one up and one down.
I turn about and see
Over the windowpane's frosted hemisphere
A small black hat sail slowly past my eyes
Into the unknown ocean of the sun at noon.

TULLYNOE: TÊTE-À-TÊTE IN THE PARISH PRIEST'S PARLOUR

'Ah, he was a grand man.'
'He was: he fell out of the train going to Sligo.'
'He did: he thought he was going to the lavatory.'
'He did: in fact he stepped out the rear door of the train.'

'He did: God, he must have got an awful fright.'
'He did: he saw that it wasn't the lavatory at all.'
'He did: he saw that it was the railway tracks going away from
    him.'
'He did: I wonder if . . . but he was a grand man.'
'He was: he had the most expensive Toyota you can buy,'
'He had: well, it was only beautiful.'
'It was: he used to have an Audi.'
'He had: as a matter of fact he used to have two Audis.'
'He had: and then he had an Avenger.'
'He had: and then he had a Volvo.'
'He had: in the beginning he had a lot of Volkses.'
'He had: he was a great man for the Volkses.'
'He was: did he once have an Escort?'
'He had not: he had a son a doctor.'
'He had: and he had a Morris Minor too.'
'He had: he had a sister a hairdresser in Kilmallock.'
'He had: he had another sister a hairdresser in Ballybunion.'
'He had: he was put in a coffin which was put in his father's cart.'
'He was: his lady wife sat on top of the coffin driving the
    donkey.'
'She did: Ah, but he was a grand man.'
'He was: he was a grand man . . .'
'Good night, Father.'
'Good night, Mary.'

THE HAULIER'S WIFE MEETS JESUS ON THE ROAD NEAR MOONE

           I live in the town of Cahir
           In the Glen of Aherlow,
           Not far from Peekaun
           In the townland of Toureen,
           At the foot of Galtee Mór
           In the County of Tipperary.
           I am thirty-three years old,
           In the prime of my womanhood:
           The mountain stream of my sex
           In spate and darkly foaming;
           The white hills of my breasts

                      290

Brimful and breathing;
The tall trees of my eyes
Screening blue skies;
Yet in each palm of my hand
A sheaf of fallen headstones.
When I stand in profile
Before my bedroom mirror
With my hands on my hips in my slip,
Proud of my body,
Unashamed of my pride,
I appear to myself a naked stranger,
A woman whom I do not know
Except fictionally in the looking-glass,
Quite dramatically beautiful.
Yet in my soul I yearn for affection,
My soul is empty for the want of affection.
I am married to a haulier,
A popular and a wealthy man,
An alcoholic and a county councillor,
Father with me of four sons,
By repute a sensitive man and he is
Except when he makes love to me:
He takes leave of his senses,
Handling me as if I were a sack of gravel
Or a carnival dummy,
A fruit machine or a dodgem.
He makes love to me about twice a year;
Thereafter he does not speak to me for weeks,
Sometimes not for months.
One night in Cruise's Hotel in Limerick
I whispered to him: Please *take* me.
(We had been married five years
And we had two children.)
Christ, do you know what he said?
Where? Where do you want me to take you?
And he rolled over and fell asleep,
Tanked up with seventeen pints of beer.
We live in a Georgian, Tudor, Classical Greek,
Moorish, Spanish Hacienda, Regency Period,
Ranch House, Three-Storey Bungalow
On the edge of the edge of town:

'Poor Joe's Row'
The townspeople call it,
But our real address is 'Ronald Reagan Hill' –
That vulturous-looking man in the States.
We're about twelve miles from Ballyporeen
Or, as the vulture flies, about eight miles.
After a month or two of silence
He says to me: Wife, I'm sorry;
I know that we should be separated,
Annulled or whatever,
But on account of the clients and the neighbours,
Not to mention the children, it is plain
As a pikestaff we are glued to one another
Until death do us part.
Why don't you treat yourself
To a weekend up in Dublin,
A night out at the theatre:
I'll pay for the whole shagging lot.

There was a play on at the time
In the Abbey Theatre in Dublin
Called *The Gigli Concert*,
And, because I liked the name –
But also because it starred
My favourite actor, Tom Hickey –
I telephoned the Abbey from Cahir.
They had but one vacant seat left!
I was so thrilled with myself,
And at the prospect of Tom Hickey
In a play called *The Gigli Concert*
(Such a euphonious name for a play, I thought),
That one wet day I drove over to Clonmel
And I went wild, and I bought a whole new outfit.
I am not one bit afraid to say
That I spent all of £200 on it
(Not, of course, that Tom Hickey would see me
But I'd be seeing myself seeing Tom Hickey
Which would be almost, if not quite,
The very next best thing):
A long, tight-fitting, black skirt
Of Chinese silk,

With matching black jacket
And lace-frilled, pearl-white blouse;
Black fishnet stockings with sequins;
Black stiletto high-heeled shoes
Of pure ostrich leather.
I thought to myself – subconsciously, of course –
If I don't transpose to be somebody's *femme fatale*
It won't anyhow be for the want of trying.

Driving up to Dublin I began to daydream
And either at Horse & Jockey or Abbeyleix
I took a wrong turn and within a quarter of an hour
I knew I was lost. I stopped the car
And I asked the first man I saw on the road
For directions:
'Follow me' – he said – 'my name is Jesus:
Have no fear of me – I am a travelling actor.
We'll have a drink together in the nearby inn.'
It turned out we were on the road near Moone.
(Have you ever been to the Cross at Moone?
Once my children and I had a picnic at Moone
When they were little and we were on one
Of our Flight into Egypt jaunts to Dublin.
They ran round the High Cross round and round
As if it were a maypole, which maybe it is:
Figure carvings of loaves and fishes, lions and dolphins.
I drank black coffee from a thermos flask
And the children drank red lemonade
And they were wearing blue duffle coats with red scarves
And their small, round, laughing, freckled faces
Looked pointedly like the faces of the twelve apostles
Gazing out at us from the plinth of the Cross
Across a thousand years.
Only, of course, their father was not with us:
He was busy – busy being our family euphemism.
Every family in Ireland has its own family euphemism
Like a heraldic device or a coat of arms.)
Jesus turned out to be a lovely man,
All that a woman could ever possibly dream of:
Gentle, wild, soft-spoken, courteous, sad;
Angular, awkward, candid, methodical;

Humorous, passionate, angry, kind;
Entirely sensitive to a woman's world.
Discreetly I invited Jesus to spend the night with me –
Stay with me, the day is almost over and it is getting dark –
But he waved me aside with one wave of his hand,
Not contemptuously, but compassionately.
'Our night will come,' he smiled,
And he resumed chatting about my children,
All curiosity for their welfare and well-being.
It was like a fire burning in me when he talked to me.
There was only one matter I felt guilty about
And that was my empty vacant seat in the Abbey.
At closing time he kissed me on both cheeks
And we bade one another goodbye and then –
Just as I had all but given up hope –
He kissed me full on the mouth,
My mouth wet with alizarin lipstick
(A tube of Guerlain 4 which I've had for twelve years).
As I drove on into Dublin to the Shelbourne Hotel
I kept hearing his Midlands voice
Saying to me over and over, across the Garden of Gethsemane –
Our night will come.

Back in the town of Cahir,
In the Glen of Aherlow,
Not far from Peekaun
In the townland of Toureen,
At the foot of Galtee Mór
In the County of Tipperary,
For the sake of something to say
In front of our four sons
My husband said to me:
Well, what was Benjamino Gigli like?
Oh, 'twas a phenomenal concert!
And what was Tom Hickey like?
Miraculous – I whispered – miraculous.
Our night will come – he had smiled – our night will come.

Around the corner from Francis Bacon
Was where we made our first nest together
On the waters of the flood;
Where we first lived in sin:
The sunniest, most virtuous days of our life.
Not even the pastoral squalor of Clapham Common,
Nor the ghetto life of Notting Hill Gate,
Nor the racial drama of Barcelona,
Nor the cliffhanging bourgeois life of Cork City
Could ever equal those initial, primeval times together
Living in sin
In the halcyon ambience of South Kensington,
A haven for peaceful revolutionaries such as Harriet Waugh
Or Francis Bacon, or ourselves.
I slept on an ironing board in the kitchen
And you slept in the attic:
Late at night when all the other flat-dwellers
Were abed and – we thought wishfully – asleep,
You crept down the attic ladder
To make love with me on the ironing board,
As if we had known each other in a previous life
So waterily did our two body-phones attune,
Underwater swimming face to face in the dark,
Francis Bacon-Cimabue style.
My body-phone was made in Dublin
But your body-phone was made in Japan.
Standing up naked on the kitchen floor,
In the smog-filtered moonlight,
You placed your hand on my little folly, murmuring:
I have come to iron you, Sir Board.
Far from the tyrant liberties of Dublin, Ireland,
Where the comedy of freedom was by law forbidden
And truth, since the freedom of the State, gone underground.
When you had finished ironing me
I felt like hot silk queuing up to be bathèd
Under a waterfall in Samarkand
Or a mountain stream in Enniskerry.
Every evening I waited for you to come home,
Nipping out only in the rush hour to the delicatessen

Where Francis Bacon, basket under arm,
Surfacing like Mr Mole from his mews around the corner,
Used be stocking up in tomato purée and curry powder
Before heading off into the night and The Colony Room Club
Into whose green dark you and I sometimes also tiptoed.
In your own way you were equally Beatrix Potter-like,
Coming home to me laden with fish fingers and baked beans.
While I read to you from Dahlberg, you taught me about the
    psyche
Of the female orang-outang caged in the zoo:
Coronation Street . . . Z Cars . . . The World in Action . . .
Then Z Cars to beat all Z Cars – our own world in action –
The baskets of your eyes chock-a-block with your unique brands
Of tomato purée and curry powder;
Or, *That Was The Week That Was*, and then, my sleeping friend,
In the sandhills of whose shoulders sloping secretly down
Into small, hot havens of pure unscathèd sands
Where the only sounds are the sounds of the sea's tidal waters
Flooding backwards and forwards,
Tonight is the night that always is forever –
Ten or twenty minutes in the dark,
And in four million years or so
My stomach will swarm again suddenly with butterflies,
As with your bowl of water and your towel,
Your candle and your attic ladder,
Your taut high wire and your balancing pole,
A green minidress over your arm, a Penguin paperback in your
    hand,
I watch you coming towards me in the twilight of rush hour
On your hands and knees
And on the wet, mauve tip of your extended tongue
The two multicoloured birds of your plumed eyes ablaze
Around the corner from Francis Bacon.

from SIX NUNS DIE IN CONVENT INFERNO

To the
happy memory of six Loreto nuns
who died
between midnight and morning of
2 June 1986

I

We resided in a Loreto convent in the centre of Dublin city
On the east side of a public gardens, St Stephen's Green.
Grafton Street – the *paseo*
Where everybody *paseo*'d, including even ourselves –
Debouched on the north side, and at the top of Grafton Street,
Or round the base of the great patriotic pebble of O'Donovan
    Rossa,
Knelt tableaus of punk girls and punk boys.
When I used pass them – scurrying as I went –
Often as not to catch a mass in Clarendon Street,
The Carmelite Church in Clarendon Street
(Myself, I never used the Clarendon Street entrance,
I always slipped in by way of Johnson's Court,
Opposite the side entrance to Bewley's Oriental Café),
I could not help but smile, as I sucked on a Fox's mint,
That for all the half-shaven heads and the martial garb
And the dyed hair-dos and the nappy pins
They looked so conventional, really, and vulnerable,
Clinging to war paint and to uniforms and to one another.
I knew it was myself who was the ultimate drop-out,
The delinquent, the recidivist, the vagabond,
The wild woman, the subversive, the original punk.
Yet, although I confess I was smiling, I was also afraid,
Appalled by my own nerve, my own fervour,
My apocalyptic enthusiasm, my other-worldly hubris:
To opt out of the world and to
Choose such exotic loneliness,
Such terrestrial abandonment,
A lifetime of bicycle lamps and bicycle pumps,
A lifetime of galoshes stowed under the stairs,
A lifetime of umbrellas drying out in the kitchens.

I was an old nun – an agèd beadswoman –
But I was no daw.
I knew what a weird bird I was, I knew that when we
Went to bed we were as eerie an aviary as you'd find
In all the blown-off rooftops of the city:
Scuttling about our dorm, wheezing, shrieking, croaking,
In our yellowy corsets, wonky suspenders, strung-out garters,
A bony crew in the gods of the sleeping city.
Many's the night I lay awake in bed
Dreaming what would befall us if there were a fire:
No fire-escapes outside, no fire-extinguishers inside;
To coin a Dublin saying,
We'd not stand a snowball's chance in hell. Fancy that!
It seemed too good to be true:
Happy death vouchsafed only to the few.
Sleeping up there was like sleeping at the top of the mast
Of a nineteenth-century schooner, and in the daytime
We old nuns were the ones who crawled out on the yardarms
To stitch and sew the rigging and the canvas.
To be sure we were weird birds, oddballs, Christniks,
For we had done the weirdest thing a woman can do –
Surrendered the marvellous passions of girlhood,
The innocent dreams of childhood,
Not for a night or a weekend or even a Lent or a season,
But for a lifetime.
Never to know the love of a man or a woman;
Never to have children of our own;
Never to have a home of our own;
All for why and for what?
To follow a young man – would you believe it –
Who lived two thousand years ago in Palestine
And who died a common criminal strung up on a tree.

As we stood there in the disintegrating dormitory
Burning to death in the arms of Christ –
O Christ, Christ, come quickly, quickly –
Fluttering about in our tight, gold bodices,
Beating our wings in vain,
It reminded me of the snaps one of the sisters took
When we took a seaside holiday in 1956
(The year Cardinal Mindszenty went into hiding

In the US legation in Budapest.
He was a great hero of ours, Cardinal Mindszenty,
Any of us would have given our right arm
To have been his nun – darning his socks, cooking his meals,
Making his bed, doing his washing and ironing).
Somebody – an affluent buddy of the bishop's repenting his
    affluence –
Loaned Mother Superior a secluded beach in Co. Waterford –
Ardmore, along the coast from Tramore –
A cove with palm trees, no less, well off the main road.
There we were, fluttering up and down the beach,
Scampering hither and thither in our starched bathing-costumes.
Tonight, expiring in the fire, was quite much like that,
Only instead of scampering into the waves of the sea,
Now we were scampering into the flames of the fire.

That was one of the gayest days of my life,
The day the sisters went swimming.
Often in the silent darkness of the chapel after Benediction,
During the Exposition of the Blessed Sacrament,
I glimpsed the sea again as it was that day.
Praying – daydreaming really –
I became aware that Christ is the ocean
Forever rising and falling on the world's shore.
Now tonight in the convent Christ is the fire in whose waves
We are doomed but delighted to drown.
And, darting in and out of the flames of the dormitory,
Gabriel, with that extraordinary message of his on his boyish lips,
Frenetically pedalling his skybike.
He whispers into my ear what I must do
And I do it – and die.
Each of us in our own tiny, frail, furtive way
Was a Mother of God, mothering forth illegitimate Christs
In the street life of Dublin city.
God have mercy on our whirring souls –
Wild women were we all –
And on the misfortunate, poor fire-brigade men
Whose task it will be to shovel up our ashes and shovel
What is left of us into black plastic refuse sacks.
Fire-brigade men are the salt of the earth.

Isn't it a marvellous thing how your hour comes
When you least expect it? When you lose a thing,
Not to know about it until it actually happens?
How, in so many ways, losing things is such a refreshing
    experience,
Giving you a sense of freedom you've not often experienced?
How lucky I was to lose – I say, lose – lose my life.
It was a Sunday night, and after vespers
I skipped bathroom so that I could hop straight into bed
And get in a bit of a read before lights out:
Conor Cruise O'Brien's new book *The Siege*,
All about Israel and superlatively insightful
For a man who they say is reputedly an agnostic –
I got a loan of it from the brother-in-law's married niece –
But I was tired out and I fell asleep with the book open
Face down across my breast and I woke
To the racket of bellowing flame and snarling glass.
The first thing I thought was that the brother-in-law's married niece
Would never again get her Conor Cruise O'Brien back
And I had seen on the price-tag that it cost £23.00:
Small wonder that the custom of snipping off the price
As an exercise in social deportment has simply died out;
Indeed a book today is almost worth buying for its price,
Its price frequently being more remarkable than its contents.

The strange Eucharist of my death –
To be eaten alive by fire and smoke.
I clasped the dragon to my breast
And stroked his red-hot ears.
Strange! There we were, all sleeping molecules,
Suddenly all giving birth to our deaths,
All frantically in labour.
Doctors and midwives weaved in and out
In gowns of smoke and gloves of fire.
Christ, like an Orthodox patriarch in his dressing-gown,
Flew up and down the dormitory, splashing water on our souls:
Sister Eucharia; Sister Seraphia; Sister Rosario;
Sister Gonzaga; Sister Margaret; Sister Edith.
If you will remember us – six nuns burnt to death –
Remember us for the frisky girls that we were,
Now more than ever kittens in the sun.

THE LATE MR CHARLES LYNCH DIGRESSES
to Síabhra

Having sat all morning at the bay window
Of the run-down boarding house on the bitch-bedecked hill
Overlooking the drowned city of Cork
With a long-stemmed wine-glass balancing on the fulcrum
Of his ladylike, crossed knees – the deceased virtuoso
In the threadbare black greatcoat and frayed white shirt
Tiptoes through the urban heat
And scrupulously digresses into the Cork School of Music
When, from next door's crucial radio studios,
A production technician, Evie, comes skittering –
'Mr Lynch, they necessitate you urgently next door.'
Without altering the adagio of his gait, or its cantabile,
The ghostly pianist, the master digresser,
Perilously whispers:
'I'm sorry, Evie – but I'm *dashing*.'

THE LEVITE AND HIS CONCUBINE AT GIBEAH

After Paul Durcan left his wife
– Actually she left him but it is more *recherché* to say
That he left her –
Would you believe it but he turned up at our villa
With a woman whom we had never heard of before,
Much less met. To *our* villa! The Kerrs of Dundalk!
I, Mrs Kerr, with a windowframe around my neck!
You will not believe it but he actually asked me
To put him up for the night – and his friend –
A slip of a thing, half his age.
I said that I would but in separate bedrooms.
This is a family home – I had to remind him.
I resented having to remind him.

The pair of them proceeded to squat in silence
In the living room for what was left of the evening
So that I could not even switch on the television.
As a consequence I missed *Twin Peaks*.

What got up my nose
Was that she sat on the step of the fireplace
On a cushion from our sofa thrown down by him
With her hands joined around his knees:
Himself sitting in my husband's armchair
As if he owned it – without so much as a 'May I?'

She was got up in a loudspoken yellow dress
And those precious little hands of hers around his knees
As if his knees were pillows;
Her face a teatowel of holy innocence
As if margarine would not melt in her tonsils.
I would go so far as to say that it was indelicate –
The way she had her hands joined around his knees.

As soon as I began to yawn, he began to speak:
Holding forth until three o'clock in the a.m.
On what he called his 'Theory of Peripeteia' –
A dog's dinner of gibberish about the philosophical significance
Of 'not caring being the secret to transforming misfortune'.
Finally I stood up and declared 'Peripeteia, Goodnight'.
I installed the pair of them in separate bedrooms.
I left my own bedroom door open.

I fell asleep about five.
When I knocked him up for breakfast
She answered the door. I was that indignant
That when they came down for breakfast
I gave them porridge – like it or lump it.
I did not utter one word to them
Until they had finished.
Then I took him aside and I let him have it:

Now listen to me Paul Durcan:
You may be a poet and a Levite
But you will not take advantage of me.
Get yourself and your – your – your concubine
Out of my Dundalk villa.
How dare a woman wear a loudspoken yellow dress –
When you set foot in Gibeah next time
Do not ever Durcan my doorstep again.

Know what his response was? To ask me
If he might borrow my Shell Guide and my donkey?
To be rid of him I gave in – more fool I.
He shimmied out the door singing to himself:
'We borrowed the loan of Kerr's big ass
To go to Dundalk with butter . . .'

Know what he did then? He went down to that old peasant
In the lane at the end of the avenue – Kavanagh –
Who goes about the town always with his socks down
Because he used play football for Mucker–Rotterdam:
Kavanagh with that – that ridiculous –
That – that vulgar –
That – that gross
Brass knocker on his front door.

BERNARD O'DONOGHUE

Born Cullen, north-west Cork, 1945. Educated at Oxford University, where he lectures in medieval literature at Magdalen College. O'Donoghue is a notable critic of contemporary poetry.

O'Donoghue's most convincing lyrics disguise his sophisticated literary self-consciousness to render aspects of rural Irish experience in a strongly idiomatic poetic language.

A NUN TAKES THE VEIL

That morning early I ran through briars
To catch the calves that were bound for market.
I stopped the once, to watch the sun
Rising over Doolin across the water.

The calves were tethered outside the house
While I had my breakfast: the last one at home
For forty years. I had what I wanted (they said
I could), so we'd loaf bread and Marie biscuits.

We strung the calves behind the boat,
Me keeping clear to protect my style:
Confirmation suit and my patent sandals.
But I trailed my fingers in the cool green water,

Watching the puffins driving homeward
To their nests on Aran. On the Galway mainland
I tiptoed clear of the cow-dunged slipway
And watched my brothers heaving the calves

As they lost their footing. We went in a trap,
Myself and my mother, and I said goodbye
To my father then. The last I saw of him
Was a hat and jacket and a salley stick,

Driving cattle to Ballyvaughan.
He died (they told me) in the county home,
Asking to see me. But that was later:
As we trotted on through the morning mist,

I saw a car for the first time ever,
Hardly seeing it before it vanished.
I couldn't believe it, and I stood up looking
To where I could hear its noise departing

But it was only a glimpse. That night in the convent
The sisters spoilt me, but I couldn't forget
The morning's vision, and I fell asleep
With the engine humming through the open window.

THE WEAKNESS

It was the frosty early hours when finally
The cow's despairing groans rolled him from bed
And into his boots, hardly awake yet.
He called 'Dan! come on, Dan!
She's calving', and stumbled without his coat
Down the icy path to the haggard.

Castor and Pollux were fixed in line
Over his head but he didn't see them,
This night any more than another.
He crossed to the stall, past the corner
Of the fairy-fort he'd levelled last May.
But this that stopped him, like the mind's step

Backward: what was that, more insistent
Than the calf's birth-pangs? 'Hold on, Dan.
I think I'm having a weakness.
I never had a weakness, Dan, before.'
And down he slid, groping for the lapels
Of the shocked boy's twenty-year-old jacket.

FRANK ORMSBY

Born Enniskillen, County Fermanagh, 1947. Educated at St Michael's College, Enniskillen, and Queen's University Belfast. Has taught since 1971 at the Royal Belfast Academical Institution, where he is head of English. Edited the *Honest Ulsterman*, 1969–89. An influential anthologist, notably of *Poets from the North of Ireland* (1979; 1990) and *A Rage for Order: Poetry of the Northern Ireland Troubles* (1992).

Precise, observant and witty, Ormsby's poems frequently interrogate the sense of place as a source both of stability and division in Northern Ireland.

PASSING THE CREMATORIUM

Someone is leaving town as clean smoke
This summer morning, too much the drifter
Now to let us know – even if he could –
His destination. Who watched, perhaps, the trail
Of jets in skies another summer
May find already that he's half-way there;
Or thinned instead into a blacker air
The factories muster. Whatever fate
Our leisured thought contrives to fit his journey
Pales with our passing;
Diverts no longer than we take to cruise
Beyond that frail thread, seawards, this summer morning.

HOME

Once, in the Giant's Ring, I closed my eyes
and thought of Ireland,
the air-wide, skin-tight, multiple meaning of here.

When I opened them I was little the wiser,
in that, perhaps, one

with the first settlers in the Lagan Valley
and the Vietnamese boat-people of Portadown.

from A PARIS HONEYMOON

L'ORANGERIE

We have floated to the surface of Monet's pond
this morning in the Orangerie, somewhere among
discarded buttonholes, bedraggled bouquets,
the wreaths of drowned sorrows.
Your face grows secret and lovely. It is a face
of many fathoms in this time and place.
I am the lover opening his eyes
in mid-kiss, as though he might surprise
the unique swirl of self, who catches instead,
buoyant and timeless and all unaware,
you crossing, perhaps, your exact instant of death,
too brimmed with love and living to yield it room
for this or many a year – or you submerged
in the not-yet-carnate moment of giving birth.
Primordial blossoms. Watery nebulae.
Blurred, breathless features in a spawny hush
gathering towards us, miming the kiss of light.

CIARAN CARSON

Born Belfast, into an Irish-speaking family, 1948. Educated at St Mary's
Christian Brothers' School and Queen's University Belfast. Worked as a
teacher and civil servant before being appointed Traditional Arts Officer
for the Arts Council of Northern Ireland, a position he combined with
that of Literature Officer in 1991. A musician as well as a poet, Carson
has published *The Pocket Guide to Irish Traditional Music* (1986).

A distrust of the facility with which he had reduplicated the modern
Irish lyric in his first collection (*The New Estate*, 1976) kept Carson silent
for more than a decade. He returned to publication on evolving a form
adequate to his suspicion of artistic closure: the circling, digressing
narratives of *The Irish for No* (1987) draw on the traditional storytelling
techniques encountered in Carson's Arts Council work to play the
literary off against the vernacular in a grim relativistic comedy. 'Dresden'
dramatises a scepticism towards high culture and towards the
mythologies alike of the militarised state and its paramilitary opponents.
Carson's method is extended in *Belfast Confetti* (1989) to offer a densely
textured, book-length map of a city in an endless process of destruction
and renewal. The Belfast of 'The Mouth', 'Hamlet' and other pieces is a
deceptive, unpredictable place, familiar yet misremembered, spookily
normal and reassuringly surreal – a labyrinth as much of mental
categories and linguistic evasions as of streets. 'Ovid: *Metamorphoses*, V,
529–550' performs one of the grittier in a series of Ovidian variations by
contemporary poets, *After Ovid* (1994). With a nod towards MacNeice,
'Bagpipe Music' deploys Carson's intimacy with traditional music to
ironic effect.

DRESDEN

Horse Boyle was called Horse Boyle because of his brother Mule;
Though why Mule was called Mule is anybody's guess. I stayed
    there once,
Or rather, I nearly stayed there once. But that's another story.
At any rate they lived in this decrepit caravan, not two miles out
    of Carrick,

Encroached upon by baroque pyramids of empty baked bean tins,
    rusts
And ochres, hints of autumn merging into twilight. Horse
    believed
They were as good as a watchdog, and to tell you the truth
You couldn't go near the place without something falling over:
A minor avalanche would ensue – more like a shop bell, really,

The old-fashioned ones on string, connected to the latch, I
    think,
And as you entered in, the bell would tinkle in the empty shop,
    a musk
Of soap and turf and sweets would hit you from the gloom,
    Tobacco.
Baling wire. Twine. And, of course, shelves and pyramids of tins.
An old woman would appear from the back – there was a sizzling
    pan in there,
Somewhere, a whiff of eggs and bacon – and ask you what you
    wanted;
Or rather, she wouldn't ask; she would talk about the weather.
    It had rained
That day, but it was looking better. They had just put in the
    spuds.
I had only come to pass the time of day, so I bought a token
    packet of Gold Leaf.

All this time the fry was frying away. Maybe she'd a daughter
    in there
Somewhere, though I hadn't heard the neighbours talk of it; if
    anybody knew,
It would be Horse. Horse kept his ears to the ground.
And he was a great man for current affairs; he owned the only TV
    in the place.
Come dusk he'd set off on his rounds, to tell the whole townland
    the latest
Situation in the Middle East, a mortar bomb attack in
    Mullaghbawn –
The damn things never worked, of course – and so he'd tell the
    story
How in his young day it was very different. Take young Flynn,
    for instance,

Who was ordered to take this bus and smuggle some sticks of
  gelignite

Across the border, into Derry, when the RUC – or was it the
  RIC? –
Got wind of it. The bus was stopped, the peeler stepped on.
  Young Flynn
Took it like a man, of course: he owned up right away. He
  opened the bag
And produced the bomb, his rank and serial number. For all
  the world
Like a pound of sausages. Of course, the thing was, the peeler's
  bike
Had got a puncture, and he didn't know young Flynn from
  Adam. All he wanted
Was to get home for his tea. Flynn was in for seven years and
  learned to speak
The best of Irish. He had thirteen words for a cow in heat;
A word for the third thwart in a boat, the wake of a boat on the
  ebb tide.

He knew the extinct names of insects, flowers, why this place was
  called
Whatever: *Carrick*, for example, was a *rock*. He was damn right
  there –
As the man said, *When you buy meat you buy bones, when you buy
  land you buy stones.*
You'd be hard put to find a square foot in the whole bloody
  parish
That wasn't thick with flints and pebbles. To this day he could
  hear the grate
And scrape as the spade struck home, for it reminded him of
  broken bones:
Digging a graveyard, maybe – or better still, trying to dig a
  reclaimed tip
Of broken delph and crockery ware – you know that sound that
  sets your teeth on edge
When the chalk squeaks on the blackboard, or you shovel ashes
  from the stove?

Master McGinty – he'd be on about McGinty then, and
    discipline, the capitals
Of South America, Moore's *Melodies*, the Battle of Clontarf, and
*Tell me this, an educated man like you: What goes on four legs when
    it's young,*
Two legs when it's grown up, and three legs when it's old? I'd pretend
I didn't know. McGinty's leather strap would come up then, stuffed
With threepenny bits to give it weight and sting. Of course, it
    never did him
Any harm: *You could take a horse to water but you couldn't make
    him drink.*
He himself was nearly going on to be a priest.
And many's the young cub left the school, as wise as when he came.

Carrowkeel was where McGinty came from – *Narrow Quarter,*
    Flynn explained –
Back before the Troubles, a place that was so mean and crabbed,
Horse would have it, men were known to eat their dinner from a
    drawer.
Which they'd slide shut the minute you'd walk in.
He'd demonstrate this at the kitchen table, hunched and furtive,
    squinting
Out the window – past the teetering minarets of rust, down the
    hedge-dark aisle –
To where a stranger might appear, a passer-by, or what was
    maybe worse,
Someone he knew. Someone who wanted something. Someone
    who was hungry.
Of course who should come tottering up the lane that instant but
    his brother

Mule. I forgot to mention they were twins. They were as like
    two –
No, not peas in a pod, for this is not the time nor the place to
    go into
Comparisons, and this is really Horse's story, Horse who – now
    I'm getting
Round to it – flew over Dresden in the war. He'd emigrated
    first, to
Manchester. Something to do with scrap – redundant mill
    machinery,

Giant flywheels, broken looms that would, eventually, be ships,
  or aeroplanes.
He said he wore his fingers to the bone.
And so, on impulse, he had joined the RAF. He became a rear
  gunner.
Of all the missions, Dresden broke his heart. It reminded him of
  china.

As he remembered it, long afterwards, he could hear, or almost
  hear
Between the rapid desultory thunderclaps, a thousand tinkling
  echoes –
All across the map of Dresden, store-rooms full of china shivered,
  teetered
And collapsed, an avalanche of porcelain, slushing and cascading:
  cherubs,
Shepherdesses, figurines of Hope and Peace and Victory, delicate
  bone fragments.
He recalled in particular a figure from his childhood, a milkmaid
Standing on the mantelpiece. Each night as they knelt down for
  the rosary,
His eyes would wander up to where she seemed to beckon to
  him, smiling,
Offering him, eternally, her pitcher of milk, her mouth of rose
  and cream.

One day, reaching up to hold her yet again, his fingers stumbled,
  and she fell.
He lifted down a biscuit tin, and opened it.
It breathed an antique incense: things like pencils, snuff, tobacco.
His war medals. A broken rosary. And there, the milkmaid's
  creamy hand, the outstretched
Pitcher of milk, all that survived. Outside, there was a scraping
And a tittering; I knew Mule's step by now, his careful drunken
  weaving
Through the tin-stacks. I might have stayed the night, but there's
  no time
To go back to that now; I could hardly, at any rate, pick up the
  thread.
I wandered out through the steeples of rust, the gate that was a
  broken bed.

COCKTAILS

Bombing at about ninety miles an hour with the exhaust
     skittering
The skid-marked pitted tarmac of Kennedy Way, they hit the
     ramp and sailed
Clean over the red-and-white guillotine of the check-point and
     landed
On the M1 flyover, then disappeared before the Brits knew what
     hit them. So
The story went: we were in the Whip and Saddle bar of the
     Europa.

There was talk of someone who was shot nine times and lived,
     and someone else
Had the inside info. on the Romper Room. We were trying to
     remember the facts
Behind the Black & Decker case, when someone ordered another
     drink and we entered
The realm of Jabberwocks and Angels' Wings, Widows' Kisses,
     Corpse Revivers.

THE MOUTH

There was this head had this mouth he kept shooting off.
     Unfortunately.
It could have been worse for us than it was for him.
     Provisionally.
But since nothing in this world is certain and you don't know
     who hears what
We thought it was time he bit off more than he could chew.
     Literally.
By the time he is found there'll be nothing much left to tell
     who he was.

But of course some clever dick from the 'Forscenic Lab'
     reconstructs
Him, what he used to be – not from his actual teeth, not his
     fingerprints,

313

But from the core – the toothmarks of the first and last bite he'd
    taken of
This sour apple. But then we would have told them anyway.
    Publicity.

HAMLET

As usual, the clock in The Clock Bar was a good few minutes fast:
A fiction no one really bothered to maintain, unlike the story
The comrade on my left was telling, which no one knew for
    certain truth:
*Back in 1922 a sergeant, I forget his name, was shot outside the
National Bank* . . .
Ah yes, what year was it that they knocked it down? Yet, its
    memory's as fresh
As the inky smell of new pound notes – which interferes with the
    beer-and-whiskey
Tang of now, like two dogs meeting in the revolutionary 69 of a
    long sniff,
Or cattle jostling shit-stained flanks in the Pound. For *pound*, as
    some wag
Interrupted, was an off-shoot of the Falls, from the Irish, *fál*, a
    hedge;
Hence, *any kind of enclosed thing*, its twigs and branches
    commemorated
By the soldiers' drab and olive camouflage, as they try to melt
Into a brick wall; red coats might be better, after all. *At any rate,*
*This sergeant's number came up; not a winning one. The bullet had his
name on it.*
Though Sergeant X, as we'll call him, doesn't really feature in
    the story:
The nub of it is, *This tin can which was heard that night, trundling
down*
*From the bank, down Balaklava Street. Which thousands heard, and no
one ever*
Saw. Which was heard for years, any night that trouble might be
Round the corner . . . and when it skittered to a halt, you knew
That someone else had snuffed it: a name drifting like an
    afterthought,

A scribbled wisp of smoke you try and grasp, as it becomes
   diminuendo, then
Vanishes. For *fál* is also *frontier, boundary*, as in *the undiscovered
   country*
For whose bourne no traveller returns, the illegible, thorny hedge of
   time itself –
Heartstopping moments, measured not by the pulse of a wrist-
   watch, nor
The archaic anarchists' alarm-clock, but a mercury tilt device
Which 'only connects' on any given bump on the road. So, by
   this wingèd messenger
The promise 'to pay the bearer' is fulfilled:

As someone buys another round, an Allied Irish Banks £10 note
   drowns in
The slops of the counter; a Guinness stain blooms on the artist's
   impression
Of the sinking of the *Girona*; a tiny foam hisses round the
   salamander brooch
Dredged up to show how love and money endure, beyond death
   and the Armada,
Like the bomb-disposal expert in his suit of salamander-cloth.
Shielded against the blast of time by a strangely mediaeval visor,
He's been outmoded by this jerky robot whose various
   attachments include
A large hook for turning over corpses that may be booby-trapped;
But I still have this picture of his hands held up to avert the
   future
In a final act of *No surrender*, as, twisting through the murky
   fathoms
Of what might have been, he is washed ashore as pearl and coral.

This *strange eruption to our state* is seen in other versions of the
   Falls:
A no-go area, a ghetto, a demolition zone. For the ghost, as it turns
   out –
All this according to your man, and I can well believe it – this tin
   ghost,
Since the streets it haunted were abolished, was never heard again.
The sleeve of Raglan Street has been unravelled; the helmet of
   Balaklava

Is torn away from the mouth. The dim glow of Garnet has gone
    out,
And with it, all but the memory of where I lived. I, too, heard
    the ghost:
A roulette trickle, or the hesitant annunciation of a downpour,
    ricocheting
Off the window; a goods train shunting distantly into a siding,
Then groaning to a halt; the rainy cries of children after dusk.
For the voice from the grave reverberates in others' mouths, as
    the sails
Of the whitethorn hedge swell up in a little breeze, and tremble
Like the spiral blossom of Andromeda: so suddenly are shrouds
    and branches
Hung with street-lights, celebrating all that's lost, as fields are
    reclaimed
By the Starry Plough. So we name the constellations, to put a
    shape
On what was there; so, the storyteller picks his way between the
    isolated stars.

But, *Was it really like that?* And, *Is the story true?*
You might as well tear off the iron mask, and find that no one,
    after all,
Is there: nothing but a cry, a summons, clanking out from the
    smoke
Of demolition. Like some son looking for his father, or the father
    for his son,
We try to piece together the exploded fragments. Let these
    broken spars
Stand for the Armada and its proud full sails, for even if
The clock is put to rights, everyone will still believe it's fast:
The barman's shouts of *time* will be ignored in any case, since
    time
Is conversation; it is the hedge that flits incessantly into the
    present,
As words blossom from the speakers' mouths, and the flotilla
    returns to harbour,
Long after hours.

OVID: *METAMORPHOSES*, V, 529-550

Persephone ate seven pomegranate seeds. So what? I'll tell you
    what –
It doesn't do to touch strange fruit, when it's forbidden by the
    Powers-
That-Be. Who put you on a hunger strike which, if you break,
    you'll stay put
In the Underworld. It doesn't do to get caught out. Watch out
    for prowlers.

She'd wandered into Pluto's murky realm; plucked the dull-
    orange bubble.
Split the cortex. Sucked. And who was salivating in the bushes'
    dark interior
But Ascalaphus. Stoolie. Pipsqueak. Mouth. He spilled the beans
    on her, he blabbed –
Straight off he shot, and knocked, knocked, knocked on
    Heaven's iron door.

But she spat back as good as she had got: unholy water from the
    Phlegethon
She slabbered on him. His eyes yellowed, drooled, and grew. His
    neb became a beak.
He sprouted spermy wings. Hooked talons shot from his fingers.
    His body dwindled
Into mostly head. All ears, all eyes: touts everywhere, potential
    freaks.

Beware. For now he is the scrake-owl, Troubles' augury for
    Auld Lang Syne,
Who to this day is harbinger of doom, the gloom of Pluto's
    no-go zone.

BAGPIPE MUSIC

He came lilting down the brae with a blackthorn stick the thick
    of a shotgun
In his fist, going *blah dithery dump a doodle scattery idle fortunoodle* –

When I saw his will-o'-the-wisp go dander through a field of
   blue flax randomly, abandonedly
Till all his dots and dashes zipped together, ripped right through
   their perforations
Like a Zephyr through the Zodiac: the way a quadrille, in its last
   configuration,
Takes on the branches of a swastika, all ribs and shanks and male
   and female chromosomes;
Till I heard his voice diminish like the corncrake's in the last
   abandoned acre –
Scrake tithery lass a laddle nation aries hiber Packie, he'd be

Oblivious to the black-and-tan, leaf-and-muck-bestrewn
   squatting figure
Whose only obvious features are the almost-blue whites of his
   two blue eyes, who crabs
From leaf to shadow, mesmerized by olive and burnt umber, the
   khaki, lion patches
Of his Cockney accent, going *hang bang a bleeper doddle doodlebug
   an asterix.*
The Pisces rod of his aerial twitched just now, as if he'd got the
   message,
That the earth itself was camouflaged. Bluebells carpeted the
   quivered glades, as,
Three fields away, the tick-tock of the grandmother reassures us
   with the long extended
Skillet of its pendulum. The wife in all of this is sidelong, poised
   Egyptian
In her fitted kitchen, though the pictograph is full of *Ireland's
   Own*-type details, Virgin
Marys, blue and white plates ranged like punctuation in the lull
   of memory.
The walls are sentences. We see the three walls and the fourth is
   glassy us.

Ocularity a moiety blah skiddery ah disparity: the shotgun made a
   kind of statement, two
Crows falling in a dead-black umlaut. *The Lucky Shot*, my man
   would say, and feed
Me yet another yarn: how you find a creeper in the undergrowth
   and yank,

And a rippled, ripped net shivers through its warp of black-damp
    earth aroma.
There's ink embedded in his two eyes blue, like children's dots.
    Listen close
Enough, you'll get the blooping of the retting dam, parturient, as
    bubbles
Pick and pock a morseway through the stench of rotting flax. For
    it seemed
The grandmother produced an alarm-clock from her
    psychobabble handbag.

That was at the check-point. Meanwhile, the trail was beginning
    to leak and waft
Away, but the sniffer dogs persevered in their rendition of *The
    Fox Chase*, lapping
And snuffling up the pepper-black stardust fibrillating on the
    paper, till
The interview was thwarted by Aquarius, a blue line on the map
    that was
Contemporaneous with its past. *Skirl girn a snaffle birdle girdle on
    the griddle howlin –*

Here a squad of black-and-white minstrels wheel in from Stage
    Right, or rather, they
Are wearing balaklavas, and it only looks like that, their grinning
Toothpaste lips, their rolling whites of eyes, their *Tipp-Ex*ed
    teeth, their *Daz* forensic
Gloves. They twirl their walking-sticks as thick as guns to
    marching tunes
That blatter in that fourth green field across the border, upstairs
    in a tent,
With Capricorn-skin drums and fifes, while Blavatsky hollers
    through a bullhorn,
Give ye thirty shillins for yer wan poun ten, yer wan poun ten, yer
Fair exchange, they say, sure six of one and half-a-dozen of the
    brother –
I get the drift of the *Bloo* in the portable loo, John, like, it's one
    ping cancels out
The pong, going *January, February, March! April, May, June, July!*

He was blabbing with his Jew-or-jaw's harp finger on his lower
    lip, when the breech
Of the gun snapped out its breach of the peace. The linen
    handkerchief had got
A brack in it, somehow, the dots and dashes of some other's red.
    I tried to pin it down
Just then, or pen it down, but the Lambegs wouldn't let me, and
    anyway, my thumb
And finger's smeared up to the wrist with *Lion* ink. My hand
    is dis-
Located. The unmarked car came quietly, enquiringly, while in a
    no-go zone
Three streets away, I heard two taxis crabbing, like Gemini in
    Gethsemane, which
Of them was black: *honk parp a bullet billet reverup and harp a ballad*
Scrake nithery lou a mackie nice wee niece ah libralassie . . .
Just before I put the thing to bed, I closed a pair of scorpion's
    inverted commas round it.
Tomorrow I would glance at the decapitated headlines, then flick
    forward to the Stars.

TOM PAULIN

Born Leeds, 1949, of English father and Northern Irish mother. Moved to Belfast, 1953. Educated at Annadale Grammar School, Belfast, the University of Hull and Lincoln College, Oxford. Taught from 1972 at the University of Nottingham, where he was briefly Professor of Poetry before being appointed lecturer in English at Hartford College, Oxford, in 1994. A founder member and director of the Field Day Theatre Company, he has published versions of Aeschylus and Sophocles, and edited two controversial anthologies, *The Faber Book of Political Verse* (1986) and *The Faber Book of Vernacular Verse* (1990). *Minotaur: Poetry and the Nation State* (1992) is the most recent of three critical books. A prominent critic in both print and broadcast media in Britain, Paulin is currently working on a life of William Hazlitt.

Paulin's poetry is perhaps best seen as a corollary of the brilliant, tendentious and ultimately equivocal critique of Protestantism elaborated in his literary essays. The decline of Calvinist individualism to the vulgar, blustering consumerism he wittily – some might say outrageously – portrays in 'Off the Back of a Lorry' is charted in a series of superb studies (of Milton, Emily Dickinson, Ted Hughes and others) in *Minotaur*. Paulin's vision of Ulster unionism in 'Desertmartin' and 'A Written Answer' rests on an aspirational reading of the 1798 rebellion: the Presbyterian United Irishmen exist for him in an innocent foretime to Protestantism's disastrous pact with imperialism. The spiky acerbity of his style counters any sentimentality in Paulin's historical conceptions. His more recent work – represented here by the Yeatsian spoof 'The Lonely Tower' – seeks to fracture the formalities of lyric utterance in the interest of a vernacular urgency.

POT BURIAL

He has married again. His wife
Buys ornaments and places them
On the dark sideboard. Year by year
Her vases and small jugs crowd out
The smiles of the wife who died.

WHERE ART IS A MIDWIFE

In the third decade of March,
A Tuesday in the town of Z—

The censors are on day-release.
They must learn about literature.

There are things called ironies,
Also symbols, which carry meaning.

The types of ambiguity
Are as numerous as the enemies

Of the state. Formal and bourgeois,
Sonnets sing of the old order,

Its lost gardens where white ladies
Are served wine in the subtle shade.

This poem about a bear
Is not a poem about a bear.

It might be termed a satire
On a loyal friend. Do I need

To spell it out? Is it possible
That none of you can understand?

DESERTMARTIN

At noon, in the dead centre of a faith,
Between Draperstown and Magherafelt,
This bitter village shows the flag
In a baked absolute September light.
Here the Word has withered to a few
Parched certainties, and the charred stubble
Tightens like a black belt, a crop of Bibles.

Because this is the territory of the Law
I drive across it with a powerless knowledge –
The owl of Minerva in a hired car.
A Jock squaddy glances down the street
And grins, happy and expendable,
Like a brass cartridge. He is a useful thing,
Almost at home, and yet not quite, not quite.

It's a limed nest, this place. I see a plain
Presbyterian grace sour, then harden,
As a free strenuous spirit changes
To a servile defiance that whines and shrieks
For the bondage of the letter: it shouts
For the Big Man to lead his wee people
To a clean white prison, their scarred bald trustful town.

Masculine Islam, the rule of the Just,
Egyptian sand dunes and geometry,
A theology of rifle-butts and executions:
These are the places where the spirit dies.
And now, in Desertmartin's sandy light,
I see a culture of twigs and bird-shit
Waving a gaudy flag it loves and curses.

OFF THE BACK OF A LORRY

A zippo lighter
and a quilted jacket,
two rednecks troughing
in a gleamy diner,
the flinty chipmarks
on a white enamel pail,
Paisley putting pen to paper
in Crumlin jail,
a jumbo double
fried peanut butter
sandwich Elvis scoffed
during the last
diapered days –

they're more than tacky,
these pured fictions,
and like the small ads
in a country paper
they build a gritty
sort of prod baroque
I must return to
like my own boke.

A WRITTEN ANSWER

This poem by Rupert Brookeborough
is all about fishing and the stout B-men
(they live for always in our hearts,
their only crime was being loyal),
there is a lough in it and stacks of rivers,
also a brave wee hymn to the sten-gun.
The poet describes Gough of the Curragh
and by his use of many metric arts
he designs a fictionary universe
which has its own laws and isn't quite
the same as this place that we call real.
His use of metonymy is pretty desperate
and the green symbolism's a contradiction,
but I like his image of the elm and chestnut,
for to me this author is a fly man
and the critics yonder say his work is alright.

THE LONELY TOWER

'WANTED – *coastal farm, site, derelict house, period house,
stable yard, outhouse, lodge, martello. Must be on sea.
Immediate cash settlement. Box Z0490.*'

Either incognito and desperate
or more likely a small developer
dreaming the obvious

they've neither the form nor the substance
only the theme
but what a theme it is
– John Melly's breezeblock bothie
in the dunes above Dooey Strand
a windy look-out post
from the Emergency
the Lone Man's House
at Ballyeriston
(baled hay in every room
blank uncurtained windows
dust sealight bullocks blurping in the fields
doggy bones on the kitchen floor)
that coastguard station
– roofless since the state's founding
set on the hillside
above Portnoo Post Office
an entire deserted village even
where the road gives up its potholed ghost
in a wilderness of scree and ironstone
– from the dead martello
down to the shed on the cement pier
most any building
in this squally clachan
could quicken into newness
– you can write them out in a verse
or jump in a lorry
rammed with cement and timber
then *bash bash bash* till the day
when you paint *Wavecrest* on the gatepost

BIDDY JENKINSON

'Biddy Jenkinson' is the pseudonym of a poet born in 1949, who is the wife of a diplomat. When 'Cáitheadh' was published in *Poetry Ireland Review* (Summer, 1988) the 'Notes on Contributors' described the author as a 'hermit' and 'pensioned bee-keeper', and credited the translator with a volume called *The Flaccid Halo*.

Jenkinson is perhaps the most stylistically assured and versatile Irish-language poet to emerge over the last decade. She has imposed a partial ban on translation of her work into English: 'It is a small rude gesture to those that think that everything can be harvested and stored without loss in an English-speaking Ireland.' I have chosen one poem from the small number she has permitted to appear in dual-language format

Dá mba mise an barruisce ghabhfainn chugham do bharraicíní
Dhéanfainn suirí le do rúitíní le cúr grian-gheal na scríbe
Dhéanfainn tathaint ar do choiscéim le haistharraingt na maidhme
is líonfainn ort na hioscaidí
le cuilithíní.

Dá mba mise an tonn shúraic dhéanfainn mán mán le do ghlúine
Chuirfinn creathánacht ag preabarnach ar fud do cheathrúna
Dhéanfainn leisbhearta dem chraiceann duit is triús dem shíoda
uaine
Brachlainn thar do bholg suas is
mórtas ort go guaillí.

Dá mba mé an mhuir iomghorm ghoidfinn uait do shúile
D'fhiarfainn chugham d'intinn le siansa is suaitheadh
Ruathuile ad tharraingt domhain domhain chugham de rúchladh
Cíocha an chuain ag borradh chughat
le mana múirne

Mar gur geal an lá, gur geal an spéir, gur dáimh liom gach dúile
is ní fhágfainn broigheall dubh ar leac
dá bhféadhfainn é mhúscailt.
Tá an fharraige ard, an ghrian go hard, mise lán de ghrásta
is feam i lár na feamainne ag rince leis go sásta.

SPRAY

If I were the spreading tide sheets I would overwhelm your
    insteps
I would fetch up round your ankles with the sunbleached wrath
    of storms
I would coax you to step closer with the swishback of the gravel
and swoosh back up behind your knees
in curls.

If I were the tugging backwash I would titter you and tease you
send waves of gooseflesh up your legs in squames
Thigh holes of my skin for you. my greenest silk to please you
High combers up your reefy ribs. your shoulders spumed
in squalls

If I were green in essence I would melt your eyes and take them
I would hold your mind suspended like the water in a wave
Down, you'd flow; deep down to me, while over you most
    blithely
The harbour's breasts would jut with intimations
of a war.

For the day is fine, the sky is bright and I am full and friendly
and I'd leave no sea shag crucified if I could plume its feathers
Swelling sea and shining sun and . . . Oh my dear, be merry
The sea staff through the sea membranes
is delicately stirring.

translated by Alex Osborne

MEDBH McGUCKIAN

Born Belfast, 1950. Educated at the Dominican College, Belfast, and
Queen's University. Worked as a secondary school teacher for some
years before becoming a full-time writer. Has been literary editor of
Fortnight, writer-in-residence at Queen's and visiting fellow at the
University of California, Berkeley. Lives in Belfast.

McGuckian's playful, enigmatic lyrics recall the work of Rilke and
Stevens in their absorption with their own processes – if not in their
sometimes coquettish tone. Critics are divided as to whether their
challenge to semantic authority issues from postmodernist relativism or
feminist radicalism. 'The Seed-Picture' and 'The Sitting' explore in
terms of picture-making the power relations involved in any act of
representation. 'The Flower Master' meditates on the inescapable
tensions of sexuality, managing in the metaphors of the closing lines to
be coy and genitally specific at the same time. 'Porcelain Bells', an
elegiac sequence on the death of the poet's father, is addressed
to her mother.

THE SEED-PICTURE

This is my portrait of Joanna – since the split
The children come to me like a dumb-waiter,
And I wonder where to put them, beautiful seeds
With no immediate application . . . the clairvoyance
Of seed-work has opened up
New spectrums of activity, beyond a second home.
The seeds dictate their own vocabulary,
Their dusty colours capture
More than we can plan,
The mould on walls, or jumbled garages,
Dead flower heads where insects shack . . .
I only guide them not by guesswork
In their necessary numbers,
And attach them by the spine to a perfect bedding,
Woody orange pips, and tear-drop apple,

The banana of the caraway, wrinkled peppercorns,
The pocked peach, or waterlily honesty,
The seamed cherry stone so hard to break.

Was it such self-indulgence to enclose her
In the border of a grandmother's sampler,
Bonding all the seeds in one continuous skin,
The sky resolved to a cloud the length of a man?
To use tan linseed for the trees, spiky
Sunflower for leaves, bright lentils
For the window, patna stars
For the floral blouse? Her hair
Is made of hook-shaped marigold, gold
Of pleasure for her lips, like raspberry grain.
The eyelids oatmeal, the irises
Of Dutch blue maw, black rape
For the pupils, millet
For the vicious beige circles underneath.
The single pearl barley
That sleeps around her dullness
Till it catches light, makes women
Feel their age, and sigh for liberation.

GATEPOSTS

A man will keep a horse for prestige
But a woman ripens best underground.
He settles where the wind
Brings his whirling hat to rest,
And the wind decides which door is to be used.

Under the hip-roofed thatch,
The bed-wing is warmed by the chimney breast;
On either side the keeping-holes
For his belongings, hers.

He says it's unlucky to widen the house
And leaves the gateposts holding up the fairies.
He lays his lazy-beds and burns the river,

331

He builds turf-castles,
And sprigs the corn with apple-mint.

She spreads heather on the floor
And sifts the oatmeal ark for thin-bread farls:
All through the blue month, July,
She tosses stones in basins to the sun,
And watches for the trout in the holy well.

THE FLOWER MASTER

Like foxgloves in the school of the grass moon
We come to terms with shade, with the principle
Of enfolding space. Our scissors in brocade,
We learn the coolness of straight edges, how
To stroke gently the necks of daffodils
And make them throw their heads back to the sun.

We slip the thready stems of violets, delay
The loveliness of the hibiscus dawn with quiet ovals,
Spirals of feverfew like water splashing,
The papery legacies of bluebells. We do
Sea-fans with sea-lavender, moon-arrangements
Roughly for the festival of moon-viewing.

This black container calls for sloes, sweet
Sultan, dainty nipplewort, in honour
Of a special guest, who summoned to the
Tea ceremony, must stoop to our low doorway,
Our fontanelle, the trout's dimpled feet.

THE SITTING

My half-sister comes to me to be painted:
She is posing furtively, like a letter being
Pushed under a door, making a tunnel with her
Hands over her dull-rose dress. Yet her coppery

332

Head is as bright as a net of lemons, I am
Painting it hair by hair as if she had not
Disowned it, or forsaken those unsparkling
Eyes as blue may be sifted from the surface
Of a cloud; and she questions my brisk
Brushwork, the note of positive red
In the kissed mouth I have given her,
As a woman's touch makes curtains blossom
Permanently in a house: she calls it
Wishfulness, the failure of the tampering rain
To go right into the mountain, she prefers
My sea-studies, and will not sit for me
Again, something half-opened, rarer
Than railroads, a soiled red-letter day.

MARCONI'S COTTAGE

Small and watchful as a lighthouse,
A pure clear place of no particular childhood,
It is as if the sea had spoken in you
And then the words had dried.

Bitten and fostered by the sea
And by the British spring,
There seems only this one way of happening,
And a poem to prove it has happened.

Now I am close enough, I open my arms
To your castle-thick walls, I must learn
To use your wildness when I lock and unlock
Your door weaker than kisses.

Maybe you are a god of sorts,
Or a human star, lasting in spite of us
Like a note propped against a bowl of flowers,
Or a red shirt to wear against light blue.

The bed of your mind has weathered
Books of love, you are all I have gathered

333

To me of otherness; the worn glisten
Of your flesh is relearned and reloved.

Another unstructured, unmarried, unfinished
Summer, slips its unclenched weather
Into my winter poems, cheating time
And blood of their timelessness.

Let me have you for what we call
Forever, the deeper opposite of a picture,
Your leaves, the part of you
That the sea first talked to.

from PORCELAIN BELLS

3 SPEAKING INTO THE CANDLES

This death you have nourished is too orderly,
its fragrance too convincing.
You wear it like an unusually free veil,
so light it flies by me;
the mirror hardly believes it.
Or as if you were living in another town,
rejoining us with a completely different
handwriting, timid and beautiful.
Leaving the room, you break off a piece of the world,
around which my life is standing,
through which my blood spreads.
Missing so much world,
you still hold out your hands for more world,
your footsteps softening like a creature
before whom doors give way.
You lie alone on a new surface,
sharp as your own edge or a strange birthday,
unsleeping early in a new darkness,
too-awake like a brightly lit house,
its prolonged and counted light.
There is a closeness of many lights in you,
like stars moving forward meaningfully.

Every flower in you is everywhere.
Even if you were outside, where summer was,
you would still be inside every leaf.
Pain opens your hands like a book
or a two-syllable word I find as unintelligible
as the windows of other people.
Yet you are continually understanding it,
though now you are drained of all meaning,
and out of politeness try to remember
how to be completely afraid.
What do you care if I, your younger mouth,
stay or leave, though your dress shone upon me
when it willed me into existence?
You cannot anymore be the blue
in my eyes. What is the year to you
when you have moved outside yourself
and endure the motion of the earth
as not being right for you,
growing dark everywhere inside you
as if your air had been driven out
far above you?
Yet even as you refuse to be understood,
like your city in which nothing
is ever forgiven, if I dare
upon your silence, you cry it out whole,
with a full, upward glance,
like a nightingale.
I will survive this late-speaking love
when morning becomes conscious
it is no longer possible –
when the eternal procession of the sky
passes over it as over nature.
It will not be the night
between yesterday and today,
but these less shaken days
I would hold like a resurrection
to my breath.
When you find your way out
of the jewel-groove of your limbs
and the used-up breeze goes past

your icy eyelid,
already no longer anyone's,
I will dive you back to earth
and pull it up with you.

PAUL MULDOON

Born Portadown, County Armagh, 1951. Brought up near the Moy, County Tyrone, and educated at St Patrick's College, Armagh, and Queen's University Belfast, where he was taught by Seamus Heaney. Worked for many years as a radio producer for the BBC in Belfast until moving to the United States in the late 1980s. Now lives in New Jersey, where he directs the creative writing programme at the University of Princeton. In addition to seven collections of poetry, Muldoon has written a libretto, *Shining Brow* (1992), and edited *The Faber Book of Contemporary Irish Poetry* (1986).

Muldoon's sardonic virtuosity extends the limits of Irish poetic endeavour even as it exposes them. Through a combination of jokes, puns, mock rhymes, hallucinatory anecdotes and parodies, his verse offers a critique of the language habits fundamental to conflicting versions of Irish cultural identity. Muldoon is one of contemporary poetry's most accomplished practitioners of the long poem, to which – in a characteristic paradox – he brings a miniaturist's eye for detail. A teasingly allusive extended work has featured as the concluding poem of each of his volumes since *Mules* (1977). The spoof sonnet sequence 'The More a Man Has the More a Man Wants' (from *Quoof*, 1983) is perhaps the most sustained of these, though the 150-page elegiac fantasy 'Yarrow' (from *The Annals of Chile*, 1994) equals it in invention and underlying seriousness. In charting the adventures of its shape-changing hero Gallogly – a figure based on the Trickster mythology of the Winnebago Indians – 'The More a Man Has . . .' sheds a phatasmagoric light on the deranged logic and ungainsayable violence of the Troubles. A knowledge of the work of Robert Frost and Seamus Heaney will take the reader a considerable way through the network of allusion which can make the poem's narrative structure difficult to discern on first encounter (the closing line of Frost's 'For Once, Then, Something' provides an indispensable key – 'Truth? A pebble of quartz? For once, then, something').

I

'Is it really a revolution, though?'
I reached across the wicker table
With another $10,000 question.
My celebrated pamphleteer,
Co-author of such volumes
As *Blood on the Rose,*
The Dream and the Drums,
And *How It Happened Here,*
Would pour some untroubled Muscatel
And settle back in his cane chair.

'Look, son. Just look around you.
People are getting themselves killed
Left, right and centre
While you do what? Write rondeaux?
There's more to living in this country
Than stars and horses, pigs and trees,
Not that you'd guess it from your poems.
Do you never listen to the news?
You want to get down to something true,
Something a little nearer home.'

I called again later that afternoon,
A quiet suburban street.
'You want to stand back a little
When the world's at your feet.'
I'd have liked to have heard some more
Of his famous revolution.
I rang the bell, and knocked hard
On what I remembered as his front door,
That opened then, as such doors do,
Directly on to a back yard.

II

Not any back yard, I'm bound to say,
And not a thousand miles away
From here. No one's taken in, I'm sure,

338

By such a mild invention.
But where (I wonder myself) do I stand,
In relation to a table and chair,
The quince-tree I forgot to mention,
That suburban street, the door, the yard –
All made up as I went along
As things that people live among.

And such a person as lived there!
My celebrated pamphleteer!
Of course, I gave it all away
With those preposterous titles.
The Bloody Rose? The Dream and the Drums?
The three-day-wonder of the flowering plum!
Or was I desperately wishing
To have been their other co-author.
Or, at least, to own a first edition
Of *The Boot Boys and Other Battles?*

'When are you going to tell the truth?'
For there's no such book, so far as I know,
As *How it Happened Here*,
Though there may be. There may.
What should I say to this callow youth
Who learned to write last winter –
One of those correspondence courses –
And who's coming to lunch today?
He'll be rambling on, no doubt,
About pigs and trees, stars and horses.

CUBA

My eldest sister arrived home that morning
In her white muslin evening dress.
'Who the hell do you think you are,
Running out to dances in next to nothing?
As though we hadn't enough bother
With the world at war, if not at an end.'
My father was pounding the breakfast-table.

'Those Yankees were touch and go as it was –
If you'd heard Patton in Armagh –
But this Kennedy's nearly an Irishman
So he's not much better than ourselves.
And him with only to say the word.
If you've got anything on your mind
Maybe you should make your peace with God.'

I could hear May from beyond the curtain.
'Bless me, Father, for I have sinned.
I told a lie once, I was disobedient once.
And, Father, a boy touched me once.'
'Tell me, child. Was this touch immodest?
Did he touch your breast, for example?'
'He brushed against me, Father. Very gently.'

ANSEO

When the Master was calling the roll
At the primary school in Collegelands,
You were meant to call back *Anseo*
And raise your hand
As your name occurred.
Anseo, meaning here, here and now,
All present and correct,
Was the first word of Irish I spoke.
The last name on the ledger
Belonged to Joseph Mary Plunkett Ward
And was followed, as often as not,
By silence, knowing looks,
A nod and a wink, the Master's droll
'And where's our little Ward-of-court?'

I remember the first time he came back
The Master had sent him out
Along the hedges
To weigh up for himself and cut
A stick with which he would be beaten.
After a while, nothing was spoken;

340

He would arrive as a matter of course
With an ash-plant, a salley-rod.
Or, finally, the hazel-wand
He had whittled down to a whip-lash,
Its twist of red and yellow lacquers
Sanded and polished,
And altogether so delicately wrought
That he had engraved his initials on it.

I last met Joseph Mary Plunkett Ward
In a pub just over the Irish border.
He was living in the open,
In a secret camp
On the other side of the mountain.
He was fighting for Ireland,
Making things happen.
And he told me, Joe Ward,
Of how he had risen through the ranks
To Quartermaster, Commandant:
How every morning at parade
His volunteers would call back *Anseo*
And raise their hands
As their names occurred.

GATHERING MUSHROOMS

The rain comes flapping through the yard
like a tablecloth that she hand-embroidered.
My mother has left it on the line.
It is sodden with rain.
The mushroom shed is windowless, wide,
its high-stacked wooden trays
hosed down with formaldehyde.
And my father has opened the Gates of Troy
to that first load of horse manure.
Barley straw. Gypsum. Dried blood. Ammonia.
Wagon after wagon
blusters in, a self-renewing gold-black dragon

341

we push to the back of the mind.
We have taken our pitchforks to the wind.

All brought back to me that September evening
fifteen years on. The pair of us
tripping through Barnett's fair demesne
like girls in long dresses
after a hail-storm.
We might have been thinking of the fire-bomb
that sent Malone House sky-high
and its priceless collection of linen
sky-high.
We might have wept with Elizabeth McCrum.
We were thinking only of psilocybin.
You sang of the maid you met on the dewy grass –
And she stooped so low gave me to know
it was mushrooms she was gathering O.

He'll be wearing that same old donkey-jacket
and the sawn-off waders.
He carries a knife, two punnets, a bucket.
He reaches far into his own shadow.
We'll have taken him unawares
and stand behind him, slightly to one side.
He is one of those ancient warriors
before the rising tide.
He'll glance back from under his peaked cap
without breaking rhythm:
his coaxing a mushroom – a flat or a cup –
the nick against his right thumb;
the bucket then, the punnet to left or right,
and so on and so forth till kingdom come.

We followed the overgrown tow-path by the Lagan.
The sunset would deepen through cinnamon
to aubergine,
the wood-pigeon's concerto for oboe and strings,
allegro, blowing your mind.
And you were suddenly out of my ken, hurtling
towards the ever-receding ground,
into the maw

of a shimmering green-gold dragon.
You discovered yourself in some outbuilding
with your long-lost companion, me,
though my head had grown into the head of a horse
that shook its dirty-fair mane
and spoke this verse:

Come back to us. However cold and raw, your feet
were always meant
to negotiate terms with bare cement.
Beyond this concrete wall is a wall of concrete
and barbed wire. Your only hope
is to come back. If sing you must, let your song
tell of treading your own dung,
let straw and dung give a spring to your step.
If we never live to see the day we leap
into our true domain,
lie down with us now and wrap
yourself in the soiled grey blanket of Irish rain
that will, one day, bleach itself white.
Lie down with us and wait.

THE MORE A MAN HAS THE MORE A MAN WANTS

At four in the morning he wakes
to the yawn of brakes,
the snore of a diesel engine.
Gone. All she left
is a froth of bra and panties.
The scum of the Seine
and the Farset.
Gallogly squats in his own pelt.
A sodium street light
has brought a new dimension
to their black taxi.
By the time they force an entry
he'll have skedaddled
among hen runs and pigeon lofts.

The charter flight from Florida
touched down at Aldergrove
minutes earlier,
at 3.54 a.m.
Its excess baggage takes the form
of Mangas Jones, Esquire,
who is, as it turns out, Apache.
He carries only hand luggage.
'Anything to declare?'
He opens the powder-blue attaché-
case. 'A pebble of quartz.'
'You're an Apache?' 'Mescalero.'
He follows the corridor's
arroyo till the signs read *Hertz*.

He is going to put his foot down
on a patch of waste ground
along the Stranmillis embankment
when he gets wind
of their impromptu fire.
The air above the once-sweet stream
is aquarium-
drained.
And six, maybe seven, skinheads
have formed a quorum
round a burnt-out heavy-duty tyre.
So intent on sniffing glue
they may not notice Gallogly,
or, if they do, are so far gone.

Three miles west as the crow flies
an all-night carry-out
provides the cover
for an illegal drinking club.
While the bar man unpacks a crate
of Coca-Cola,
one cool customer
takes on all comers in a video game.
He grasps what his two acolytes
have failed to seize.
Don't they know what kind of take-away

this is, the glipes?
Vietmanese. Viet-ma-friggin'-*knees*.
He drops his payload of napalm.

Gallogly is wearing a candy-stripe
king-size sheet,
a little something he picked up
off a clothes line.
He is driving a milk van
he borrowed from the Belfast Co-op
while the milkman's back
was turned.
He had given the milkman a playful
rabbit punch.
When he stepped on the gas
he flooded the street
with broken glass.
He is trying to keep a low profile.

The unmarked police car draws level
with his last address.
A sergeant and eight constables
pile out of a tender
and hammer up the stairs.
The street bristles with static.
Their sniffer dog, a Labrador bitch,
bursts into the attic
like David Balfour in *Kidnapped*.
A constable on his first dawn swoop
leans on a shovel
He has turned over a
new leaf in her ladyship's herb patch.
They'll take it back for analysis.

All a bit much after the night shift
to meet a milkman
who's double-parked his van
closing your front door after him.
He's sporting your
Donegal tweed suit and your
Sunday shoes and politely raises your

hat as he goes by.
You stand there with your mouth open
as he climbs into the still-warm
driving seat of your Cortina
and screeches off towards the motorway,
leaving you uncertain
of your still-warm wife's damp tuft.

Someone on their way to early Mass
will find her hog-tied
to the chapel gates –
O Child of Prague –
big-eyed, anorexic.
The lesson for today
is pinned to her bomber jacket.
It seems to read *Keep off the Grass*.
Her lovely head has been chopped
and changed.
For Beatrice, whose fathers
knew Louis Quinze,
to have come to this, her *perruque*
of tar and feathers.

He is pushing the maroon Cortina
through the sedge
on the banks of the Callan.
It took him a mere forty minutes
to skite up the M1.
He followed the exit sign
for Loughgall and hared
among the top-heavy apple orchards.
This stretch of the Armagh/Tyrone
border was planted by Warwickshiremen
who planted in turn
their familiar quick-set damson hedges.
The Cortina goes to the bottom.
Gallogly swallows a plummy-plum-plum.

'I'll warrant them's the very pair
o' boys I seen abroad
in McParland's bottom, though where

in under God –
for thou art so possessed with murd'rous hate –
where they come from God only knows.'
'They were mad for a bite o' mate,
I s'pose.'
'I doubt so. I come across a brave dale
o' half-chawed damsels. Wanst wun disappeared
I follied the wun as yelly as Indy male.'
'Ye weren't afeared?'
'I follied him.' 'God save us.'
'An' he driv away in a van belongin' t'*Avis*.'

The grass sprightly as Astroturf
in the September frost
and a mist
here where the ground is low.
He seizes his own wrist
as if, as if
Blind Pew again seized Jim
at the sign of the 'Admiral Benbow'.
As if Jim Hawkins led Blind Pew
to Billy Bones
and they were all one and the same,
he stares in disbelief
at an Asprin-white spot he pressed
into his own palm.

Gallogly's thorn-proof tweed jacket
is now several sizes too big.
He has flopped
down in a hay shed
to ram a wad of hay into the toe
of each of his ill-fitting
brogues, when he gets the drift
of ham and eggs.
Now he's led by his own wet nose
to the hacienda-style
farmhouse, a baggy-kneed animated
bear drawn out of the woods
by an apple pie
left to cool on a windowsill.

347

She was standing at the picture window
with a glass of water
and a Valium
when she caught your man
in the reflection of her face.
He came
shaping past the milking parlour
as if he owned the place.
Such is the integrity
of their quarrel
that she immediately took down
the legally held shotgun
and let him have both barrels.
She had wanted only to clear the air.

Half a mile away across the valley
her husband's UDR patrol
is mounting a check-point.
He pricks up his ears
at the crack
of her prematurely arthritic hip-
joint,
and commandeers one of the jeeps.
There now, only a powder burn
as if her mascara had run.
The bloody puddle
in the yard, and the shilly-shally
of blood like a command wire
petering out behind a milk churn.

A hole in the heart, an ovarian
cyst.
Coming up the Bann
in a bubble.
Disappearing up his own bum.
Or, running on the spot
with all the minor aplomb
of a trick-cyclist.
So thin, side-on, you could spit
through him.
His six foot of pump water

bent double
in agony or laughter.
Keeping down-wind of everything.

White Annetts. Gillyflowers. Angel Bites.
When he names the forgotten names
of apples
he has them all off pat.
His eye like the eye of a travelling rat
lights on the studied negligence
of these scraws of turf.
A tarpaulin. A waterlogged pit.
He will take stock of the Kalashnikov's
filed-down serial number,
seven sticks of unstable
commercial gelignite
that have already begun to weep.
Red Strokes. Sugar Sweet. Widows Whelps.

Buy him a drink and he'll regale you
with how he came in for a cure
one morning after the night before
to the *Las Vegas* Lounge and Cabaret.
He was crossing the bar's
eternity of parquet floor
when his eagle eye
saw something move on the horizon.
If it wasn't an Indian.
A Sioux. An ugly Sioux.
He means, of course, an Oglala
Sioux busily tracing the family tree
of an Ulsterman who had some hand
in the massacre at Wounded Knee.

He will answer the hedge-sparrow's
Littlebitofbreadandnocheese
with a whole bunch
of freshly picked watercress,
a bulb of garlic,
sorrel,
with many-faceted blackberries.

Gallogly is out to lunch.
When his cock rattles its sabre
he takes it in his dab
hand, plants one chaste kiss
on its forelock,
and then, with a birl and a skirl,
tosses it off like a caber.

The UDR corporal had come off duty
to be with his wife
while the others set about
a follow-up search.
When he tramped out just before twelve
to exercise the greyhound
he was hit by a single high-velocity
shot.
You could, if you like, put your fist
in the exit wound
in his chest.
He slumps
in the spume of his own arterial blood
like an overturned paraffin lamp.

Gallogly lies down in the sheugh
to munch
through a Beauty of
Bath. He repeats himself, *Bath,*
under his garlic-breath.
Sheugh, he says. *Sheugh.*
He is finding that first 'sh'
increasingly difficult to manage.
Sh-leeps. A milkmaid sinks
her bare foot
to the ankle
in a simmering dung hill
and fills the slot
with beastlings for him to drink.

In Ovid's conspicuously tongue-in-cheek
account of an eyeball
to eyeball

between the goddess Leto
and a shower of Lycian reed cutters
who refuse her a cup of cloudy
water
from their churned-up lake,
Live then forever in that lake of yours,
she cries, and has them
bubble
and squeak
and plonk themselves down as bullfrogs
in their icy jissom.

A country man kneels on his cap
beside his neighbour's fresh
grave-mud
as Gallogly kneels to lap
the primrose-yellow
custard.
The knees of his hand-me-down duds
are gingerish.
A pernickety seven-
year-old girl-child
parades in her mother's trousseau
and mumbles a primrose
Kleenex tissue
to make sure her lipstick's even.

Gallogly has only to part the veil
of its stomach wall
to get right under the skin,
the spluttering heart
and collapsed lung,
of the horse in *Guernica.*
He flees the Museum of Modern Art
with its bit between his teeth.
When he began to cough
blood, Hamsun rode the Minneapolis/
New York night train
on top of the dining-car.
One long, inward howl.
A porter-drinker without a thrapple.

A weekend trip to the mountains
North of Boston
with Alice, Alice A.
and her paprika hair,
the ignition key
to her family's Winnebago camper,
her quim
biting the leg off her.
In the oyster bar
of Grand Central Station
she gobbles a dozen Chesapeakes –
'Oh, I'm not particular as to size' –
and, with a flourish of tabasco,
turns to gobble him.

A brewery lorry on a routine delivery
is taking a slow,
dangerous bend.
The driver's blethering
his code name
over the Citizens' Band
when someone ambles
in front of him. Go, Johnny, Go, Go, Go.
He's been dry-gulched
by a sixteen-year-old numb
with Mogadon,
whose face is masked by the seamless
black stocking filched
from his mum.

When who should walk in but Beatrice,
large as life, or larger,
sipping her one glass of lager
and singing her one song.
If he had it to do all over again
he would let her shave his head
in memory of '98
and her own, the French, Revolution.
The son of the King of the Moy
met this child on the Roxborough
estate. *Noblesse,* she said. *Noblesse*

oblige. And her tiny nipples
were bruise-bluish, wild raspberries.
The song she sang was 'The Croppy Boy'.

Her *grand'mère* was once asked to tea
by Gertrude Stein,
and her *grand'mère* and Gertrude
and Alice B., *chère* Alice B.
with her hook-nose,
the three of them sat in the nude
round the petits fours
and repeated *Eros is Eros is Eros.*
If he had it to do all over again
he would still be taken in
by her Alice B. Toklas
Nameless Cookies
and those new words she had him learn:
hash, hashish, *lo perfido assassin.*

Once the local councillor straps
himself into the safety belt
of his Citroën
and skids up the ramp
from the municipal car park
he upsets the delicate balance
of a mercury-tilt
boobytrap.
Once they collect his smithereens
he doesn't quite add up.
They're shy of a foot, and a calf
which stems
from his left shoe like a severely
pruned-back shrub.

Ten years before. The smooth-as-a-
front-lawn at Queen's
where she squats
before a psilocybin god.
The indomitable gentle-bush
that had Lanyon or Lynn
revise their elegant ground plan

for the university quad.
With calmness, with care,
with breast milk, with dew.
There's no cure now.
There's nothing left to do.
The mushrooms speak through her.
Hush-hush.

'Oh, I'm not particular as to size,'
Alice hastily replied
and broke off a bit of the edge
with each hand
and set to work very carefully,
nibbling
first at one
and then the other.
On the Staten Island Ferry
two men are dickering
over the price
of a shipment of Armalites,
as Henry Thoreau was wont to quibble
with Ralph Waldo Emerson.

That last night in the Algonquin
he met with a flurry
of sprites,
the assorted shades
of Wolfe Tone, Napper Tandy,
a sanguine
Michael Cusack
brandishing his blackthorn.
Then, Thomas Meagher
darts up from the Missouri
on a ray
of the morning star
to fiercely ask
what has become of Irish hurling.

Everyone has heard the story of
a strong and beautiful bug
which came out of the dry leaf

of an old table of apple-tree wood
that stood
in a farmer's kitchen in Massachusetts
and which was heard gnawing out
for several weeks –
When the phone trills
he is careful not to lose his page –
Who knows what beautiful and winged life
whose egg
has been buried for ages
may unexpectedly come forth? 'Tell-tale.'

Gallogly carries a hunting bow
equipped
with a bow sight
and a quiver
of hunting arrows
belonging to her brother.
Alice has gone a little way off
to do her job.
A timber wolf,
a caribou,
or merely a trick of the light?
As, listlessly,
he lobs
an arrow into the undergrowth.

Had you followed the river Callan's
Pelorus Jack
through the worst drought
in living memory
to the rains of early Autumn
when it scrubs its swollen,
scab-encrusted back
under a bridge, the bridge you look down from,
you would be unlikely to pay much heed
to yet another old banger
no one could be bothered to tax,
or a beat-up fridge
well-stocked with gelignite,
or some five hundred yards of Cortex.

He lopes after the dribs of blood
through the pine forest
till they stop dead
in the ruins of a longhouse
or hogan.
Somehow, he finds his way
back to their tent.
Not so much as a whiff of her musk.
The girl behind the Aer Lingus
check-in desk
at Logan
is wearing the same scent
and an embroidered capital letter *A*
on her breast.

Was she Aurora, or the goddess Flora,
Artemidora, or Venus bright,
or Helen fair beyond compare
that Priam stole from the Grecian sight?
Quite modestly she answered me
and she gave her head one fetch up
and she said I am gathering musheroons
to make my mammy ketchup.
The dunt and dunder
of a culvert-bomb
wakes him
as it might have woke Leander.
And she said I am gathering musheroons
to make my mammy ketchup O.

Predictable as the gift of the gab
or a drop of the craythur
he noses round the six foot deep
crater.
Oblivious to their Landrover's
olive-drab
and the Burgundy berets
of a snatch-squad of Paratroopers.
Gallogly, or Gollogly,
otherwise known as Golightly,
otherwise known as Ingoldsby,

otherwise known as English,
gives forth one low cry of anguish
and agrees to come quietly.

They have bundled him into the cell
for a strip-
search.
He perches
on the balls of his toes, my my,
with his legs spread
till both his instep arches
fall.
He holds himself at arm's
length from the brilliantly Snowcem-ed
wall, a game bird
hung by its pinion tips
till it drops, in the fullness of time,
from the mast its colours are nailed to.

They have left him to cool his heels
after the obligatory
bath,
the mug shots, fingerprints
et cetera.
He plumps the thin bolster
and hints
at the slop bucket.
Six o'clock.
From the A Wing of Armagh jail
he can make out
the Angelus bell
of St Patrick's cathedral
and a chorus of 'For God and Ulster'.

The brewery lorry's stood at a list
by the *Las Vegas*
throughout the afternoon,
its off-side rear tyres down.
As yet, no one has looked agog
at the smuts and rusts
of a girlie mag

in disarray on the passenger seat.
An almost invisible, taut
fishing line
runs from the Playmate's navel
to a pivotal
beer keg.
As yet, no one has risen to the bait.

I saw no mountains, no enormous spaces,
no magical growth and metamorphosis
of buildings, nothing remotely like
a drama or a parable
in which he dons these lime-green
dungarees,
green Wellingtons,
a green helmet of aspect terrible.
The other world to which mescalin
admitted me was not the world of visions;
it existed out there, in what I could see
with my eyes open.
He straps a chemical pack on his back
and goes in search of some Gawain.

Gallogly pads along the block
to raise his visor
at the first peep-hole.
He shamelessly
takes in her lean piglet's
back, the back
and boyish hams
of a girl at stool.
At last. A tiny goat's-pill.
A stub of crayon
with which she has squiggled
a shamrock, yes,
but a shamrock after the school
of Pollock, Jackson Pollock.

I stopped and stared at her face to face
and on the spot a name came to me,
a name with a smooth, nervous sound:

Ylayali.
When she was very close
I drew myself up straight
and said in an impressive voice,
'Miss, you are losing your book.'
And Beatrice, for it is she, she squints
through the spy-hole
to pass him an orange,
an Outspan orange some visitor has spiked
with a syringe-ful
of vodka.

The more a man has the more a man wants,
the same I don't think true.
For I never met a man with one black eye
who ever wanted two.
In the *Las Vegas* Lounge and Cabaret
the resident group –
pot bellies, Aran knits –
have you eating out of their hands.
Never throw a brick at a drowning man
when you're near to a grocer's store.
Just throw him a cake of Sunlight soap,
let him wash himself ashore.
You will act the galoot, and gallivant,
and call for another encore.

Gallogly, Gallogly, O Gallogly
juggles
his name like an orange
between his outsize baseball glove
paws,
and ogles
a moon that's just out of range
beyond the perimeter wall.
He works a gobbet of Brylcreem
into his quiff
and delves
through sand and gravel,
shrugging it off
his velveteen shoulders and arms.

Just
throw
him
a
cake
of
Sunlight
soap,
let
him
wash
him-
self
ashore.

Into a picture by Edward Hopper
of a gas station
in the mid-West
where Hopper takes as his theme
light, the spooky
glow of an illuminated sign
reading Esso or Mobil
or what-have-you –
into such a desolate oval
ride two youths on a motorbike.
A hand gun. Balaclavas.
The pump attendant's grown so used
to hold-ups he calls after them:
Beannacht Dé ar an obair.

The pump attendant's not to know
he's being watched by a gallowglass
hot-foot from a woodcut
by Derricke
who skips across the forecourt
and kicks the black
plastic bucket
they left as a memento.
Nor is the gallowglass any the wiser.
The bucket's packed with fertilizer
and a heady brew

of sugar and paraquat's
relentlessly gnawing its way through
the floppy knot of a Durex.

It was this self-same pump attendant
who dragged the head and torso
clear
and mouthed an Act of Contrition
in the frazzled ear
and overheard
those already-famous last words
Moose . . . Indian.
'Next of all wus the han'.' 'Be Japers.'
'The sodgers cordonned-off the area
wi' what-ye-may-call-it tape.'
'Lunimous.' 'They foun' this hairy
han' wi' a drowneded man's grip
on a lunimous stone no bigger than a . . .'

'Huh.'

SOMETHING ELSE

When your lobster was lifted out of the tank
to be weighed
I thought of woad,
of madders, of fugitive, indigo inks,

of how Nerval
was given to promenade
a lobster on a gossamer thread,
how, when a decent interval

had passed
(son front rouge encor du baiser de la reine)
and his hopes of Adrienne

proved false,
he hanged himself from a lamp-post
with a length of chain, which made me think

of something else, then something else again.

CAULIFLOWERS

Plants that glow in the dark have been developed
through gene-splicing, in which light-producing
bacteria from the mouths of fish are introduced to
cabbage, carrots and potatoes.
The National Enquirer

More often than not he stops at the headrig to light
his pipe
and try to regain
his composure. The price of cauliflowers
has gone down
two weeks in a row on the Belfast market.

From here we can just make out
a platoon of Light
Infantry going down
the road to the accompaniment of a pipe-
band. The sun glints on their silver-
buttoned jerkins.

My uncle, Patrick Regan,
has been leaning against the mud-guard
of the lorry. He levers
open the bonnet and tinkers with a light
wrench at the hose-pipe
that's always going down.

Then he himself goes down
to bleed oil into a jerry-can.
My father slips the pipe
into his scorch-marked

breast pocket and again makes light
of the trepanned cauliflowers.

All this as I listened to lovers
repeatedly going down
on each other in the next room . . . 'light
of my life . . .' in a motel in Oregon.
All this. Magritte's
pipe

and the pipe-
bomb. White Annetts. Gillyflowers.
Margaret,
are you grieving? My father going down
the primrose path with Patrick Regan.
All gone out of the world of light.

All gone down
the original pipe. And the cauliflowers
in an unmarked pit, that were harvested by their own light.

NUALA NÍ DHOMHNAILL

Born Lancashire, 1952. Grew up in Nenagh, County Tipperary, and in
west Kerry Gaeltacht. Educated at University College Cork.
Spent most of the 1970s in Turkey. Now lives in Dublin.

In abundance and variety Nuala Ní Dhomhnaill's work surpasses that of
any other modern poet in Irish. Though much of her imagery is drawn
from communal sources such as folklore and Catholic symbology, it
serves a questioning, roguishly heterodox point of view. Earthy,
generous and democratic, Ní Dhomhnaill's poems are also graceful and
sophisticated. She cites John Berryman as a liberating influence and her
writing shares something of the American poet's delight in mixing
registers and in juggling high and low cultural references. An unfussy
experimentalism can be seen alike in her employment of a range of lyric
and narrative modes and in her approach to the poetic line. While many
of her poems invite a feminist interpretation, others (deliberately?) resist
it. 'Caitlín' offers a rare excursion into political commentary, its
uproarious spirit inventively caught in Paul Muldoon's translation.
As the versions of Montague, Hartnett and Muldoon testify,
Ní Dhomhnaill has been a key figure in continuing the dialogue
between the poetries of Ireland's two languages.

SCÉALA

Do chuimhnigh sí
go deireadh thiar
ar scáil an aingil
sa teampall,
cleitearnach sciathán
ina timpeall;
is dúiseacht le dord colúr
is stealladh ga gréine
ar fhallaí aolcloch
an lá a fuair sí an scéala.

É siúd
d'imigh
is n'fheadar ar chuimhnigh riamh
ar cad a d'eascair
óna cheathrúna,
dhá mhíle bliain
d'iompar croise
de dhóiteán is deatach,
de chlampar chomh hard
le spící na Vatacáine.

Ó, a mhaighdean rócheansa,
nár chuala trácht ar éinne riamh
ag teacht chughat sa doircheacht
cosnocht, déadgheal
is a shúile lán de rógaireacht.

FÉAR SUAITHINSEACH

Nuair a bhís i do shagart naofa
i lár an Aifrinn, faoi do róbaí corcra
t'fhallaing lín, do stól, do chasal,
do chonnaicis m'aghaidhse ins an slua

ANNUNCIATIONS

She remembered to the very end
the angelic vision
in the temple:
the flutter of wings
about her –
noting the noise of doves,
sun-rays raining
on lime-white walls –
the day she got the tidings.

He
he went away
and perhaps forgot
what grew from his loins –
two thousand years
of carrying a cross
two thousand years
of smoke and fire
of rows that reached a greater span
than all the spires of the Vatican.

Remember
o most tender virgin Mary
that never was it known
that a man came to you
in the darkness alone,
his feet bare, his teeth white
and roguery swelling in his eyes.

translated by Michael Hartnett

MIRACULOUS GRASS

There you were in your purple vestments
half-way through the Mass, an ordained priest
under your linen alb and chasuble and stole:
and when you saw my face in the crowd

a bhí ag teacht chun comaoineach chughat
is thit uait an abhlainn bheannaithe.

Mise, ní dúrt aon ní ina thaobh.
Bhí náire orm.
Bhí glas ar mo bhéal.
Ach fós do luigh sé ar mo chroí
mar dhealg láibe, gur dhein sé slí
dó fhéin istigh im ae is im lár
gur dhóbair go bhfaighinn bás dá bharr.

Ní fada nó gur thiteas 'on leabaidh;
oideasaí leighis do triaileadh ina gcéadtaibh,
do tháinig chugham dochtúirí, sagairt is bráithre
is n'fhéadadar mé a thabhairt chun sláinte
ach thugadar suas i seilbh bháis mé.

Is téigí amach, a fheara,
tugaíg libh rámhainn is speala
corráin, grafáin is sluaiste.
Réabaíg an seanafhothrach,
bearraíg na sceacha, glanaíg an luifearnach,
an slámas fáis, an brus, an ainnise
a fhás ar thalamh bán mo thubaiste.

Is ins an ionad inar thit
an chomaoine naofa féach go mbeidh
i lár an bhiorlamais istigh
toirtín d'fhéar suaithinseach.

Tagadh an sagart is lena mhéireanna
beireadh sé go haiclí ar an gcomaoine naofa
is tugtar chugham í, ar mo theanga
leáfaidh sí, is éireod aniar sa leaba
chomh slán folláin is a bhíos is mé i mo leanbh.

for Holy Communion
the consecrated host fell from your fingers.

I felt shame, I never
mentioned it once,
my lips were sealed.
But still it lurked in my heart
like a thorn under mud, and it
worked itself in so deep and sheer
it nearly killed me.

Next thing then, I was laid up in bed.
Consultants came in their hundreds,
doctors and brothers and priests,
but I baffled them all. I was
incurable, they left me for dead.

So out you go, men,
out with the spades and scythes,
the hooks and shovels and hoes.
Tackle the rubble,
cut back the bushes, clear off the rubbish,
the sappy growth, the whole straggle and mess
that infests my green unfortunate field.

And there where the sacred wafer fell
you will discover
in the middle of the shooting weeds
a clump of miraculous grass.

The priest will have to come then
with his delicate fingers, and lift the host
and bring it to me and put it on my tongue.
Where it will melt, and I will rise in the bed
as fit and well as the youngster I used to be.

translated by Seamus Heaney

A bhábóigín bhriste ins an tobar,
caite isteach ag leanbh ar bhogshodar
anuas le fánaidh, isteach faoi chótaí a mháthar.
Ghlac sé preab in uaigneas an chlapsholais
nuair a léim caipíní na bpúcaí peill chun a bhéil,
nuair a chrom na méaracáin a gceannaibh ina threo
is nuair a chuala sé uaill chiúin ón gceann cait ins an dair.
Ba dhóbair nó go dtitfeadh an t-anam beag as nuair a ghaibh
easóg thar bráid is pataire coinín aici ina béal,
na putóga ar sileadh leis ar fuaid an bhaill
is nuair a dh'eitil an sciathán leathair ins an spéir.

Theith sé go glórach is riamh ó shin
tánn tú mar fhinné síoraí ar an ghoin
ón tsaighead a bhuail a chluais; báite sa láib
t'fhiarshúil phlaisteach oscailte de ló
is d'oíche, chíonn tú an madra rua is a hál
ag teacht go bruach na féithe raithní taobh lena bpluais
is iad ag ól a sáith; tagann an broc chomh maith ann
is níonn a lapaí; sánn sé a shoc san uisce is lá
an phátrúin tagann na daoine is casann siad seacht n-uaire
ar deiseal; le gach casadh caitheann siad cloch san uisce.

Titeann na clocha beaga seo anuas ort.
Titeann, leis, na cnónna ón gcrann coill atá ar dheis
an tobair is éireoir reamhar is feasach mar bhreac
beannaithe sa draoib. Tiocfaidh an spideog bhroinndearg
de mhuintir Shúilleabháin is lena heireabaillín
déanfaidh sí leacht meala de uiscí uachtair an tobair
is leacht fola den íochtar, fós ní bheidh corraí asat.
Taoi teanntaithe go síoraí ins an láib, do mhuineál tachtaithe
le sreanganna *lobelia*. Chím do mhílí ag stánadh orm
gan tlás as gach poll snámha, as gach lochán, Ophelia.

THE BROKEN DOLL

O little broken doll, dropped in the well,
thrown aside by a child, scampering downhill
to hide under the skirts of his mother!
In twilight's quiet he took sudden fright
as toadstool caps snatched at his tongue,
foxgloves crooked their fingers at him
and from the oak, he heard the owl's low call.
His little heart almost stopped when a weasel
went by, with a fat young rabbit in its jaws,
loose guts spilling over the grass while
a bat wing flicked across the evening sky

He rushed away so noisily and ever since
you are a lasting witness to the fairy arrow
that stabbed his ear; stuck in the mud
your plastic eyes squinny open from morning
to night: you see the vixen and her brood
stealing up to lap the ferny swamphole
near their den, the badger loping to wash
his paws, snuff water with his snout. On
Pattern days people parade seven clockwise
rounds; at every turn, throwing in a stone.

Those small stones rain down on you.
The nuts from the hazel tree that grows
to the right of the well also drop down:
you will grow wiser than any blessed trout
in this ooze! The redbreasted robin
of the Sullivans will come to transform
the surface to honey with her quick tail,
churn the depths to blood, but you don't move.
Bemired, your neck strangled with lobelias,
I see your pallor staring starkly back at me
from every swimming hole, from every pool, Ophelia.

translated by John Montague

FÁILTE BHÉAL NA SIONNA DON IASC

Léim an bhradáin
Sa doircheacht
Lann lom
Sciath airgid,
Mise atá fáiltiúil, líontach
Sleamhain,
Lán d'fheamnach,
Go caise ciúin
Go heireaball eascon.

Bia ar fad
Is ea an t-iasc seo
Gan puinn cnámh
Gan puinn putóg
Fiche punt teann
De mheatáin iata
Dírithe
Ar a nead sa chaonach néata.

Is seinim seoithín
Do mo leannán
Tonn ar thonn
Leathrann ar leathrann,
Mo thine ghealáin mar bhairlín thíos faoi
Mo rogha a thoghas féin ón iasacht.

AN BHEAN MHÍDHÍLIS

Do phioc sé suas mé
ag an gcúntúirt
is tar éis beagáinín cainte
do thairg deoch dom
nár eitíos uaidh
is do shuíomair síos
ag comhrá.

THE SHANNON ESTUARY WELCOMES THE FISH

The salmon's leap
In the darkness –
Bare blade
Silver shield;
And me welcoming, net-
Draped and slippery
Full of seaweed
Of quiet eddies
And eel-tails.

All meat
Is this fish
Almost nothing of bone
Less of entrail
Twenty packed pounds
Of tensed muscle
Straining
Towards its nest among the neat mosses.

And I sing a lullaby
To my darling
Wave on wave
Verse after verse,
My phosphorescence a sheet beneath him
My chosen one, drawn from afar.

translated by Patrick Crotty

THE UNFAITHFUL WIFE

He started coming on to me
at the spirit-grocer's warped and wonky counter
and after a preliminary spot of banter
offered to buy me a glass of porter;
I wasn't one to demur
and in no time at all we were talking
the hind leg off a donkey.

Chuamair ó dheoch go deoch
is ó *joke* go *joke*
is do bhíos-sa sna trithí aige
ach dá mhéid a bhíos ólta
ní dúrt leis go rabhas pósta.

Dúirt sé go raibh carr aige
is ar theastaigh síob abhaile uaim
is ní fada ar an mbóthar
nó gur bhuail an teidhe é.
Do tharraing sé isteach ag *lay-by*
chun gurbh fhusaide mé a phógadh.
Bhí málaí plaisteacha ar na sceacha
is bruscar ag gabháilt lastuas dóibh
is nuair a leag sé a lámh idir mo cheathrúna
ní dúrt leis go rabhas pósta.

Bhí sé cleachtaithe deaslámhach
ag oscailt chnaipí íochtair mo ghúna,
ag lapadáil go barr mo stocaí
is an cneas bog os a gcionnsan
is nuair a bhraith sé
nach raibh bríste orm
nach air a tháinig giúmar
is cé thógfadh orm ag an nóiméad sin
ná dúrt leis go rabhas pósta.

Do bhain sé do a threabhsar
leis an éirí a bhuail air
is do shleamhnaigh sall im shuíochánsa
is do tharraing sé anuas air mé
is nuair a shuíos síos air go cúramach
is gur mharcaíos thar an sprioc é
ba é an chloch ba shia im phaidrín
a rá leis go rabhas pósta.

Bhí mus úr a cholainne
mar ghairdín i ndiaidh báistí
is bhí a chraiceann chomh slim
chomh síodúil sin lem chneas féin
agus is mór an abairt sin

A quick succession of snorts and snifters
and his relentless repartee
had me splitting my sides with laughter.
However much the drink had loosened my tongue
I never let on I was married.

He would ask if he could leave me home
in his famous motoring-car,
though we hadn't gone very far down that road
when he was overtaken by desire.
He pulled in to a lay-by
the better to heap me with kisses.
There were plastic bags bursting with rubbish
stacked against the bushes.
Even as he slipped his hand between my thighs
I never let on I was married.

He was so handy,
too, when it came to unbuttoning my dress
and working his way past my stocking-tops
to the soft skin just above.
When it dawned on him
that I wasn't wearing panties
things were definitely on the up and up
and it hardly seemed the appropriate moment
to let on I was married.

By this time he had dropped his trousers
and, with his proper little charlie,
manoeuvred himself into the passenger-seat
and drew me down until, ever so gingerly,
I might mount.
As I rode him past the winning-post
nothing could have been further from my mind
than to let on I was married.

For his body was every bit as sweet
as a garden after a shower
and his skin was as sheer-delicate as my own
– which is saying rather a lot –
while the way he looked me straight in the eye

is nuair a bhíos ag tabhairt
pléisiúrtha dhó
d'fhéach sé sa dá shúil orm
is fuaireas mothú pabhair is tuisceana
nár bhraitheas ó táim pósta.

Bhí boladh lofa ós na clathacha
is dramhaíl ag bun na gcrann
is bhí an port féarach taobh liom
breac le cac gadhar na gcomharsan
is nuair a thráigh ar an éirí air
tháinig aithis is ceann faoi air
is nár dhomh ba mhaith an mhaise ansan
ná dúrt leis go rabhas pósta.

Do bhuaileas suas an casán
lem scol amhráin is lem phort feadaíle
is níor ligeas orm le héinne
an eachtra a bhí laistiar díom
is má chastar orm arís é
i ndioscó nó i dteach tábhairne
ar ghrá oinigh nó réitigh
ní admhód riamh bheith pósta.

An ndéanfása?

CEIST NA TEANGAN

Cuirim mo dhóchas ar snámh
i mbáidín teangan
faoi mar a leagfá naíonán
i gcliabhán
a bheadh fite fuaite
de dhuilleoga feileastraim
is bitiúman agus pic
bheith cuimilte lena thóin

as he took such great delight
gave me a sense of power and the kind of insight
I'd not had since I was married.

There was this all-pervasive smell
from the refuse-sacks lying under the hedge
while the green, grassy slope beyond
was littered with dog-shit.
Now, as the groundswell of passion
began to subside,
he himself had a hang-dog, coy expression
that made me think it was just as well
I never let on I was married.

As I marched up my own garden-path
I kicked up a little dust.
I burst into song and whistled a tune
and vowed not to breathe a word
to a soul about what I'd done.
And if, by chance, I run into him again
at a disco or in some shebeen
the only honourable course – the only decent thing –
would be to keep faith and not betray his trust
by letting on I was married.

Don't you think?

translated by Paul Muldoon

THE LANGUAGE ISSUE

I place my hope on the water
in this little boat
of the language, the way a body might put
an infant

in a basket of intertwined
iris leaves,
its underside proofed
with bitumen and pitch,

ansan é a leagadh síos
i measc na ngiolcach
is coigeal na mban sí
le taobh na habhann,
féachaint n'fheadaraís
cá dtabharfaidh an sruth é,
féachaint, dála Mhaoise,
an bhfóirfidh iníon Fharoinn?

CAITLÍN

Ní fhéadfá í a thabhairt in aon áit leat,
do thabharfadh sí náire is aithis duit.
Díreach toisc go raibh sí an-mhór ina *vamp*
thiar ins na fichidí, is gur dhamhas sí an Searlastan
le tonntracha méiríneacha ina gruaig dhualach thrilseánach;
gur phabhsae gléigeal í thiar i naoi déag sé déag,
go bhfacthas fornocht i gConnachta í, mar áille na háille,
is ag taisteal bhóithre na Mumhan, mar ghile na gile;
go raibh sí beo bocht, gan locht,
a píob mar an eala, ag teacht taobh leis an dtoinn
is a héadan mar shneachta,

ní théann aon stad uirthi ach ag maíomh
as na seanlaethanta, nuair a bhíodh sí ag ionsaí
na dúthaí is an drúcht ar a bróga,
maidin Domhnaigh is í ag dul go hEochaill
nó ar an mbóthar cothrom idir Corcaigh agus Dúghlas.
Na rudaí iontacha a dúirt an Paorach fúithi
is é mar mhaor ar an loing. Is dúirt daoine eile
go mbeadh an Éirne ina tuilte tréana, is go réabfaí
cnoic. Murab ionann is anois nuair atá sí ina baintreach tréith
go raibh sí an tráth san ina maighdean mhómhar, chaoin, shéimh
is díreach a dóthain céille aici chun fanacht i gcónaí
ar an dtaobh thall den dteorainn ina mbítear de shíor.

then set the whole thing down amidst
the sedge
and bulrushes by the edge
of a river

only to have it borne hither and thither,
not knowing where it might end up;
in the lap, perhaps,
of some Pharaoh's daughter.

translated by Paul Muldoon

CATHLEEN

You can't take her out for a night on the town
without her either showing you up or badly letting you down:
just because she made the Twenties roar
with her Black and Tan Bottom – O Terpsichore –
and her hair in a permanent wave;
just because she was a lily grave
in nineteen sixteen; just because she once was spotted
quite naked in Cannought, of beauties most beautied,
or tramping the roads of Moonstare, brightest of the bright;
just because she was poor, without blemish or blight,
high-stepping it by the ocean with her famous swan's prow
and a fresh fall of snow on her broadest of broad brows –

because of all that she never stops bending your ear
about the good old days of yore
when she crept through the country in her dewy high heels
of a Sunday morning, say, on the road to Youghal
or that level stretch between Cork and Douglas.
There was your man Power's ridiculous
suggestion when he was the ship's captain, not to speak
of the Erne running red with abundance and mountain-peaks
laid low. She who is now a widowed old woman
was a modest maiden, meek and mild, but with enough
    gumption
at least to keep to her own
side of the ghostly demarcation, the eternal buffer-zone.

Ba dhóigh leat le héisteacht léi nár chuala
sí riamh gur binn béal ina thost, is nach mbíonn
in aon ní ach seal, go gcríonnann an tslat le haois
is fiú dá mba dhóigh le gach spreasán an uair úd
go mba leannán aige féin í, go bhfuil na laethanta san thart.
Cuirfidh mé geall síos leat nár chuala sí leis
mar tá sé de mhórbhua aici agus de dheis
gan aon ní a chloisint ach an rud a 'riúnaíonn í féin.
Tá mil ar an ógbhean aici, dar léi, agus rós breá
ina héadan. Is í an sampla í is fearr ar m'aithne
de bhodhaire Uí Laoghaire.

For you'd think to listen to her she'd never heard
that discretion is the better part, that our names are writ
in water, that the greenest stick will wizen:
even if every slubberdegullion once had a dream-vision
in which she appeared as his own true lover,
those days are just as truly over.
And I bet Old Gummy Granny
has taken none of this on board because of her uncanny
knack of hearing only what confirms
her own sense of herself, her honey-nubile form
and the red nose, proud rose or canker
tucked behind her ear, in the head-band of her blinkers.

translated by Paul Muldoon

MATTHEW SWEENEY

Born Donegal, 1952. Lives in London, where he is currently writer-in-residence at the South Bank Centre. Has published a well-received book of children's verse, *The Flying Spring Onion* (1992).

Sweeney is a miniaturist of estrangement. The account of the last hours of a victim of the King's Cross fire in 'Tube Ride to Martha's' is typical of his brief, discommoding tales of contemporary urban life and death.

TO THE BUILDING TRADE

Here's to the building trade,
to the renovations and facelifts,
the fake Victorian façades;
to the dust-muffled din
that stops on Sundays;
to the men that make it,
especially one from Dalston
who, after a pint or two
and a ploughman's, fell –
but the scaffolding stayed up
till the flats were clean.
Here's to the offduty cabbie
in the first-floor kitchen
who saw him splatter
on the pavement; to the mate
with the trowel, staring down,
his question unanswered;
to the rent increase
and the officer who set it.
Here's to the young widow
whose home's in this city
where migrant scaffolding,
wherever she moves,
will find her walls sometime.

Before the sirens started, he was late –
late for a dinner at his woman's,
but he'd managed to find a good Rioja
and an excellent excuse: his cat
had burned her tail in the toaster
(this was true) and he'd brought her
to the vet and back in a cab.
He thought about a third cab to Martha's
but funds were low, and the tube ride
was four stops, a half hour with the walks.
He had a thriller in his carrier-bag,
a Ross McDonald, long out of print,
which he opened on the escalator, wanting
it finished tonight. When the smoke came
he hardly noticed, till the black guard
tried to hustle everyone upstairs,
and trains rushed by, without stopping,
and people pushed and screamed.
As the smoke got thicker and blacker
with flames growing fast, he realised
it was over, almost before it had begun.

MAURICE RIORDAN

Born Lisgoold, County Cork, 1953. Educated at St Colman's College, Fermoy, University College Cork and McMaster University, Ontario. Taught briefly at UCC. Lives in London as a freelance writer.

'The mature paradigm of a good poem for me would be something like Robert Frost's "Birches" – a spoken language which seems simpler than it actually is.' Riordan's unsentimental narratives of shadow-lives parallel to those we actually live share something of the astutely colloquial quality he admires in Frost. Again like those of the American poet, his lyrics communicate a sense of a lurking grimness in the everyday.

MILK

This notebook in which he used to sketch
has, on its expensive-looking black cover,

a sprinkle of whitish stains: of the sort
sure to detain the unborn biographer.

Could they be the miniaturist's impression
of the northern sky, his Starry Night?

Or might lab-tests point to something else?
That they are, in fact, human milk-stains,

the effect of lactic acid on cheap skin,
and date from five years earlier –

a time when his wife's hyperactive glands
used to lob milk right across the room

to the wing-chair in which he dozed,
the sketchbook (it seems) closed in his hands.

Though he felt its light lash on his skin
many a night, he never took to that milk

and wished only for a wider room.
A failure of imagination, you might claim,

though it could be he needed more
of human kindness from that source then.

You could even say that the milk stopped,
but the acid didn't. That he replied in kind.

And thus it began: the pointless unstoppable game
across a room, in which a child grew

less small, and became the mesmerized umpire
looking now one way, now the other.

TIME OUT

Such is modern life
Stephen Dobyns

The two young ones fed, bathèd, zippered, read to and sung to.
   Asleep.
Time now to stretch on the sofa. Time for a cigarette.
When he realizes he's out. Clean out of smokes.
He grabs a fistful of coins, hesitates to listen before
Pulling the door softly to. Then sprints for the cornershop.

When he trips on a shoelace, head first into the path of a
   U-turning cab.
The screech of brakes is coterminous with his scream.
The Somalian shopkeeper, who summons the ambulance, knows
   the face,
But the name or address? No – just someone he remembers
Popping in, always with kids (this he doesn't say).

Casualty is at full stretch and the white thirtyish male,
Unshaven, with broken runners, is going nowhere. Is cleanly
   dead.

Around midnight an orderly rummages his pockets: £2.50 in
    change,
A latchkey, two chestnuts, one mitten, scraps of paper,
Some written on, but no wallet, cards, licence, or address book.

Around 2 a.m. he's put on ice, with a numbered tag.
Around 3 a.m. a child wakes, cries, then wails for attention.
But after ten minutes, unusually, goes back to sleep.
Unusually his twin sleeps on undisturbed till six o'clock,
When they both wake together, kicking, calling out *dada, dada*

Happily: well slept, still dry, crooning and pretend-reading in the
    half-light.
Then one slides to the floor, toddles to the master bedroom
And, seeing the empty (unmade) bed, toddles towards the stairs,
Now followed by the other, less stable, who stumbles halfway
    down
And both roll the last five steps to the bottom, screaming.

To be distracted by the post plopping onto the mat: all junk,
Therefore bulky, colourful, glossy, illicit. Time slips.
Nine o'clock: hungry, soiled, sensing oddness and absence,
Edgy together and whimpering now, when they discover the TV
Still on, its 17-channel console alive to their touch.

The Italian Parliament, sumo wrestling, the Austrian Grand Prix,
Opera, the Parcel Force ad, see them through to half past nine
When distress takes hold and the solid stereophonic screaming
    begins,
Relentless and shrill enough to penetrate the attention
Of the retired French pharmacist next door

Who at, say ten o'clock, pokes a broomstick through her rear
    window
To rattle theirs: magical silencing effect, lasting just so long
As it takes for the elderly woman to draw up her shopping list,
To retrieve two tenners from the ice-compartment, dead-lock
    her front doors,
Shake her head at the sunning milk, and make it to the bus.

Let us jump then to 10 p.m., to the nightmare dénouement . . .
No, let us duck right now out of this story, for such it is:
An idle, day-bed, Hitchcockian fantasy (though prompted by a
    news item,
A clockwork scenario: it was five days before that three-year-old
Was discovered beside the corpse of his Irish dad in Northolt).

Let us get *this* dad in and out of the shop, safely across the street,
Safely indoors again, less a couple of quid, plus the listings mags
And ten Silk Cut, back on board the sofa: reprieved, released,
    relaxed,
Thinking it's time for new sneakers, for a beard trim, for an
    overall
Rethink in the hair department. Time maybe to move on from
    the fags.

A WORD FROM THE LOKI

    The Loki tongue does not lend itself
    to description along classical lines.
    Consider the vowels: there are just four,
    including one produced by inspiration
    (i.e. indrawn breath), which then requires
    an acrobatic feat of projection
    to engage with its troupe of consonants.
    The skilled linguist can manage, at best,
    a sort of tattoo; whereas the Loki
    form sounds of balletic exactness.
    Consider further: that the tribe has evolved
    this strenuous means of articulation
    for one word, a defective verb
    used in one mood only, the optative.

    No semantic equivalent can be found
    in English, nor within Indo-European.
    Loosely, the word might be glossed as *to joke*,
    provided we cite several other usages,
    such as *to recover from snakebite*;
    to eat fish with the ancestors;

387

to die at home in the village, survived
by all of one's sons and grandsons.
It is prohibited in daily speech,
and the Loki, a moderate people
who abjure physical punishments,
are severe in enforcing this taboo,
since all offenders, of whatever age
or status, are handed over to *mouri*

– sent, in effect, to a gruesome death:
for the victim is put on board a raft,
given a gourd of drinking water, a knife,
and one of those raucous owl-faced
monkeys as companion, then towed
to midstream and set loose on the current.
Yet the taboo is relaxed at so-called
'joke parties': impromptu celebrations
that can be provoked by multiple births
or by an out-of-season catch of bluefish.
They are occasions for story-telling
and poetry, and serve a useful end
in allowing the young to learn this verb
and to perfect its exact delivery.

For the word is held to have come down
from the ancestral gods, to be their one gift.
And its occult use is specific: to ward off
the Loordhu, a cannibalistic horde,
believed to roam the interior forest,
who are reputed to like their meat
fresh and raw, to keep children in lieu of pigs,
and to treat eye and tongue as delicacies.
The proximity of danger is heralded
by a despondency that seems to strike
without visible cause but which effects
a swift change among a people by nature
brave and practical, bringing to a stop
in a matter of hours all work, play, talk.

At such crises, the villagers advance
to the riverbank and, as night falls,

they climb into the trees, there to recite
this verb throughout the hours of darkness.
But since, in the memory of the village,
the Loordhu have never yet attacked,
one has reason to doubt the existence
of an imminent threat to the Loki –
who nonetheless continue, in suspense, their chant.
At once wistful and eerie, it produces
this observable result: that it quells
the commotion of the guenon monkeys
and lulls, within its range, the great forest.

THOMAS McCARTHY

Born Cappoquin, County Waterford, 1954. Educated at St Anne's
Secondary School, Cappoquin, and University College Cork.
Member of International Writing Program at the University of Iowa,
1977–8. Works in City Library, Cork. McCarthy has published two
novels of political life in Munster, *Without Power* (1991) and
Asya and Christine (1992).

McCarthy's teenage experience as a Fianna Fáil activist throws a long
shadow over his work in verse and prose alike. His poems register the
tedium and self-delusion of lower-middle-class rural life in the Republic
while sympathetically observing its impulses towards grace and
generosity. McCarthy's lyrics are at their stongest when they resist a
prettifying aestheticism to look directly at unprepossessing realities:
'Persephone, 1978' confronts the trauma of a road disaster the poet
survived, while 'The Standing Trains' finds an emblem of declining
political idealism in the railway shutdowns of the 1960s. 'Mr Nabokov's
Memory', a cunning tessellation of details from the novelist's *Speak,
Memory*, represents the more literary side of McCarthy's sensibility.

STATE FUNERAL

Parnell will never come again, he said.
He's there, all that was mortal of him.
Peace to his ashes.
James Joyce, *Ulysses*

That August afternoon the family
Gathered. There was a native *déjà vu*
Of Funeral when we settled against the couch
On our sunburnt knees. We gripped mugs of tea
Tightly and soaked the TV spectacle;
The boxed ritual in our living-room.

My father recited prayers of memory,
Of monster meetings, blazing tar-barrels
Planted outside Free-State homes, the Broy-
Harriers pushing through a crowd, Blueshirts;

And, after the war, de Valera's words
Making Churchill's imperial palette blur.

What I remember is one decade of darkness,
A mind-stifling boredom; long summers
For blackberry picking and churning cream,
Winters for saving timber or setting lines
And snares: none of the joys of here and now
With its instant jam, instant heat and cream:

It was a landscape for old men. Today
They lowered the tallest one, tidied him
Away while his people watched quietly.
In the end he had retreated to the first dream,
Coming truth. I think of his austere grandeur;
Taut sadness, like old heroes he had imagined.

MR NABOKOV'S MEMORY

For my first poem there are specific images
herded like schoolchildren into a neat row.
There is an ear and human finger hanging
from the linden tree in the Park north of
Maria Square and, between there and Morskaya
Street, other images of defeat. Such
as a black article in a Fascist newspaper
blowing along the footpath, or an old soldier
throwing insults at lovers out walking.
Even the *schveitsar* in our hallway
sharpens pencils for my father's meeting
as if sharpening the guillotine of the future.
There is only Tamara, who arrives with the poem
as something good; her wayward hair tied back
with a bow of black silk. Her neck,
in the long light of summer, is covered
with soft down like the bloom on almonds.
When winter comes I'll miss school to listen
to her minor, uvular poems, her jokes,
her snorting laughter in St Petersburg museums.

I have all this; this luxury of love; until
she says: 'a flaw has appeared in us,
it's the strain of winters in St Petersburg' –
and like a heroine from a second-rate
matinée in Nevski Street she steps into the womb
of the Metro to become a part of me forever.

So many things must happen at once in this,
this single chrysalis of memory, this poem.
While my son weeps by my side at a border
checkpoint, a caterpillar ascends
the stalk of a campanula, a butterfly comes to rest
on the leaf of a tree with an unforgettable
name; an old man sighs in an orchard
in the Crimea, an even older housekeeper
loses her mind and the keys to our kitchen.
A young servant is sharpening the blade
of the future, while my father leaps
into the path of an assassin's bullet
at a brief August lecture in Berlin.
All these things must happen at once
before the rainstorm clears, leaving one
drop of water pinned down by its own weight.
When it falls from the linden leaf I shall
run to my mother, forever waiting forever
waiting, with maternal Russian tears,
to listen to her son's one and only poem.

PERSEPHONE, 1978

The late March mist is an angry Cerberus,
sniffing debris, sniffing the helpless
with its moist noses. The dead are bunched together:
a woman decapitated by a flying wheel-rim,
her daughter screaming 'Help me! Help Mama!'
I crawl through a shattered windscreen
to taste diesel fumes, pungent scattered grain
from the overturned distillery truck.
Arc-lights go on everywhere although

it's still daylight. My eyes hurt. My arms.
My neck is wet, a bloody mist thickening,
a soft March day. There's blood and rain
on the tarmac. Bodies lie stone-quiet
after the catapult of speed.
Even the injured snore deeply. Some will never
come back, never grow warm again.
My mind fills with the constant mutilated dead,
the Ulster dead, the perennial traffic-accident
of Ireland. Here are funerals being made.
A priest walks among the wounded,
Christian stretcher-bearer, helper
and scavenger. My mind fills with hatred.
I race before him to the comatose,
shouting 'You'll be fine! Just keep warm!'
and cover a mother with my duffle-coat.
It is my will against his,
I want to shroud the woman's soul with love,
hesitant, imperfect, but this side of Paradise.
Everywhere is the sound of wailing pain.
A surgeon hurries past, sweating,
his tattered gown is purple with blood,
his face a dark blue narcissus.
I have only words to offer, nothing
like pethidine or the oils of Extreme Unction.
Beside me the woman dies, peppered with barley –
plucked from the insane world like Persephone.

THE STANDING TRAINS

. . . and I thought how wonderful to miss
one's connections;
soon I shall miss them
all the time
Louis MacNeice: *The Strings are False*

From the windows of a standing train
you can judge the artwork of our poor Republic.
The prominent ruins that make Limerick Junction
seem like Dresden in 1945

and the beaten-up coaches at Mallow Station,
the rusted side-tracks at Charleville,
have taken years of independent thought.
It takes decades to destroy a system
of stations. On the other hand, a few
well-placed hand-signals can destroy a whole
mode of life, a network of happiness.
This is our own Republic! O Memory,
O Patria, the shame of silenced junctions.
Time knew we'd rip the rails apart, we'd sell
emigrant tickets even while stripping
the ticket-office bare. The standing trains
of the future were backed against a wall.

Two hens peck seed from the bright platform,
hens roost in the signal-box.
Bilingual signs that caused a debate in the Senate
have been unbolted and used as gates:
it's late summer now in this dead station.
When I was twelve they unbolted the rails.
Now there's only the ghost of my father,
standing by the parcel-shed with his ghostly
suitcase. When he sees me walking towards him
he becomes upset. *Don't stop here!* he cries.
Keep going, keep going! This place is dead.

IAN DUHIG

Born into Irish family in Hammersmith, London, 1954. A worker on homelessness projects in London, Belfast and Yorkshire, he now lives in Leeds.

Seeking out the brutalities behind the euphemisms of history, Duhig's poems exhibit a Browningesque delight in distortion. An author's note on 'I'r Hen Iaith A'i Chaneuon' reads: 'The title is Welsh and means "To the Old Tongue and Its Songs". The Irish translates roughly as: Speak not to me of the foreign prelate/ Nor of his creed with neither truth nor faith/ For the foundation stone of his temple/ Is the bollocks of King Henry VIII.'

I'R HEN IAITH A'I CHANEUON

If the tongue only speak all that the mind knows
There wouldn't be any neighbours
The Red Book of Hergest

When I go down to Wales for the long bank holiday
to visit my wife's grandfather who is teetotal,
who is a non-smoker, who does not approve
of anyone who is not teetotal and a non-smoker,
when I go down to Wales for the long, long bank holiday
with my second wife to visit her grandfather
who deserted Methodism for The Red Flag,
who won't hear a word against Stalin,
who despite my oft-professed socialism
secretly believes I am still with the Pope's legions,
receiving coded telegrams from the Vatican
specifying the dates, times and positions I should adopt
for political activity and sexual activity,
who in his ninetieth year took against boxing,
which was the only thing I could ever talk to him about,
when I visit my second wife's surviving grandfather,
and when he listens to the football results in Welsh
I will sometimes slip out to the pub.

I will sometimes slip out to the pub
and drink pint upon pint of that bilious whey
they serve there, where the muzak will invariably be
The Best of the Rhosllanerchrugog Male Voice Choir
and I will get trapped by some brain donor from up the valley
who will really talk about 'the language so strong and so beautiful
that has grown out of the ageless mountains,
that speech of wondrous beauty that our fathers wrought',
who will chant to me in Welsh his epileptic verses
about Gruffudd ap Llywellyn and Daffydd ap Llywellyn,
and who will give me two solid hours of slaver
because I don't speak Irish and who will then bring up religion,
then I will tell him I know one Irish prayer about a Welsh king
on that very subject, and I will recite for him as follows:
'Ná thrácht ar an mhinistéir Ghallda
Ná ar a chreideimh gan bheann gan bhrí,
Mar ní'l mar bhuan-chloch dá theampuill
Ach magairle Annraoi Rí.' 'Beautiful,'
He will say, as they all do, 'It sounds quite beautiful.'

REFORMA AGRARIA

In 1936,
Falange or Carlist priests
showed wounded men,
republicans,
rojoseperatistas,
an extreme unction,
a cristazio limpio,
a blow with the crucifix
between the eyes,
a blessed paseo,
the light oil of the gun
like watchmaker's oil,
or sunflower oil,
ran from the Lugers,
ran from Berettas
down into the eyes
of wounded land-leaguers,

who closed them knowing
even then they'd won
two square metres,
room for the red rose tree.

PAULA MEEHAN

Born Dublin, 1955. Educated at Trinity College Dublin and Eastern
Washington University. Lives in Dublin. A popular reader of
her work, Meehan runs writing workshops in prisons, schools
and community groups.

Meehan's poems are remarkable for their unaffected confidence and
directness of address and for their sudden, intense bursts of lyricism.
Many of them celebrate the resilience of women in adversity.

THE PATTERN

Little has come down to me of hers,
a sewing machine, a wedding band,
a clutch of photos, the sting of her hand
across my face in one of our wars

when we had grown bitter and apart.
Some say that's the fate of the eldest daughter.
I wish now she'd lasted till after
I'd grown up. We might have made a new start

as women without tags like *mother*, *wife*,
sister, *daughter*, taken our chances from there.
At forty-two she headed for god knows where.
I've never gone back to visit her grave.

★

First she'd scrub the floor with Sunlight soap,
an armreach at a time. When her knees grew sore
she'd break for a cup of tea, then start again
at the door with lavender polish. The smell
would percolate back through the flat to us,
her brood banished to the bedroom.

And as she buffed the wax to a high shine
did she catch her own face coming clear?
Did she net a glimmer of her true self?
Did her mirror tell what mine tells me?
I have her shrug and go on
knowing history has brought her to her knees.

She'd call us in and let us skate around
in our socks. We'd grow solemn as planets
in an intricate orbit about her.

★

She's bending over crimson cloth,
the younger kids are long in bed.
Late summer, cold enough for a fire,
she works by fading light
to remake an old dress for me.
It's first day back at school tomorrow.

★

'Pure lambswool. Plenty of wear in it yet.
You know I wore this when I went out with your Da.
I was supposed to be down in a friend's house,
your Granda caught us at the corner.
He dragged me in by the hair - it was long as yours then -
in front of the whole street.
He called your Da every name under the sun,
cornerboy, lout; I needn't tell you
what he called me. He shoved my whole head
under the kitchen tap, took a scrubbing brush
and carbolic soap and in ice-cold water he scrubbed
every spick of lipstick and mascara off my face.
Christ but he was a right tyrant, your Granda.
It'll be over my dead body anyone harms a hair of your head.'

★

She must have stayed up half the night
to finish the dress. I found it airing at the fire,

three new copybooks on the table and a bright
bronze nib, St Christopher strung on a silver wire,

as if I were embarking on a perilous journey
to uncharted realms. I wore that dress
with little grace. To me it spelt poverty,
the stigma of the second hand. I grew enough to pass

it on by Christmas to the next in line. I was sizing
up the world beyond our flat patch by patch
daily after school, and fitting each surprising
city street to city square to diamond. I'd watch

the Liffey for hours pulsing to the sea
and the coming and going of ships,
certain that one day it would carry me
to Zanzibar, Bombay, the Land of the Ethiops.

★

There's a photo of her taken in the Phoenix Park
alone on a bench surrounded by roses
as if she had been born to formal gardens.
She stares out as if unaware
that any human hand held the camera, wrapped
entirely in her own shadow, the world beyond her
already a dream, already lost. She's
eight months pregnant. Her last child.

★

Her steel needles sparked and clacked,
the only other sound a settling coal
or her sporadic mutter
at a hard part in the pattern.
She favoured sensible shades:
Moss Green, Mustard, Beige.

I dreamt a robe of a colour
so pure it became a word.

Sometimes I'd have to kneel
an hour before her by the fire,
a skein around my outstretched hands,
while she rolled wool into balls.
If I swam like a kite too high
amongst the shadows on the ceiling
or flew like a fish in the pools
of pulsing light, she'd reel me firmly
home, she'd land me at her knees.

Tongues of flame in her dark eyes,
she'd say,'One of these days I must
teach you to follow a pattern.'

CHILD BURIAL

Your coffin looked unreal,
fancy as a wedding cake.

I chose your grave clothes with care,
your favourite stripey shirt,

your blue cotton trousers.
They smelt of woodsmoke, of October,

your own smell there too.
I chose a gansy of handspun wool,

warm and fleecy for you. It is
so cold down in the dark.

No light can reach you and teach you
the paths of wild birds,

the names of the flowers,
the fishes, the creatures.

Ignorant you must remain
of the sun and its work,

my lamb, my calf, my eaglet,
my cub, my kid, my nestling,

my suckling, my colt. I would spin
time back, take you again

within my womb, your amniotic lair,
and further spin you back

through nine waxing months
to the split seeding moment

you chose to be made flesh,
word within me.

I'd cancel the love feast
the hot night of your making.

I would travel alone
to a quiet mossy place,

you would spill from me into the earth
drop by bright red drop.

LABURNUM

You walk into an ordinary room
on an ordinary evening, say
mid-May, when the laburnum

hangs over the railings of the Square
and the city is lulled by eight o'clock,
the traffic sparse, the air fresher.

You expect to find someone
waiting, though now you live
alone. You've answered none

of your calls. The letters pile
up in the corner. The idea
persists that someone waits while

you turn the brass handle and knock
on the light. Gradually
the dark seeps into the room, you lock

out the night, scan a few books.
It's days since you ate.
The plants are dying – even the cactus,

shrivelled like an old scrotum,
has given up the ghost. There's
a bit of wine in a magnum

you bought, when? The day
before? The day before that?
It's the only way

out. The cold sweats
begin. You knock back a few.
You've no clean clothes left.

He is gone. Say it.
Say it to yourself, to the room.
Say it loud enough to believe it.

You will live breath
by breath. The beat of your own heart
will scourge you. You'll wait

in vain, for he's gone from you.
And every night is a long
slide to the dawn you

wake to, terrified in your ordinary room
on an ordinary morning, say
mid-May, say the time of laburnum.

SEÁN DUNNE

Born Waterford, 1956. Educated at Mount Sion Christian Brothers'
School, Waterford, and University College Cork. Worked as a journalist
on the *Cork Examiner*. Edited *Poets of Munster* (1985) and *The Cork
Anthology* (1993). *In My Father's House*, a memoir of Dunne's
childhood, appeared in 1991, and *The Road to Silence*, a spiritual
autobiography, in 1994. Seán Dunne died suddenly in 1995.

Domestic harmony achieved or disrupted serves as an icon for a
range of wider concerns in Dunne's poems, many of which
share the muted elegiac tone of 'Sydney Place', with its
portrait of a disintegrating marriage.

from SYDNEY PLACE

BEANS

What must they have grown to now,
Secrets sprouting in the dark?
My arm resting on a windowsill,
I flicked mung beans at ivy
As if next morning I'd wake
To a beanstalk ripe with solutions.

THE MOBILE

It jangles in a mild breeze
Above my son tucked in his cot.
Each morning he wakes and strains
To reach its impossible height,
But misses always those turning birds,
Plastic fish swimming in the sky.

RAILINGS

My son swings from black railings
Where once a horse was tethered.
Snow settles on his woollen hat,

Crystals dissolve in strands.
In a photograph he squints ahead
To a future from which we've gone.

THE DEAD PIANIST

The pianist's funeral passes
Terraces at evenings, his long
Fingers joined on a still stomach.
I think of John Field dead in Moscow
And hear a nocturne settling
In leaves from trees on Wellington Road.

THE BUS STATION

The passport photo booth flashes
In the bus station near the river.
I watch it from my high window:
A message sent with a mirror
From desperate souls in a valley,
Frantic for answers in the far hills.

THE POET UPSTAIRS

The poet is working upstairs.
I can hear his typewriter clattering
Between our arguments, poems made
Among shouts and accusations:
Our fierce anger a dust that clogs
The bright needle of his work.

TEA

Endless infusions, silver strainers.
Teapots, bags dangling from strings
In cups where dried leaves darken.
Rosehip and hibiscus, camomile, mint,
And lapsang souchong with its smell
Of woodsmoke from a forest hearth.

THE LOST WIFE

A poet by the fireside cries
For his dead wife. Whiskey draws
Sadness from him like a keen.
He talks of voice, hair, skin,
Holds a ring up to the light
And frames the space where she has been.

THE OLD SCHOOL

The school is gone from Belgrave Place,
Rats scramble in briars near the wall.
A light burns in a closed classroom
Where I sense the ghosts of children,
Their pinafores pressed and the lost
Future a blackboard at which they stand.

THE NIGHT SKY

A moon you could hang a coat on,
A pantomime curve in the sky.
Smog rises above roofs of the city
From homes rife with offerings
To appease it before it disappears:
The last god going in a sliver of light.

CATHAL Ó SEARCAIGH

Born Meenala, County Donegal, 1956. Educated at National Institute for Higher Education, Limerick. Has worked as radio producer for RTE. Writer-in-residence at the University of Ulster at Coleraine and Queen's University Belfast, 1992–3. Lives on small farm in County Donegal.

Ó Searcaigh is a productive poet who brings a variety of moods to his exploration of the relationship of his native Gaeltacht area of Donegal to modern mass culture. Though the somewhat self-conscious elegance of his poems on Dublin and London is not without its attractions, the plainer, more elevated mode of 'Na Píopaí Créafóige' and 'Caoineadh' is finally more convincing. Translation cannot do justice to the despairing recourse to English as the language of personal freedom in 'Bó Bhradach'.

BÓ BHRADACH
do Liam Ó Muirthile

D'éirigh sé dúthuirseach déarfainn
den uaigneas a shníonn anuas i dtólamh
fríd na maolchnocáin is fríd na gleanntáin
chomh malltriallach le *hearse* tórraimh;
de bhailte beaga marbhánta na mbunchnoc
nach bhfuil aos óg iontu ach oiread le créafóg;
de na seanlaochra, de lucht roiste na dtortóg
a d'iompaigh an domasach ina deargfhód
is a bhodhraigh é *pink* bliain i ndiaidh bliana
ag éisteacht leo ag maíomh as seanfhóid an tseantsaoil;

de na *bungalows* bheaga bhána atá chomh gránna
le *dandruff* in ascaill chíbeach an Ghleanna;
de na daoine óga gafa i g*cage* a gcinniúna
dálta ainmhithe allta a chaill a ngliceas;
de thrí thrua na scéalaíochta i dtruacántas
lucht na dífhostaíochta, den easpa meanmna,
den iargúltacht, den chúngaigeantacht ar dhá thaobh an
    Ghleanna;
de na leadhbacha breátha thíos i dTigh Ruairí
a chuir an fear ag bogadaigh ann le fonn
ach nach dtabharfadh túrálú ar a raibh de shú ann;

de theorainneacha treibhe, de sheanchlaíocha teaghlaigh,
de bheith ag mún a mhíshástachta in éadan na mballaí
a thóg cine agus creideamh thart air go teann.
D'éirigh sé dúthuirseach de bheith teanntaithe sa Ghleann
is le rúide bó bradaí maidin amháin earraigh
chlearáil sé na ballaí is *hightailáil* anonn adaí.

NA PÍOPAÍ CRÉAFÓIGE

Ní chasfaidh tusa thart do chloigeann
agus an bás ag rolladh chugat mar an t-aigéan.

A RUNAWAY COW
for Liam Ó Muirthile

I'd say he'd had too much
of the desolation that trickles down
through the glens and the hillocks
steadily as a hearse;
of the lifeless villages in the foothills
as bare of young folk as of soil;
of the old codgers, the hummock-blasters
who turned the peat into good red earth
and who deafened him pink year after year
with their talk of the grand sods of the old days;

of the little white bungalows, attractive
as dandruff in the hairy armpit of the Glen;
of the young people trapped in their destinies
like caged animals out of touch with their instinct;
of the Three Sorrows of Storytelling
in the pity of unemployment, of low morale,
and of the remoteness and narrow-mindedness
of both sides of the Glen;
of the fine young things down in Rory's
who woke the man in him
but wouldn't give a curse for his attentions;

of clan boundaries, of old tribal ditches,
of pissing his frustration against the solid walls
race and religion built round him.
He'd had too much of being stuck in the Glen
and with a leap like a runaway cow's one spring morning
he *cleared* the walls and *hightailed* away.

translated by Patrick Crotty

THE CLAY PIPES

You won't be the one to turn away when death
rolls in towards you like the ocean.

Coinneoidh tú ag stánadh air go seasta
agus é ag scuabadh chugat isteach ina spraisteacha geala
ó fhíor na síoraíochta.
Coinneoidh tú do chiall
agus do chéadfaí agus é ag siollfarnaigh
thar chladaí d'inchinne
go dtí go mbeidh sé ar d'aithne
go huile agus go hiomlán
díreach mar a rinne tú agus tú i do thachrán
ar thránna Mhachaire Rabhartaigh
agus tonnta mara an Atlantaigh
ag sealbhú do cholainne.
Ach sula ndeachaigh do shaol ar neamhní
shroich tusa ciumhais an chladaigh.
Tarlóidh a mhacasamhail anseo.
Sroichfidh tú domhan na mbeo
tar éis dul i dtaithí an duibheagáin le d'aigne;
ach beidh séala an tsáile ort go deo,
beidh doimhneacht agat mar dhuine:
as baol an bháis tiocfaidh fírinne.

Ní thabharfainn de shamhail duit i mo dhán
ach iadsan i gcoillte Cholumbia
ar léigh mé fá dtaobh daofa sa leabharlann:
dream a chaitheann píopaí daite créafóige, píopaí
nár úsáideadh riamh lena ndéanamh
ach scaobóga créafóige
a baineadh i mbaol beatha
i ndúichí sean-namhad, gleann scáthach
timepallaithe le gaistí, gardaí agus saigheada nimhe.
Dar leo siúd a deir an t-alt tuairisce
nach bhfuil píopaí ar bith iomlán,
seachas na cinn a bhfuil baol
ag baint le soláthar a gcuid créafóige.

You will hold to your steadfast gaze,
as it comes tiding in, all plash and glitter
from the rim of eternity.
You will keep your head.
You will come to your senses again as it
foams over the ridged beaches of your brain
and you will take it all in
and know it completely:
you will be a child again, out on the strand
at Magheraroarty, your body
abandoned altogether
to the lift of the Atlantic.
But before you went the whole way then away
into nothingness, you would touch the bottom.
And this will be what happens to you here:
you'll go through a black hole of initiation,
then reach the land of the living;
but the seal of the brine will be on you forever
and you'll have depth as a person:
you'll walk from danger of death into the truth.

Here is the best image I can find:
you are like the forest people of Columbia
I read about in the library,
a tribe who smoke clay pipes, coloured pipes
that used to have to be made from this one thing:
basketfuls of clay
scooped out in fatal danger
in enemy country, in a scaresome place
full of traps and guards and poisoned arrows.
According to this article, they believe
that the only fully perfect pipes
are ones made out of the clay
collected under such extreme conditions.

translated by Seamus Heaney

CAOINEADH

i gcuimhne mo mháthar

Chaoin mé na cuileatacha ar ucht mo mháthara
An lá a bhásaigh Mollie – peata de sheanchaora
Istigh i gcreagacha crochta na Beithí.
Á cuartú a bhí muid lá marbhánta samhraidh
Is brú anála orainn beirt ag dreasú na gcaorach
Siar ó na hailltreacha nuair a tímid an marfach
Sna beanna dodhreaptha. Préacháin dhubha ina scaotha
Á hithe ina beatha gur imigh an dé deiridh aisti
De chnead choscrach amháin is gan ionainn iarraidh
Tharrthála a thabhairt uirthi thíos sna scealpacha.
Ní thiocfaí mé a shásamh is an tocht ag teacht tríom;
D'fháisc lena hucht mé is í ag cásamh mo chaill liom
Go dtí gur chuireas an racht adaí ó íochtar mo chroí.
D'iompair abhaile mé ansin ar a guailneacha
Ag gealladh go ndéanfadh sí ceapairí arán préataí.

Inniu tá mo Theangaidh ag saothrú an bháis.
Ansacht na bhfilí – teangaidh ár n-aithreacha
Gafa i gcreagacha crochta na Faillí
Is gan ionainn í a tharrtháil le dásacht.
Cluinim na smeachannaí deireanacha
Is na héanacha creiche ag teacht go tapaidh,
A ngoba craosacha réidh chun feille.
Ó dá ligfeadh sí liú amháin gaile – liú catha
A chuirfeadh na creachadóirí chun reatha,
Ach seo í ag creathnú, seo í ag géilleadh;
Níl mo mháthair anseo le mé a shuaimhniú a thuilleadh
Is ní dhéanfaidh gealladh an phian a mhaolú.

LAMENT

in memory of my mother

I cried on my mother's breast, cried sore
The day Mollie died, our old pet ewe
Trapped on a rockface up at Beithí.
It was sultry heat, we'd been looking for her,
Sweating and panting, driving sheep back
From the cliff-edge when we saw her attacked
On a ledge far down. Crows and more crows
Were eating at her. We heard the cries
But couldn't get near. She was ripped to death
As we suffered her terrible, wild, last breath
And my child's heart broke. I couldn't be calmed
No matter how much she'd tighten her arms
And gather me close. I just cried on
Till she hushed me at last with a piggyback
And the promise of treats of potato-cake.

To-day it's my language that's in its throes,
The poets' passion, my mothers' fathers'
Mothers' language, abandoned and trapped
On a fatal ledge that we won't attempt.
She's in agony, I can hear her heave
And gasp and struggle as they arrive,
The beaked and ravenous scavengers
Who are never far. Oh if only anger
Came howling wild out of her grief,
If only she'd bare the teeth of her love
And rout the pack. But she's giving in,
She's quivering badly, my mother's gone
And promises now won't ease the pain.

translated by Seamus Heaney

PETER SIRR

Born Waterford, 1960. Educated at Trinity College Dublin. Lived for a number of years in Italy and Holland. Now lives in Dublin, where he is director of the Irish Writers' Centre. A frequent poetry reviewer for the *Irish Times*.

Sirr's poems are notable for their rapid movement and, at their best, reveal a restless, penetrating intelligence.

A FEW HELPFUL HINTS

Tell them what you like. Tell them
the world is flat and when you get to the edge you fall
into the usual darkness, hell if you like
but anywhere will do, any storied space
mythical returners have whined of, salty
and smelling of loss. Tell them the rain falls
and steals slyly up and falls, and falls –
tell them everything twice for emphasis
and then again the next day for revision.
Set them tests on the same thing time and time again.
Tell them most of life is repetitive
and this will stand them in good stead.
Tell them about gravity and love,
drop the whole world on their heads
if you have to, the broad curriculum
of hatred and desire and the need for money
and love, tell them some things are permissible
and some less so, though ideally we'd prefer it
if you left that to us. Above all
don't be heavyhanded, keep a light tone,
encourage them to laugh, encourage them to believe
they are getting away with something when they do.
Encourage them to see you as a fragile
merely human being. Forget things, mix up names
and be occasionally unfair in the allotment of marks.

Tell them about yourself if it helps. Allow your emotions
to enter the syllabus, when reading a poem, or telling them
things that have happened. Break down if you have to,
rail against the world and its mindless cruelties.
Tell them we could all be blown out of it
or the sun might go out or too much of it get through.
Tell them not to use aerosols, organise a project
on it. Projects are good. We like to stress
the need to work together. Harmony
is the oil in the machinery, or something
like that. Tell them about the men who came to save us
with beautiful voices and a poetry
we would like to have found time for, we may yet
retire to. Tell them about those
who have still to come, shuffling in awkwardness and anger
from the cardboard slums that tremble even now
on the outskirts, whose poems
may already be struggling in our blood
or hurtling through the dark cathedral spaces
achieved and pure, unsettling the stars.

PETER McDONALD

Born Belfast, 1962. Educated at Methodist College, Belfast, and University College, Oxford. Lectures in English at the University of Bristol. A critic of distinction, McDonald has published *Louis MacNeice: The Poet in his Contexts* (1991).

McDonald's is a cerebral, self-aware, resolutely unshowy poetry. 'Sunday in Great Tew' explores an exiled northern Protestant's response to the Remembrance Day massacre at Enniskillen in 1987, an event the poem never directly mentions.

SUNDAY IN GREAT TEW
8th November 1987

1

It's time to get back to the car. Already, at half-past three,
the light's three-quarters gone, and back across the green
you can watch the shifting greys of a subtle fog by now
coming over to freeze the steps we leave, our ghosts' footprints,

to slight marks in November grass, and that's the last
of us this afternoon, this year, in this model village
a half-hour's drive from Oxford, where we come in summer
like the other tourists, to drink decent beer, sniff woodsmoke,

and admire thatched roofs on sturdy, stone-built houses,
as though the whole place were a replica of some England,
an idea on show, unchanging, glassy, not quite touchable.
But this is November, and Sunday. It is Sunday in Great Tew.

2

Every visit nowadays is an act of remembrance,
measuring changes in us against some other summer
when we sat here drinking, and swapped our random gossip
– friends, work and books, hard politics or love –

across a wooden table in an always busy pub
with proper beer on sale, not the watery Oxford slops,
and where, as their speciality, they sell hand-made pipes,
briars and clay-pipes, every one the genuine article,

(though these, admittedly, we never got around to buying);
one year we're talking about that headstrong, happy girl
you'd chased unluckily for months; another, and we're discussing
far-off acts of war, the real thing, here in the Falkland Arms.

3

The manor house, concealed behind thick trees and hedges,
might well be home now for some eccentric millionaire
who seldom shows his face; from the road going uphill
to the church, you can see through gaps down to the house itself,

heavy and strong, like the brash history it suggests,
having and holding so much; was it here since the Civil War,
when the bookish man who owned the place, Lord Falkland,
was a loyalist who found himself outmanoeuvred?

Once he played patron here to the poet Abraham Cowley
– outmanoeuvred himself, in his way, by Parliament's
staunch worker Milton, true to different lights, but blind,
po-faced, pig-headed and holy, almost an Ulsterman.

4

Names of the wars change, and of course the protagonists change:
the church contains its various slabs of memorial stone
with names of the dead men, where today a single wreath
of poppies does its duty, pays them its stiff homage

of glaring red flowers for death, rootless and papery,
bunched together in grief or pride, or with indifference,
on a Sunday like any other Sunday in November;
there's a smell of damp mixed with the smell of genteel ladies

and the cold slips forward from the walls and the dark floor
so that here, too, we must become aliens, shut out

from whatever we might be tempted to call our own, reminded
that the dead are close, that here the poppy is an English flower.

5

There are no words to find for the dead, and no gestures,
no sermons to be turned, no curses to lay now and for ever
on one house, or the other, or on both; there is no need
to rerun the scalding images they have left in our keeping,

or pitch hot misery into this cold comfort, as though
one ill-bred outburst here might make sense of it;
there is no need to watch television in the afternoon
to understand that nobody has ever died with a good reason,

and see the Irish slaughter one another like wogs;
there is no need, only now a blinding appetite,
this afternoon, tomorrow, the day after; so tonight in the
    Killyhevlin
Hotel the team from ITN will be ordering champagne.

6

One drink today, one pint of beer, and one short walk
in the sober afternoon around an English village,
a conversation jumping from one silence to another
in ripe Oxonian vowels, two figures on their own

in some pretend backwater with picture-postcard views,
slipping discreetly into a proper country churchyard
and quoting poetry, and laughing now that everything's
too late, imagining the right history for the place,

inglorious, largely mute: two generals discussing terms,
their fists set hard on the oak table that's between them,
where neither will say the word 'defeat', though both return
with different names for victory to their beaten people.

7

Even in the middle of winter, the sky is everywhere,
folded above us as we walk with hands sunk in our pockets,

our fingers worrying over cold coins and key-rings;
it covers us completely as a numbing anaesthetic

so that every time we might look up, the two of us,
the trees we can see with fog trailing in their branches,
the scarecrow standing up in its one blank field
(or what looks from here like a scarecrow), the row of old houses

snug and expensive and empty, even the pub behind us,
all become incidental, oblique marks set in the margin,
swept out to the edges of a single, clear perspective,
the one that matters most, or least, and never changes.

8

A flower of crumpled paper with its button of black plastic
has fallen from somebody's coat, and is lying here beside
a vacant phone-box opposite the village school
along with an empty packet of twenty Benson and Hedges

and what looks like a bus-ticket; such modest litter
might be the last thing you notice, and for all the cars parked
there's nobody here but us walking out in the open,
and even we are making our way back to a car,

opening, closing doors, clicking in seat-belts, switching on
dipped headlights and starting the engine; turning around
and taking a right at the deserted school,
on our way home, leaving absolutely nothing behind us.

PEACETIME

Half-way down you lose the sense of falling,
call off hostilities between things and the soul
and wave perhaps, now time is to spare,
on the clear road from here to wherever;
for everyone is crying in relief
and congratulation, historians and survivors
discuss their grievous memories on air,

dizzy in this late reprieve and freedom,
and it all hurts like a childbirth, crazy
with drugs and news and people and champagne.

This is all happening before its time
or after; this is weekend leave;
these are the experts and the blonde children
ready to sing, like a happy army;
this is a good day for flying;
this is the cat's–
cradle of the bridge and the excellent sky;
this is the safe end of everything;
this is the beard and the dropping
smile of John Berryman going to heaven.

MARTIN MOONEY

Born Belfast, 1964. Grew up in Newtownards, County Down.
Educated at Queen's University Belfast. Lived in London for a number
of years before returning to Belfast. Works as a member of faculty at the
Poets' House, Portmuck, County Antrim.

Mooney's is perhaps the most quirky, interesting talent among an
emergent generation of northern poets uneasily negotiating the
influence of Paul Muldoon. The macabre satire of his low-life
London sequence *Grub* (1993) yields to a cautious lyricism in
'Anna Akhmatova's Funeral'.

ANNA AKHMATOVA'S FUNERAL

It looks to me like a hero's welcome,
as they carry you on their shoulders
to the grave, with no more delicacy
than they would cheap furniture,
like a slender matchwood wardrobe
full of old clothes and coat hangers
or an incomplete dinner service
packed in shavings and newsprint.
If I took it at face value I'd say
the untidiness of it all sits easily
with poetry, suggesting a life
lived according to nobody's rules
among messy bookshelves, tables
buried under an avalanche of drafts
in a house that's a home for anyone
who happens to knock on the door.
In the kitchen a pan of milk boils
over, smoke burps from the samovar,
a month's salads turn bitter . . . And,
in the same way, you might never
have bothered to dress yourself
or put on make-up, to answer letters

or pay the bills. The ragged edge
unravels back from the graveside
into any number of possible lives,
each one less orderly, less disciplined,
and already, so soon after them all,
history is learning to ignore you,
despite the presence of the film crew
and the mourners, who might as well
be spectators filling a stadium
or the night shift on its way home.
Admit it, it has its attractions, this
rough-handed slovenliness of things:
you could slip to one side unnoticed
and watch, suppressing a smile
that says, 'How light she is, how easily
they hold her up above their heads,
no heavier than a child or a poem,
no more solid than the priest's sermon
or the crumbling laws of gravity.'
Weightless, you tiptoe backwards
out of the cemetery, like a shy guest
still distrusting her invitation,
go home to any of the lives you led
without leaving so much as a thumbprint
or a stray eyelash to be picked up
by the unsteady gaze of the camera
skirting the edge of absence.

ACKNOWLEDGEMENTS

Grateful acknowledgement is made to:

Anvil Press Poetry for permission to reprint the following poems by Thomas McCarthy: 'Mr Nabokov's Memory' from *The Non-Aligned Storyteller* (1984); 'Persephone, 1978' and 'The Standing Trains' from *Seven Winters in Paris* (1989)

Blackstaff Press for permission to reprint the following poems by Paul Durcan: 'The Late Mr Charles Lynch Digresses' and 'Six Nuns Die in Convent Inferno' (extract) from *Going Home to Russia* (1987); for permission to reprint the following poems by John Hewitt: 'Freehold' (extract), 'The Ram s Horn', 'The Colony', 'Substance and Shadow', 'An Irishman in Coventry' and 'A Local Poet' from *Collected Poems* (1991), for permission to reprint the following poem by Martin Mooney: 'Anna Akhmatova's Funeral' from *Grub* (1993)

Bloodaxe Books for permission to reprint the following poems by Ian Duhig: 'I'r Hen Iaith A'i Chaneuon' and 'Reforma Agraria' from *The Bradford Count* (1991); for permission to reprint the following poems by Brendan Kennelly: 'Three Tides' and 'Vintage' from *Cromwell* (1987); for permission to reprint the following poem by Peter McDonald: 'Sunday in Great Tew' from *Biting the Wax* (1989)

The Calder Educational Trust, London, and the Samuel Beckett Estate for the following poems: 'Cascando' and 'Roundelay' by Samuel Beckett and 'my way is in the sand flowing' and 'what would I do without this world faceless incurious' by Samuel Beckett and translated from the French by Samuel Beckett, from *Collected Poems 1930-1978*, published by John Calder (Publishers) Ltd, London. Copyright © Samuel Beckett 1936, 1948, 1976, 1984 and copyright © the Samuel Beckett Estate 1994

Carcanet Press for permission to reprint the following poems by Padraic Fallon: 'A Flask of Brandy', 'Kiltartan Legend', 'Yeats at Athenry Perhaps', 'Three Houses' (extract) and 'A Bit of Brass' from *Collected Poems* (1990); for permission to reprint the following poems by Eavan Boland: 'Listen. This Is the Noise of Myth' and 'Fond Memory' from *Selected Poems* (1989); 'The Black Lace Fan My Mother Gave Me', 'The Latin Lesson' and 'Midnight Flowers' from *Outside History* (1990); 'Anna Liffey' from *In a Time of Violence* (1994)

Chatto and Windus for permission to reprint the following poems by Bernard O'Donoghue: 'A Nun Takes the Veil' and 'The Weakness' from *The Weakness* (1991)

R. Dardis Clarke, 21 Pleasants Street, Dublin 8, for permission to reprint the following poems by Austin Clarke: 'The Lost Heifer', 'The Young Woman of Beare' (extract), 'The Planter's Daughter', 'Celibacy', 'Martha Blake', 'The Straying Student', 'Penal Law', 'St Christopher', 'Early Unfinished Sketch', 'Martha Blake at Fifty-One' and 'Tiresias' (extract) from *Collected Poems* (1974)

An Clóchomhar Teoranta for permission to reprint the following poems by Máirtín Ó Direáin: 'Deireadh Ré', 'Cuimhne an Domhnaigh' and 'Cranna Foirtil' from *Dánta 1939-1979* (1980); all poems translated by Patrick Crotty

Cló Iar-Chonnachta Teo for permission to reprint the following poems by Cathal Ó Searcaigh: 'Bó Bhradach' (translated by Patrick Crotty), 'Na Píopaí Créafóige' (translated by Seamus Heaney) and 'Caoineadh' (translated by Seamus Heaney) from *Homecoming/An Bealach 'na Bhaile* (1993)

The estate of Brian Coffey for permission to reprint the following poems: 'Death of Hektor' (extract) and 'For What for Whom Unwanted' (extracts) from *Poems and Versions 1929-1990* (1991)

Dedalus Press for permission to reprint the following poems by Denis Devlin: 'Ank'hor Vat', 'Little Elegy' and 'Memoirs of a Turcoman Diplomat: Oteli Asia Palas, Inc.' (extract) from *Collected Poems* (1989)

The estate of Denis Devlin for permission to reprint the following poem: 'Renewal by Her Element' from *Collected Poems* (1964)

Paul Durcan for permission to reprint the following poems: 'The Hat Factory' and 'Tullynoe: Tête-à-Tête in the Parish Priest's Parlour' from *The Selected Paul Durcan* (2nd ed., 1985); 'The Haulier's Wife Meets Jesus on the Road Near Moone' and 'Around the Corner from Francis Bacon' from *The Berlin Wall Café* (1985); 'The Levite and His Concubine at Gibeah' from *Crazy About Women* (1991)

Faber and Faber for permission to reprint the following poems by Fergus Allen: 'Elegy for Faustina' and 'The Fall' from *The Brown Parrots of Providencia* (1993); for permission to reprint the following poem by Samuel Beckett: 'Words and Music' (extract) from *Collected Shorter Plays* (1984); for permission to reprint the following poems by Seamus Heaney: 'Churning Day' from *Death of a Naturalist* (1966); 'Broagh' and 'The Tollund Man' from *Wintering Out* (1972); 'Sunlight' and 'Funeral Rites' from *North* (1975); 'Casualty', 'Badgers' and 'The Harvest Bow' from *Field Work* (1979); 'The Birthplace' and 'The Cleric' from *Station Island* (1984); 'From the Frontier of Writing' and 'From the Canton of Expectation' from *The Haw Lantern* (1987); 'Wheels within Wheels', 'Lightenings VIII' and 'Lightenings IX' from *Seeing Things* (1991); for permission to reprint the following poems by Louis MacNeice: 'Mayfly', 'Snow', 'Autumn Journal XVI', 'Meeting Point', 'Autobiography', 'The Libertine', 'Western Landscape', 'Autumn Sequel XX' (extract), 'The Once-in-Passing', 'House on a Cliff', 'Soap Suds', 'The Suicide' and 'Star-gazer' from *Collected Poems* (1966); for permission to reprint the following poems by Paul Muldoon: 'Lunch with Pancho Villa', 'Cuba', 'Anseo', 'Gathering Mushrooms' and 'The More a Man Has the More a Man Wants' from *Selected Poems 1968-1983* (1986); 'Something Else' from *Meeting the British* (1987); 'Cauliflowers' from *Madoc* (1990); for permission to reprint the following poems by Tom Paulin: 'Pot Burial' and 'Where Art Is a Midwife' from *The Strange Museum* (1980); 'Desertmartin', 'Off the Back of a Lorry' and 'A Written Answer' from *Liberty Tree* (1983); 'The Lonely Tower' from *Walking a Line* (1994); for permission to reprint the following poems by Maurice Riordan: 'Milk', 'Time Out' and 'A Word from the Loki' from *A Word from the Loki* (1995)

Farrar, Straus and Giroux, Inc., for permission to reprint the following poems: 'Broagh', 'Churning Day', 'Funeral Rites', 'Sunlight' and 'The Tollund Man' from *Poems 1965–1975* by Seamus Heaney. Copyright © 1980 by Seamus Heaney; 'Badgers', 'Casualty', 'From the Canton of Expectation', 'From the Frontier of Writing' and 'The Harvest Bow' from *Selected Poems 1966–1987* by Seamus Heaney. Copyright © 1990 by Seamus Heaney; 'The Birthplace' and 'The Cleric' from *Station Island* by Seamus Heaney. Copyright © 1985 by Seamus Heaney; 'Wheels within Wheels', 'Lightenings VIII' and 'Lightenings IX' from *Seeing Things* by Seamus Heaney. Copyright © 1991 by Seamus Heaney

Gallery Press for permission to reprint the following poem by Seán Dunne: 'Sydney Place' (extracts) from *The Sheltered Nest* (1992); for permission to reprint the following poems by Eamon Grennan: 'Totem' and 'Four Deer' from *What Light There Is* (1987); 'Breaking Points' from *As If It Matters* (1991); for permission to reprint the following poems by Michael Hartnett: 'Bread', 'I have exhausted the delighted range . . .', 'For My Grandmother, Bridget Halpin', 'A Farewell to English' (extract), 'Lament for Tadhg Cronin's Children' and 'The Man who Wrote Yeats, the Man who Wrote Mozart' from *Selected and New Poems* (1994); 'Sneachta Gealaí '77' and 'Moonsnow '77' from *A Necklace of Wrens* (1987); for permission to reprint the following poems by Pearse Hutchinson: 'Málaga' and 'Gaeltacht' from *Selected Poems* (1982); 'Sometimes Feel' from *Watching the Morning Grow* (1972); for permission to reprint the following poems by Medbh McGuckian: 'The Seed-picture', 'Gateposts' and 'The Flower Master' from *The Flower Master and Other Poems* (1993); 'The Sitting' from *Venus and the Rain* (1984, 1994 revised edition); 'Marconi's Cottage' from *Marconi's Cottage* (1991); 'Porcelain Bells' (extract) from *Captain Lavender* (1994); for permission to reprint the following poems by Ciaran Carson: 'Dresden' and 'Cocktails' from *The Irish for No* (1987); 'The Mouth' and 'Hamlet' from *Belfast Confetti* (1989); 'Ovid: *Metamorphoses*, V, 529–550' and 'Bagpipe Music' from *First Language* (1993); for permission to reprint the following poems by Paula Meehan: 'The Pattern' and 'Child Burial' from *The Man Who Was Marked by Winter* (1991); 'Laburnum' from *Pillow Talk* (1994); for permission to reprint the following poems by John Montague: 'Like Dolmens Round My Childhood, the Old People', 'The Trout', 'A Chosen Light' (extract), 'The Same Gesture', 'Last Journey', 'Dowager' and 'Herbert Street Revisited' from *New Selected Poems* (1989); 'Small Secrets' from *Collected Poems* (1995); for permission to reprint the following poems by Eiléan Ní Chuilleanáin: 'The Second Voyage' and 'Deaths and Engines' from *The Second Voyage* (1977, 1986); 'The Informant' from *The Magdalene Sermon* (1990); 'The Real Thing' and 'Saint Margaret of Cortona' from *The Brazen Serpent* (1994); for permission to reprint the following poems by Nuala Ní Dhomhnaill: 'Féar Suaithinseach' (translated by Seamus Heaney), 'An Bhábóg Bhriste' (translated by John Montague), 'An Bhean Mhídhílis' (translated by Paul Muldoon) and 'Ceist na Teangan' (translated by Paul Muldoon) from *Pharoah's Daughter* (1990); 'Caitlín' (translated by Paul Muldoon) from *The Astrakhan Cloak* (1992); for permission to reprint the following poems by Frank Ormsby: 'Passing the Crematorium' from *A Store of Candles* (1977, 1986); 'Home' from *A Northern Spring* (1986); for permission to reprint the following poems by

W.R. Rodgers: 'Lent', 'The Net' and 'Stormy Night' from *Poems* (1993) and 'Snow'; for permission to reprint the following poems by James Simmons: 'One of the Boys', 'West Strand Visions' and 'From the Irish' from *Poems 1956–1986* (1986); for permission to reprint the following poem by Peter Sirr: 'A Few Helpful Hints' from *Ways of Falling* (1991)

Grove/Atlantic, Inc., for permission to reprint the following poems by Samuel Beckett: 'Cascando', 'my way is in the sand flowing', 'what would I do without this world faceless incurious' and 'Roundelay' from *Collected Poems in English and French* (1977); 'Words and Music' (extract) from *Collected Shorter Plays* (1984)

Seamus Heaney for permission to reprint the following poem: 'Keeping Going'

Sheila Iremonger for permission to reprint the following poems by Valentin Iremonger: 'This Houre Her Vigill', 'Clear View in Summer' and 'Icarus' from *Sandymount, Dublin* (1988)

Biddy Jenkinson for permission to reprint the following poem: 'Cáitheadh'

The trustees of the estate of Patrick Kavanagh, c/o Peter Fallon, Literary Agent, Loughcrew, Oldcastle, County Meath, Ireland, for kind permission to reprint the following poems: 'To the Man After the Harrow', 'Stony Grey Soil', 'The Great Hunger' (extracts), 'The Twelfth of July', 'Tarry Flynn', 'A Christmas Childhood', 'Father Mat', 'Elegy for Jim Larkin', 'Epic', 'Innocence', 'Kerr's Ass' and 'The Hospital'

Thomas Kinsella for permission to reprint the following poems: 'Chrysalides' from *Selected Poems 1956–1968* (1973); 'Notes from the Land of the Dead' (extracts) from *New Poems 1973* (1973); 'One' (extracts) and 'Anniversaries' (extract) from *One and Other Poems* (1979); 'The Messenger' (extract) and 'Out of Ireland' (extract) from *Blood and Family* (1988); 'One Fond Embrace' (extract) from *One Fond Embrace: Peppercanister 13* (1988)

Michael Longley for permission to reprint the following poems: 'Phemios and Medon' and 'River & Fountain'

Thomas McCarthy for permission to reprint the following poem: 'State Funeral' from *The First Convention* (1978)

Peter McDonald for permission to reprint the following poem: 'Peacetime'

The estate of Thomas MacGreevy for permission to reprint the following poems: 'Homage to Hieronymous Bosch' and 'Recessional' from *Collected Poems* (1991)

John Montague for permission to reprint the following poems: 'A Drink of Milk', 'Family Conference' and 'The Cave of Night' (extract) from *Selected Poems* (1982)

Richard Murphy for permission to reprint the following poems: 'Sailing to an Island' and 'The Poet on the Island' from *Sailing to an Island* (1963); 'The Battle of Aughrim' (extract) from *The Battle of Aughrim* (1968); 'Seals at High Island' and 'Stormpetrel' from *High Island* (1974); 'Morning Call' and 'The Price of Stone' (extracts) from *The Price of Stone* (1985)

New Island Books for permission to reprint the following translation by

Michael Hartnett: 'Annunciations' from Nuala Ní Dhomhnaill, *Selected Poems: Rogha Dánta* (1988)

Nuala Ní Dhomhnaill for permission to reprint the following poems: 'Scéala' (translated by Michael Hartnett) and 'Fáilte Bhéal na Sionna don Iasc' (translated by Patrick Crotty) from *An Dealg Droighin* (1981)

W.W. Norton and Company, Inc., for permission to reprint the following poems by Eavan Boland: 'Listen. This Is the Noise of Myth' and 'Fond Memory' reprinted from *Outside History: Selected Poems 1980–1990* by Eavan Boland with the permission of W.W. Norton and Company Inc. Copyright © 1990 by Eavan Boland; 'The Black Lace Fan My Mother Gave Me', 'The Latin Lesson', 'Midnight Flowers' and 'Anna Liffey' reprinted from *In a Time of Violence* by Eavan Boland with the permission of W.W. Norton and Company, Inc. Copyright © 1994 by Eavan Boland

Frank Ormsby for permission to reprint the following poem. 'A Paris Honeymoon' (extract)

Alan Jenkins for permission to reprint the following translation. 'Spray'

Oxford University Press for permission to reprint the following poems by Derek Mahon: 'A Dying Art', 'Ecclesiastes', 'An Image from Beckett', 'Lives', 'The Snow Party', 'A Refusal to Mourn' and 'A Disused Shed in Co. Wexford' from *Poems 1962–1978* (1979), © Derek Mahon 1979; 'Courtyards in Delft', 'Rathlin' and 'Tractatus' from *The Hunt by Night* (1982), © Derek Mahon 1982

Peters, Fraser and Dunlop for permission to reprint the following poems by Michael Longley: 'In Memoriam', 'Caravan', 'Wounds', 'Ghost Town', 'Man Lying on a Wall', 'Wreaths', 'Mayo Monologues (extract) and 'The Linen Industry' from *Poems 1963–1983* (1991)

Sairséal ★ Ó Marcaigh Tta for permission to reprint the following poems by Máire Mhac an tSaoi: 'Caoineadh' and 'Ceathrúintí Mháire Ní Ógáin' from *An Cion Go Dtí Seo* (1987); for permission to reprint the following poems by Seán Ó Ríordáin: 'Adhlacadh Mo Mháthar', 'Malairt', 'Cnoc Mellerí' and 'Siollabadh' from *Eireaball Spideoige* (1952); 'Claustrophobia', 'Reo' and 'Fiabhras' from *Brosna* (1964); all poems translated by Patrick Crotty

Martin Secker and Warburg for permission to reprint the following poems by Michael Longley: 'In Memoriam', 'Caravan', 'Wounds', 'Ghost Town', 'Man Lying on a Wall', 'Wreaths', 'Mayo Monologues' (extract) and 'The Linen Industry' from *Poems 1963–1983* (1991); 'Between Hovers', 'Laertes', 'Argos' and 'The Butchers' from *Gorse Fires* (1991); for permission to reprint the following poems by Matthew Sweeney: 'To the Building Trade' and 'Tube Ride to Martha's' from *Blue Shoes* (1989)

Wake Forest University Press for permission to reprint the following poems by Ciaran Carson: 'Dresden' and 'Cocktails' from *The Irish for No* (1987); 'The Mouth' and 'Hamlet' from *Belfast Confetti* (1989); 'Ovid: Metamorphoses, V, 529–550' and 'Bagpipe Music' from *First Language* (1993); for permission to reprint the following poems by Michael Longley: 'Between Hovers', 'Laertes', 'Argos' and 'The Butchers' from *Gorse Fires* (1991); for permission to reprint the following poems by Medbh McGuckian: 'Marconi's Cottage' from *Marconi's Cottage* (1991); 'Porcelain Bells' (extract) from *Captain Lavender* (1994); for permission to reprint the following poems by John Montague: 'Like Dolmens Round My Childhood, the Old People', 'The Trout', 'A Chosen Light' (extract), 'The Same Gesture', 'Last Journey', 'Small Secrets', 'Dowager' and 'Herbert Street Revisited' from *Selected Poems* (1982); for permission to reprint the following poems by Paul Muldoon: 'Lunch with Pancho Villa' from *Mules and Early Poems* (1985); 'Cuba' and 'Anseo' from *Why Brownlee Left* (1981); 'Gathering Mushrooms' and 'The More a Man Has the More a Man Wants' from *Quoof* (1983); 'Something Else' from *Meeting the British* (1987); for permission to reprint the following poems by Eiléan Ní Chuilleanáin: 'The Second Voyage', and 'Deaths and Engines' from *The Second Voyage* (1977, 1986); 'The Informant' from *The Magdalene Sermon* (1990); 'The Real Thing' and 'Saint Margaret of Cortona' from *The Brazen Serpent* (1994); for permission to reprint the following poems by Nuala Ní Dhomhnaill: 'Féar Suaithinseach' (translated by Seamus Heaney), 'An Bhábóg Bhriste (translated by John Montague), 'An Bhean Mhídhílis' (translated by Paul Muldoon) and 'Ceist na Teangan' (translated by Paul Muldoon) from *Pharoah's Daughter* (1990); 'Caitlín' (translated by Paul Muldoon) from *The Astrakhan Cloak* (1992)

The publishers have made every effort to trace and acknowledge copyright holders. We apologise for any omissions in the above list and we will welcome additions or amendments to it for inclusion in any reprint edition.

INDEX OF POETS AND TRANSLATORS

INDEX OF TITLES

431

INDEX OF FIRST LINES